'In this book, Dr Steward presents a manifesto for his method of school improvement: slow, steady, and above all, sustained. As the long-standing head teacher of a highly successful school, he clearly knows what he is talking about. I found myself nodding in agreement to much of what Steward proposed, but I was repeatedly brought up short with a provocation or argument that challenged my thinking. This is where the book has real value: it challenges the orthodoxy and presents a compelling, proven alternative. Highly recommended.'

Chris Hildrew, head teacher of Churchill Academy & Sixth Form and author of *Becoming a Growth Mindset School*

The Gradual Art of School Improvement

School improvement in recent years has largely focused on rapid improvement and quick fixes. Yet, genuine and sustainable school improvement is complex, gradual and incremental. It requires developing a culture and focusing relentlessly on teaching and learning.

The Gradual Art of School Improvement is a comprehensive practical guide to school improvement, covering aspects such as improvement planning, staff development, the learning environment, dealing with outside pressures including inspection, curriculum design and the role of leaders at all levels. It includes:

- Detailed accounts of the steps that can be taken to create a positive learning culture over time
- Case studies and worked examples, concentrating on the practical aspects of school improvement from the perspective of an experienced and successful head teacher
- Ready-to-use practitioner resources that readers can adapt and use in their own settings

Accessibly written and entertaining, this book is an invaluable resource for leaders at all levels and stages of their career.

Richard Steward is an educational consultant with 16 years' experience as a head teacher. He has taught in a variety of schools in a 30-year career and has worked as a part-time lecturer with The Open University. He regularly publishes articles in the educational press.

The Gradual Art of School Improvement

A Practical Guide

Richard Steward

LONDON AND NEW YORK

First published 2020
by Routledge
2 Park Square, Milton Park, Abingdon, Oxon OX14 4RN

and by Routledge
52 Vanderbilt Avenue, New York, NY 10017

Routledge is an imprint of the Taylor & Francis Group, an informa business

© 2020 Richard Steward

The right of Richard Steward to be identified as author of this work has been asserted by him in accordance with sections 77 and 78 of the Copyright, Designs and Patents Act 1988.

All rights reserved. No part of this book may be reprinted or reproduced or utilised in any form or by any electronic, mechanical, or other means, now known or hereafter invented, including photocopying and recording, or in any information storage or retrieval system, without permission in writing from the publishers.

Trademark notice: Product or corporate names may be trademarks or registered trademarks, and are used only for identification and explanation without intent to infringe.

British Library Cataloguing-in-Publication Data
A catalogue record for this book is available from the British Library

Library of Congress Cataloging-in-Publication Data
Names: Steward, Richard, 1961– author.
Title: The gradual art of school improvement : a practical guide / Richard Steward.
Description: Abingdon, Oxon ; New York, NY : Routledge, 2019. | Includes index.
Identifiers: LCCN 2019006993 (print) | LCCN 2019013672 (ebook) | ISBN 9780429028076 (Ebook) | ISBN 9780367136895 (hardback) | ISBN 9780367136918 (pbk.)
Subjects: LCSH: School improvement programs—Handbooks, manuals, etc.
Classification: LCC LB2822.8 (ebook) | LCC LB2822.8 .S73 2019 (print) | DDC 371.2/07—dc23
LC record available at https://lccn.loc.gov/2019006993

ISBN: 978-0-367-13689-5 (hbk)
ISBN: 978-0-367-13691-8 (pbk)
ISBN: 978-0-429-02807-6 (ebk)

Typeset in Melior
by Apex CoVantage, LLC

Wisely and slow; they stumble that run fast.
                    —William Shakespeare, *Romeo and Juliet*

I always listen to what I can leave out.
                                        —Miles Davis

Contents

Acknowledgements xii
Introduction xiii

1   Creating a learning culture 1
    Acceleration 1
    Quick fix versus slow burn 2
    Towards a definition of a learning culture 4
    Beyond the classroom 5
    Politics 7
    Avoiding distractions 9
    Head of teaching and learning 11
    The head teacher in the classroom 13
    Behaviour for learning 14
    Open classrooms, open leadership 15

2   Leadership for learning 20
    The myth of the hero head 20
    Leaders as teachers 22
    Working with the system 24
    Innovation 26
    Two examples 29
    The leadership team 32
    The whole team 35
    Appointing leaders 37
    The digital leader 41
    Improvising 43

3   Real improvement planning 47
    The vision 47
    The self-evaluation form (SEF) 48

	What should an SEF include?	*49*
	What to include in a learning plan	*50*
	An example plan	*51*
	The learning plan cycle	*55*
	Line management	*56*
	Embedding the plan	*57*
4	Staff development	60
	Teachers as researchers	*62*
	Trios	*63*
	Challenge coordinators	*64*
	Classroom to classroom	*66*
	A planned programme	*68*
	Departmental reviews	*70*
	Department reviews – an example method	*71*
	Reluctant staff	*74*
	Staff forum	*76*
	Teaching schools	*77*
5	The curriculum	83
	What do we mean by the curriculum?	*84*
	Playing the game	*87*
	Broad and balanced	*89*
	Choice	*92*
	Standing up for the arts	*95*
	Vocational education	*97*
	Putting it all together	*100*
	The importance of narrative	*101*
6	The myth of governance	106
	The role of governors	*106*
	Who are the governors?	*109*
	How qualified are governors?	*111*
	Governance in practice	*113*
	New governors	*114*
	Reporting to governors	*117*
	The importance of policies	*118*
	Critical friends	*121*
	Inviting governors into school	*123*
	Accountability and trust	*125*

7	Inspection	128
	The need for inspection	*129*
	The dangers of being satisfactory	*131*
	The dangers of being outstanding	*132*
	The limitations of inspection	*132*
	Preparing for inspection	*134*
	Over-preparing	*136*
8	Pupils, not systems	140
	The Alternative School Council	*141*
	Teaching and learning and the school council	*143*
	The school council classroom code	*144*
	Pupils as leaders of learning	*145*
	Parents	*148*
	Academic pupils, happy pupils	*150*
	Appendix	153
	Endnote	190
	Index	191

Acknowledgements

Much of the content of this book has been developed over the 16 years I have been a head teacher. I would therefore like to acknowledge the work and dedication of all the staff I have worked with and who have played such a large part in the school improvement journey outlined in these pages. In particular, I would like to thank Paul Rowe and Adam Shelley, the school's outstanding deputies, who have worked alongside me to develop a shared understanding of what school improvement is all about. Much of the success of the work we have done together is down to their involvement.

I would also like to thank the editors of the *TES* for allowing me to include here adaptations of two of the articles I wrote for them – one on teaching schools (November 2017) and one on the curriculum as a narrative (August 2017). Similarly, my thanks go to the editors of Forum Media for also allowing me to use articles previously published by them: one on the role of the finance manager in the February 2019 edition of *The Business Manager* and one on challenge coordinators from the November 2018 edition of *The School Inspection and Improvement Magazine*.

Introduction

As long ago as 1797, William Godwin, in *Reflections on Education, Manners and Literature*, said, 'Let us not, in the eagerness of our haste to educate, forget all the ends of education.' In the context of today's chaotic and fragmented educational landscape, it is perhaps time for us to think more deeply about 'all the ends of education,' and it is certainly time to focus on what goes on in the classroom rather than what goes on in the 'system.' In the past few years, schools have undergone a period of unprecedented change, leaving us with a national education system which is creaking at the seams.

We now have maintained schools, academies, free schools, city technology colleges, studio schools, multi-academy trusts, cooperative trusts and a powerful independent sector. Education has become a commercial marketplace, where large academy chains compete to take over failing schools. In addition, underfunding has led to low teacher morale, recruitment issues, crumbling schools and a real sense of uncertainty about the future in almost every school in the country. Performance tables and accountability measures dominate school life in ways we have never seen before, and, despite the fact that teachers are better trained, better qualified and more highly skilled than ever before, the teaching profession is still regarded by politicians, the media and, sadly, parents with suspicion at best and, at times, downright contempt.

It is important, in these dark times, to focus on what really matters and what goes on in the classroom. This is a book, therefore, about pupils and not systems. It is a book intended to reflect on improving education in ordinary classrooms up and down the country. It is intended to be both practical and polemical. It suggests real-world examples of school improvement in action but challenges the status quo where necessary. There is a lot of common sense involved here, though I am acutely aware that one person's common sense is another's madness. In George R. R. Martin's *Fire and Blood*, Septon Barth's book *Dragons, Wyrms, and Wyverns: Their Unnatural History* is condemned as 'provocative and unsound.' I hope there will be aspects of this book which will be regarded as provocative but that not too many will be considered unsound. There is a degree of challenge, however.

Essentially, the book is a comprehensive, practical guide to school improvement. Its aim is to offer a detailed account of the ways in which steps can be taken to create a positive learning culture over time. It therefore covers all aspects of school improvement with practical examples throughout, including improvement planning, staff development, the learning environment, dealing with outside pressures including inspection, curriculum design and the role of leaders at all levels. Each section is illustrated, where possible, with practical examples, and I have included resources which readers can adapt and use in their own settings.

Although there are occasional references to academic research, the book is essentially practical. It is anecdotal at times and, on occasion, controversial. It challenges concepts such as system leadership and the self-improving system, it debunks the myth of governance and it demonstrates fundamental flaws in the teaching and learning leadership role popular in so many schools nowadays. I hope it is both accessible and entertaining, the contents practical and useful.

Above all, this is a book which recognizes that genuine school improvement takes time. It is indeed a gradual art.

Creating a learning culture

Acceleration

We live in an age of acceleration. Thanks largely to technological innovation, changes in society seem to take place at an ever-increasing rate. We sweep through our days in a constant state of panic, clutching our smartphones just as tightly as Lewis Carroll's White Rabbit hangs on to his pocket watch. Sophisticated communication devices have created a world where we can communicate instantly but where finding time to think or simply switch off is becoming harder and harder. A phrase I hear more and more often lately is 'I'd really like to think about that, but I simply don't have the time.'

In all walks of life, things are changing faster than they have ever done before, but it could convincingly be argued that in education the pressure to accelerate is even more evident. Education deals with the future, with young people who have grown up in the digital world and for whom constant change is a given. School leaders have to keep up, respond to the needs of their students and learn to deal with changes which seem to happen at an ever-increasing rate.

In addition to dealing with changes in society generally, school leaders now find themselves working in an environment of extreme accountability. Their work in schools and colleges is driven by performance tables, exacting inspection regimes and the increasingly high expectations of parents. Successive governments have made education a key feature of their manifesto pledges and promised parents the ability to choose only the very best schools for their children. Anything less than the best is not good enough. Consequently, very few schools are considered good enough, and change is not only expected but demanded. Policy after policy is rolled out from the centre, and schools are expected to respond. School leaders now exist in what can only be described as a state of permanent revolution, something S.J. Ball has described as the 'unstoppable flood of reform'[1] or, as Benjamin Levin put it, 'a policy epidemic.'[2] Ian Stronach went one step further and called it 'policy hysteria.'[3]

School leaders, therefore, are forced to focus on rapid improvement. The short-termism of the political world, where governments have only a few years to effect change, is now played out in education where improvements have to be immediate and changes put in place straight away. It is the job of the school leader to drive up standards as quickly as possible. But are rapid changes really effective, and will they last?

League tables and inspection grades have undoubtedly led to a quick-fix culture where schools deemed to be failing are subject to rigorous scrutiny and required to move from inadequate to good in a matter of months. And, of course, school leaders have become good at this. There are dozens of examples of schools where standards have risen rapidly and a whole panoply of school improvement techniques has been introduced, if not perhaps perfected, and these have been marketed to enable other school leaders to emulate such successes. How effective many of these techniques are in the long term remains to be seen, but it is becoming increasingly clear that too many schools where rapid improvement has taken place quickly slide back to where they were before.

Increasing fragmentation in the system is often blamed for the poor performance of many schools, even if policy makers insist that the introduction of academies and Free Schools has led to more choice and better outcomes for pupils across the country. The jury is still out on the effectiveness of academization, but it is undoubtedly true to say that the new systems are more fluid and less stable than previous local authority provision. This, too, has had an accelerating effect. Schools which are deemed to be failing are taken over by academy sponsors, and if they continue to fail, sponsorships are re-brokered and another quick-fix regime instituted. In my visits to other schools, I have seen this scenario played out far too often.

The effect of all this is a professional development culture which encourages school leaders to focus on learning how to bring about rapid change. The notion of gradual development is almost inimical to a system which demands instant results. Moreover, the head teacher, with the emphasis on the word *teacher*, is becoming a thing of the past. The first step on the way was 'principal,' but now we have CEOs and 'system leaders,' titles which almost seem to exclude 'teaching' so that teaching becomes something of an outmoded concept not really worthy of the attention of those who, like powerful spiders, sit at the heart of the system webs.

The culture of rapid improvement could well be as illusory as Alice's Wonderland. Genuine and sustainable school improvement is complex, gradual and incremental. It is about developing a culture and focusing relentlessly on teaching and learning. It is not about systems; it is about what goes on in the classroom.

Quick fix versus slow burn

The rapid improvement toolbox is becoming something of a cliché and its contents surely familiar to everybody. It can easily be caricatured.

First, change the name of the school. The switch from Dotheboys Hall to The Elysian Academy serves two purposes: to announce the arrival of a new regime and to imply that pupils will be entering an unfamiliar world of academic excellence. The aim is to create an impression of sparkling novelty, even if the change of name hides the obvious fact that, in essence, the school is exactly the same. The appointment of a new leadership team is the second step. If part of a multi-academy trust, there will be a CEO or an executive head, the titles giving an appropriate sense of gravitas to the new undertaking. Since both posts will involve hours and hours of committee meetings and time spent travelling between schools, a head teacher, or more often a head of teaching and learning, will be required. It is this person's job to 'turn around' the school as quickly as possible.

So, quick wins are vital. Uniform is usually the place to start. A smart, new uniform underpinned by a strong uniform code gives the school a new sense of pride and signals a new ethos to parents. Such changes inevitably lead to endless conflicts with those who find it hard to adapt to much stricter rules, but this is where the discipline code is brought to bear. If children are to make progress, discipline must be strict. This is an idea which is always supported by parents and the wider community until the rules begin to bite. Children are sent home, detentions soar and exclusions become endemic. For a while, newness and novelty preside, but when the blazers become torn, the skirts are hitched back up and the ties shortened; cracks begin to show in what was clearly a model discipline policy.

Much is made in the media of the excessive use of exclusions, but the easiest way to establish a new era of calm in a school is to lose those pupils who cause the most trouble. It is not uncommon to see a change of leadership which results in 20 or 30 children excluded almost immediately. Such exclusions inevitably have the support of the staff, and they send a message to the community which says that the new team means business. However, excluded children have to go somewhere, they have to be taught and more often than not, they end up back where they started. Problem children do not always go away. Exclusion is quick, but it may not always be the answer.

The multi-academy trust approach is often based on the principle that what works in one school is bound to work in another. Although, as we shall see, this ignores complexities such as local context and, to some, the awkward notion that not all children are the same, nevertheless the pre-prepared school improvement package is often regarded as highly effective and sure to bring about rapid change.

With the addition of new buildings, an option seemingly only available to Free Schools nowadays, the quick-fix package is complete: a new name, a new uniform, a set of policies and practices borrowed from another school and an executive head.

This is obviously an extreme caricature, but it is a caricature many school leaders and educationalists may recognize. However, it is not hard to see that the model, although appealing, is fundamentally flawed. Making rapid change stick is very difficult indeed and changing the culture of a school is a complex undertaking.

A new culture cannot be bought in and imposed; it takes years to develop. It depends on local context, on the nature of the pupils, on the support and attitudes of parents, on economic circumstances and, above all, on approaches to learning and the attitudes to learning shared by everyone in the school.

Schools where teachers have been working steadily for a number of years to bring about gradual improvements, and those which, in the language of inspection, can be described as consistently good or better have become the Cinderellas of recent educational thinking. They rarely make the news, and they are rarely made the subject of case studies or journal articles, but they are often the places where the most effective examples of genuine school improvement are to be found. They may not have an executive head, nor can they evidence a sudden transformation from good to outstanding, but they are clearly getting a lot right and therefore having a profound impact on the children in their care. These are the 'ordinary schools.' They are certainly not the 'bog standard schools' of the Blair era because many of them are remarkable – but they are quietly remarkable and largely ignored by politicians and academics. It is in these schools where the effectiveness of the 'slow burn' is most apparent. In these schools, staff have been improving and refining their methods and practices over a number of years; it is in these schools where strong learning cultures have really taken hold, cultures which are complex, sophisticated and, unfortunately for those who seek to categorize the essential elements of successful school cultures, exceptionally hard to define. What is obvious in all of them, however, is an intense, unremitting focus on teaching and learning.

Towards a definition of a learning culture

Critics and philosophers struggle to agree on a clear definition of *culture*. A learning culture is perhaps even harder to define.

The critic Raymond Williams, in *Keywords*, writes that *culture* has three divergent meanings: there's culture as a process of individual enrichment, for example when we say that someone is 'cultured'; culture as a group's 'particular way of life,' when we talk about French culture, company culture or multiculturalism; and culture as an activity, pursued by means of museums, concerts, books and films.[4] These three versions of culture are actually quite different, and as Williams writes, they compete with one another. He explains that each time we use the word *culture*, we incline toward one or another of its aspects: the 'culture' that's imbibed through osmosis or the 'culture' that's learned at museums, the 'culture' that makes you a better a person or the 'culture' that just inducts you into a group. In schools, the tension among these three definitions is at the heart of the learning culture.

Pupils attend school for individual enrichment; they are there to learn. For teachers and parents, becoming 'cultured,' in the sense of learning how to access key works of literature, important historical facts, a good understanding of science, an appreciation of art and music and so on, is an important element of the school experience. For children in school, however, the most significant feature of school life is group culture or, more basically, interaction with their peers. Parents and teachers are often very disappointed to learn that the most powerful influence on teenagers is other teenagers.

A successful school achieves a balance among Williams's three cultures: individual enrichment is the goal, but the complex dynamics of school life are acknowledged, while a shared belief in the power and importance of developing children as cultured individuals in the traditional sense is carefully retained.

It is almost impossible to codify the essential elements of a successful school culture; its constituents are many and varied, and they differ from school to school. This doesn't mean we shouldn't try, however, and a key part of a successful school improvement agenda involves discussing what makes the school work, what makes it different, and what needs to change. These are discussions which involve all aspects of school life and discussions which must be underpinned by an appreciation of the impact of the various aspects of school life on teaching and learning. What goes on in the classroom is powerfully influenced by what goes on outside of the classroom. Learning will be at the heart of any sophisticated school culture, but it will be surrounded and supported by a complex web of activities which together form part of the experience of attending school.

It is important for leadership teams to spend time considering the extent and nature of the school's activities beyond the classroom and to assess their impact on learning as part of the wider, ongoing discussion of teaching and learning in the school.

Beyond the classroom

Let us begin, therefore, by discussing what goes on beyond the classroom before addressing directly the role and importance of classroom practice. Schools often create lists of activities to impress parents or present to inspectors but how often are these lists considered as part of the school improvement agenda? It is all too easy to regard extra-curricular activities as something other, as beyond the curriculum and therefore having only a minimal impact on school culture. In reality, they play a vital part: instead of extra-curricular, a better name might be co-curricular as they sit alongside the academic curriculum, supporting and enhancing it. Any genuine discussion of the learning culture in school must attempt to address the co-curricular aspects of what goes on in school as they often have a significant but sometimes hidden impact on academic progress. They should not be simply regarded as something that happens in school but questioned and discussed. Sometimes the results are surprising.

Sport is a good example. What is the impact of sport in school? It is easy to enumerate the number of clubs and fixtures which take place but how often do leaders consider the ethos of the physical education (PE) department and its impact on the school as a whole. Does competitive sport engender feelings of competitiveness in the classroom; does fair play and sportsmanship influence behaviour? Do pupils spend enough time exercising, and does their fitness make them ready to learn? Such a discussion could well uncover less positive features of sports provision: Is there an ultra-competitive environment which alienates some pupils and pushes them towards isolation or withdrawal? Above all, does the approach of the PE department support the academic and social aspirations of the school, or does it subtly undermine them? In too many schools, the notion that sport is a good thing is a given. How often is its impact openly explored? I have had dozens of conversations with middle and senior leaders who have never really questioned the value and importance of PE in school. It is one of the subjects we must accept as a 'good thing.' It may well be a good thing but that shouldn't stop us thinking about it.

Similarly, most schools offer a wide range of trips and visits, and again, these are used as evidence to present the school as a vibrant and exciting place. However, do they all add to the ethos of the school? Do some of them have a deleterious effect or are there simply too many of them? An objective analysis of the number of trips, their nature and duration and the time spent out of the classroom for the pupils who take part can result in really challenging discussions about what the school is trying to achieve and what really is in pupils' best interests.

Simple matters like the nature of the displays around the school can have a profound impact on learning. Many of us will have had experience of visiting schools where there is nothing to see but bare walls or carefully curated display boards used for information purposes, and the effect of such places can be quite chilling. Primary schools generally work hard to create bright and stimulating environments, but secondary schools are often guilty of assuming that colourful displays are for younger pupils only. When Specialist School Status was first introduced, the first step taken by schools that chose to become arts colleges was often to cover the walls in artwork. Despite the warnings of the doom-mongers on the staff that the work would quickly be ruined by passing crowds or simply vandalized, it quickly became evident that, in the majority of cases, pupils responded incredibly well to their new surroundings, not only valuing the displays but also protecting them.

How pupils respond to display work is well worth exploring. Is it simply a matter of bright displays which improve the atmosphere, or is it their nature which matters most? A drab corridor enlivened by some dazzling artwork is bound to lift the spirits, but how often do leaders consider how much attention is paid to the artwork itself? Do pupils look and learn, do they read the work proudly displayed by other classes and how do they respond? Leadership teams in schools where great emphasis is put on the use of displays would argue that pupils are stimulated by the art itself, that they read work on the walls because there is often nothing else to do when they are standing outside classrooms, and, most important of all, that they think about it. They respect the work because it is often done by their friends or because they hope that their work, if displayed, will be respected too. Above all, art in the corridors, words on the walls and records of the successes of other pupils may simply convey a sense of participation and achievement which is an essential ingredient in a strong learning culture.

More mundane matters should also be considered. How conducive to learning is the school environment? Often there is not much school leaders can do about ageing buildings or rooms desperately in need of refurbishment, but it is easy to ask whether pupils are warm enough, whether they can see the boards clearly in poorly lit rooms, whether they are happy to use the loos and, above all, do they feel safe?

Of course, there are bound to be aspects of school life that appear hostile to the development of a powerful learning culture, and to some extent, these are becoming more and more difficult to deal with every day. Twenty-first-century schools face problems almost completely unknown to previous generations: social media, drugs, violence and, above all, mental health issues. However, some of the negative effects on learning cultures are far less obvious. How involved in classroom practice are senior leaders? Are parents combative, supportive or disengaged? Do governors really understand the school and have an impact on its development? All these questions need to be considered to get a true understanding of the culture of the school.

Politics

One of the most interesting aspects of school development is the impact and influence of political and societal preoccupations on the learning culture in schools. It is here where school leaders often find themselves particularly put to the test. Ideas which are readily accepted as 'a good thing' are often responded to with unthinking readiness, and it is probably true to say that too many of us adopt the latest ideas with relatively little thought. I am often surprised by the eagerness of senior colleagues to get involved in projects and activities which, on the face of it, seem to be of little value, simply because they are promoted by the Regional Schools Commissioner or the Department for Education (DfE). However, an idea developed by politicians, endorsed by the press, supported by parents and made the theme of dozens and dozens of professional development programmes can be difficult to resist. But is it right for every school?

Many of us would perhaps admit to being suspicious of the Fundamental British Values (FBV) agenda, not because we don't support the idea of promoting strong values but because the very idea of a set of particularly British values is a concept which is fundamentally flawed. It is also overtly political and therefore jars with the feeling that schools should be non-political and free from such direct governmental interference. However, with FBV part of the inspection framework, it would be a brave school leader who does not decide to keep his or head down and go along with it.

A less obvious example is the recent obsession with science, technology, engineering and maths (STEM). This is an idea generated by politicians in conjunction with vested interests in industry and science. It is also partly a reaction to the apparent pre-eminence of other countries in these fields, despite the fact that Britain has some of the best universities in the world specializing in science and technology. It also draws on UK pupils' performance in the deeply flawed and controversial Programme for International Student Assessment tests and is predicated on the idea that Britain needs more scientists and mathematicians to compete globally. This is a powerful idea, and compelling arguments are put forward to ensure that schools 'get with the programme' and put a great deal of effort into promoting STEM subjects.

Such is the power of the STEM agenda that politicians have interfered directly in the day-to-day running of schools to ensure that their ideas are not only adopted but fully absorbed into the curriculum as well. The creation of the English Baccalaureate (Ebacc) meant that schools were strongly encouraged to insist that all pupils spend more time on maths and science, and the calculations underpinning Progress 8 scores privilege maths and the EBacc subjects. As a result, maths began to spread out across the curriculum to the detriment of other, supposedly less important subjects. Incidentally, politicians were aided in their endeavours to convince schools of the importance of the STEM agenda by the less-than-helpful list of facilitating subjects supplied by the Russell Group universities. On top of this, grants were made available, industry placements opened and the importance of STEM promoted almost universally in the press.

It takes a confident head teacher to go against such a powerful tide, but how many leadership teams have actually discussed the impact of STEM on their schools, and how many have been bold enough to take a different view? In some of the best schools, however, political agendas are acknowledged but rarely allowed to distort or dominate pre-existing learning cultures. It is true to say that feigned compliance is alive and well in many of our most effective academic institutions.

With more and more people expressing concern about the loss of arts subjects in schools, the devaluing of religious education, the dramatic decline in language learning and absurdly snobbish approaches to subjects such as media studies and psychology, the tide is perhaps turning. But the schools that focused wholeheartedly on the promotion of STEM subjects at the expense of other equally valuable areas of the curriculum may find it hard to change track, and they may find that a strong learning culture has become diluted.

It is also perhaps worth turning back to Raymond Williams's definitions of culture with regard to the STEM phenomenon. It may provide individual enrichment, but does it really add much to the notion of a 'cultured individual'? Cultured in the sense of scientifically, mathematically and technology confident, but what about traditional definitions of culture relating to the arts and literature?

The rise of STEM as a vital ingredient in the curriculum of mainstream schools prompts another question which is fundamental to the creation of a learning culture: what is education for? This is a huge question but how often is it asked in schools? Consideration of the role of STEM subjects provides a useful way in.

The focus on mathematics and science suggests that the real purpose of schools is to prepare pupils for the world of work. It is vital that schools equip pupils with the skills and attributes they need to work in industry and the financial markets of the future. Putting aside the doubtful assertion that the majority of jobs will require scientific or technical skills, there is the much more challenging question of whether education should be about more than preparation for work. And this is a question which often sits at the heart of the learning culture in schools. More and more pupils, encouraged by their parents, are beginning to think of the curriculum in terms of its usefulness in preparing them for job opportunities. The idea of learning for learning's sake strikes them as desperately old fashioned. The intensity of this focus is also reflected in what goes on in the classroom when pupils ask what I regard as possibly the most annoying question teachers encounter on a daily basis: Is this in the syllabus?

Of course, school leaders cannot be expected to answer the question, What is education for? But they can be encouraged to consider what they think it is for and how they can shape the curriculum accordingly. Some would argue that the curriculum is largely shaped for us by government diktats and the tyranny of the league tables, but subtle changes can have significant effects. If school leaders want their schools to focus on broader notions of cultural awareness, then they should not necessarily be afraid to challenge orthodoxies and, where necessary, go against the tide of political or populist thinking. Obviously, it would be foolish in the case of STEM to abandon these subjects altogether but far from impossible to introduce them with care so as not to impact adversely on other curriculum areas which are considered equally valuable.

Avoiding distractions

The culture of a school is undoubtedly complex and multifaceted. Any thorough discussion of a school's culture and ethos must necessarily consider many of the areas discussed earlier: the extra-curricular programme; the local area; the socio-economic circumstances of the pupils and their parents; the school environment; negative influences such as social media, drugs and gang culture; and, above all, guidance from the top in the form of political directives, league tables and the demands of inspection. All these things influence the direction and the ethos of individual schools. The most effective schools, however, recognize that the most powerful way to ensure that the multifarious demands, pressures and, of course, opportunities of school life are kept in balance is to insist that teaching and learning sit at the heart of the school and influence every decision that is made.

It is becoming increasingly difficult for school leaders to avoid distractions. There is no such thing as a typical day for a senior leader and during a day he or she has to consider hundreds of things that contribute to the successful running of the school, from frozen pipes to new legislation. In addition, schools have become the places politicians go first to solve all the nation's ills, and heads are expected to ensure that they prepare children for virtually everything life has to throw at them, from sex education to drug taking, from economic literacy to environmental awareness and so on.

I recently kept a daily record of the issues presented in the media which schools were expected to solve (see Appendix 1). After two months, I gave up because I was simply overwhelmed by the sheer number of demands for schools to sort out problems in society. The list is comprehensive, to say the least; all of life is there. It covers everything from the vital topics which plague us in the modern world – racism, mental health issues and poverty, among others – to the truly bizarre: pigeon racing clubs, for example. From Darcy Bussell stressing the importance of PE to Prince Harry warning us about the dangers of Fortnite, it seems as if everyone is entitled to a view on what schools should be doing. It is, of course, impossible for schools to satisfy society's demands and madness for any head teacher to attempt to respond to most of them. It is, however, important for leaders to be aware of the sheer level of distraction and the need to deal with it all appropriately in order simply to get on with the day job. I find it quite stressful just reading down the list of things society would like us to do; how much more stressed would I be if I attempted to respond to all of them. It is simply not possible for schools to do everything. It's a shame that the media, and politicians, in particular, don't appreciate that.

The level of reporting in schools is another potential area of distraction. Heads have to report to the local authority, to academy trusts, to governors, to the DfE and so on. Online forms are the latest menace. I have yet to see one that is properly designed. If you manage to get them to work in the first place, most of them crash after a few minutes losing all your data and forcing you to start again. Most irritating of all are the forms that don't allow you to say what you want or need to say and ask questions which you can't answer. More often than not, an unanswerable question prevents you from progressing further with the form so that you then have to ring the helpline to seek assistance. And they all require passwords, most of which you will have forgotten, if you ever had them in the first place. The DfE is currently a world leader in confusing and impossible-to-complete online forms. It is always comforting to note, however, that when you eventually track down the number for the helpline and get through to someone supposedly responsible for the form in question (and this can take days), they rarely understand the forms either.

Distractions come in so many forms that senior leaders become bewildered by the sheer impossibility of their roles. The trick, however, is to consider everything from the point of view of its impact on the classroom, and this gives every task and every distraction one clear aim. It allows for the creation and preservation of a beating heart at the centre of the chaos, a heart which beats to the rhythm of learning.

A culture which does not focus unremittingly on teaching and learning in this way is not a learning culture. The focus, therefore, of every senior leader must be the development of learning across the school. All other aspects of a school's culture are contingent on and contribute to this one overriding function of the school system. School leaders who opt for the quick fix often fail to consider the complexities of school cultures outlined earlier and, in doing so, end up neglecting the very thing they are employed to do: improve the quality of education in their schools.

Head of teaching and learning

It would be very hard to find a head teacher or principal who would not support the notion that the development of teaching and learning is absolutely fundamental to his or her role. All senior leaders talk spiritedly about their commitment to learning and the intensity of their interest in what goes on in the classroom. Is it possible, however, that there is sometimes a gap between the philosophy and the rhetoric?

If senior leaders are honest about how they spend their days, they will usually admit that a huge amount of their time is spent on administrative activities or, in some cases, dealing with behavioural issues. The distractions outlined earlier which divert leadership teams from focusing on the more important aspects of their school's learning culture are equally apparent in their day-to-day activities. This is easily confirmed by compiling a leadership log.

Anyone who writes down what he or she does in a day – and does so during the course of a week – will find such a log both surprising and dispiriting. Most senior leaders spend hours on administrative tasks, hours dealing with parents, hours addressing staff concerns and hours in meetings that seem to go on forever and achieve very little. The time spent in the classroom or the time spent directly engaged with improving teaching and learning is often minimal. The impact of the rapid improvement agenda is particularly evident here because leaders are often far too busy implementing new policies and practices to stand back and evaluate their impact. So, too, is the effect of financial constraints: leadership teams often take the brunt of budget reductions, and this inevitably increases the number of management tasks they need to take on.

When pressed, head teachers will often point out that teaching and learning are discussed at every leadership team meeting or in every staff meeting, proclaiming proudly that the team has just been away for a two-day planning meeting where nothing but learning was discussed. However, if they were to be really honest, they might acknowledge nevertheless that the majority of their time is actually spent on management. If they are reluctantly forced to admit that there is some truth in this assertion, they may then go on to ask how can it be otherwise. There is so much to do. Running a school is a uniquely complex operation, and keeping it going on a day-to-day basis is a superhuman task. Long discussions about teaching and learning have become a luxury, and there is less and less time for that sort of thing. The simple truth, however, is that in order to bring about genuine, long-lasting improvement, leaders must make time.

Heads and principals too busy themselves to focus on learning, but who nevertheless acknowledge its fundamental importance, often turn to a simple expedient: the appointment of a member of the leadership team with responsibility for teaching and learning. This is a neat but deeply flawed solution, and I must confess that when I am introduced in schools to the leader of teaching and learning, my heart sinks.

I find the idea that one person can be put in charge of teaching and learning distinctly odd. Learning should be at the heart of any effective school culture, and to assign one person to oversee it is fraught with difficulties. This is a view which is bound to raise eyebrows across the profession, but there are strong arguments to suggest that such a role may not be in the best interest of schools and their pupils.

First, there is the problem of exclusivity. Give a member of the leadership team the responsibility for teaching and learning and there is the danger that other members of the team think that teaching and learning is not something they need to think about. They are then free to focus on whichever leadership responsibilities have been assigned to them.

Second, there is status to be considered. Learning is absolutely the most important aspect of school life; should it therefore be confined to the job description of one member of the leadership team? Such a role dilutes the importance of learning in the school. If there is a need for a leader here, it surely must be the head teacher or principal.

Third, is the problem of the job description. In far too many schools, the leader of teaching and learning is often a manager responsible for the timetable or data or even cover. His or her involvement in pedagogy and the leadership of staff development may therefore be minimal.

Schools where learning is truly embedded in the culture insist that teaching and learning is a fundamental feature of every role. Schools where responsibility for learning is given to only one individual run the serious risk of lessening its importance and, above all, its impact.

The traditional distinction between pastoral and academic duties is a useful analogy. At the start of my career, there was a clear distinction between those responsible for the academic attainment of pupils (and it was attainment then – nobody discussed progress) and those who looked after discipline and support, with the emphasis firmly on discipline. Most schools had a curriculum deputy and a pastoral deputy. Year heads or house heads were responsible for keeping children in order, liaising with parents and social services and ensuring that their charges turned up on time in the appropriate uniform. As recently as the seventies or even the eighties, the idea that colleagues with pastoral responsibilities should be discussing academic progress would have been seen as quite bizarre.

Heads of year and heads of house nowadays are fully aware that their role in the development of the learner, which involves both intensive support and a relentless focus on academic progress. To assign only one part of this approach to a senior leader is therefore particularly illogical, particularly in schools where year heads and house heads play such pivotal roles in both the academic and the pastoral development of their pupils.

The head teacher in the classroom

If every member of the leadership team, and indeed every member of the school, should consider teaching and learning as at the very core of their duties, then this must be doubly true of the head teacher. Personally, I lament the decline of the title 'head teacher' because I strongly believe that's what the head of a school should be – a teacher first and foremost. John Tomsett, in his passionate account of headship, *This Much I Know about Love over Fear*, explains very clearly why all head teachers should actually teach:

- Teaching is *the thing* for all teachers, isn't it?
- A teaching head teacher has more authenticity in the eyes of her colleagues than a non-teaching head teacher
- It is pretty difficult to lead teachers' learning if you don't lead yourself
- What you learn when you teach as a head teacher enables you to help others improve their teaching
- When head teachers teach, we really are all in it together.[5]

And, as any experienced head knows, the classroom is a great place to escape when the day-to-day business of headship becomes overwhelming. It is also a place of calm and stability where the gradual nature of school improvement can most clearly be seen.

Most senior leaders would agree that the head teacher should teach, but, in practice, far too many allow themselves to be persuaded either that they haven't got the time to teach or, more perniciously, that they will be called away from the classroom far too often. In reality, heads get called away only if they allow it. Head teachers who commit themselves to the classroom make it clear that they are unavailable unless it's an absolute emergency. Ironically, this is far easier for heads to do in secondary schools where there are other senior staff to deputize for them, but it is probably true to say that the majority of secondary heads no longer teach. And how many executive heads teach? Has the age of acceleration driven too many head teachers out of the classroom into committee rooms?

The phrase 'the leadership of learning' is often used as a kind of misdirection. Instead of getting involved directly in classroom practice, some head teachers convince themselves that they are deeply involved in learning because they are directing others. This may work for a while, but a head teacher who leaves the classroom behind quickly loses touch. His or her teaching skills diminish, or in some cases atrophy, and the ability to lead effective staff development fades.

As Thomsett points out, a teaching head garners enormous credibility amongst the staff and is far more likely to be listened to in staff meetings and continuing professional development (CPD) sessions if he or she is able to draw directly on very recent classroom experience. Moreover, a head teacher who regularly sees teaching, who talks about learning in assemblies and who regularly visits other lessons to observe and learn sends a powerful message to pupils in the school. We are indeed all here to learn – even the head.

There is no more powerful symbol of a learning culture than a head teacher who teaches and gets actively involved in the development of pedagogy. A head teacher is also head learner, and his or her pupils need to see that. As John Dunford puts it,

> [i]n a learning community, it should be unthinkable that anyone might not put learning at the centre of their work, so it should be a priority for every member of the teaching and support staff to continue to be a learner, with senior leaders creating the climate for this and setting an example through their own learning.[6]

Behaviour for learning

A strong discipline policy is a key element of a quick-fix regime. Schools where behaviour has deteriorated to such an extent that teaching becomes almost impossible clearly need behaviour sorted out as soon as possible. However, once behaviour begins to improve, a discipline system which is too strict can begin to have a negative effect. The fundamental issue in schools where classroom discipline is poor is always poor teaching. Pupils are not daft; they know when they are not being taught properly, and they respond accordingly.

Media coverage of education delights in stories about poor behaviour, and it takes even greater delight in those schools where exceptionally strict rules are applied. Even the BBC, usually known for a sense of perspective, gleefully reported the rebellion of a group of parents against the new set of rules introduced by the Great Yarmouth Charter Academy.

Admittedly some of the rules did sound somewhat draconian:

> *Everyone will sit up extra straight, eyes front, looking at the teacher. You will follow their instructions first time, every time.*

It is the phrase, 'first time, every time' which is most disconcerting. Absolute obedience seems to be required before the teacher can begin. It overlooks the fact that the teacher's lesson should be sufficiently engaging for such a demand. I don't know anything about this particular school, so I cannot comment on the veracity of the BBC's report, but it serves as a useful example of what can happen when the key point is forgotten. Teachers should be respected, but if the lesson is well taught and engaging, that respect will follow naturally. It may be that in this particular school, discipline had broken down to such an extent that this kind of super-strict behaviour policy was essential in order to restore order, but it could only be a temporary fix. The only long-lasting solution to poor behaviour is good teaching. Schools where a strict behaviour policy has recently been introduced often have a brittle atmosphere as if something is about to snap.

There is an important subtext here, especially when leaders argue that strict discipline systems create ordered environments where pupils make progress and examination results improve. It could well be that results improve, but that doesn't necessarily mean learning improves. This sounds like something of a paradox: If the results improve surely pupils have learned more? This could be the case but a more subtle point is about the nature of the learning. Pupils can be hot-housed and schooled to pass exams; teaching pupils how to learn is a much harder task. The quick-fix approach may get the grades, but it is unlikely to inculcate a love of learning or equip students with the learning behaviours they will need in the sixth form, at university or, indeed, in later life.

Compliance without respect doesn't last long. A simple trick I teach trainee teachers makes the point. If they express concerns about behaviour when settling a class, I advise them to try the following: walk into the class, stand at the front, look at them and don't say anything. Don't be tempted to start talking as the noise levels drop; wait for complete silence. And then pause a few moments longer. Then, in a quiet voice, calmly begin. This works like magic, and more often than not, the trainees are amazed at the sudden power they seem to have gained. The key point here is that the starting point for the majority of pupils is respect for their teachers. A moment's assertion of authority is often enough to convince them that the respect is deserved, and the lesson can proceed.

However, that respect must be retained, and that can only be done by means of good teaching. Good teaching stimulates interest, keeps pupils on task and engages them in their learning. The trainee trick makes the point easily enough, but I then go on to explain that once you have gained respect the only way of sustaining it is by working with the class until respect is complemented by a genuine desire to learn. And like all aspects of school improvement, that takes time. Teachers get better at it as they learn more and, as they encounter more pupils, their reputation for good teaching spreads across the school. As more and more teachers improve their classroom skills, more and more pupils engage with their learning and a strong learning culture begins to take shape.

Open classrooms, open leadership

Encouraging high-quality teaching to spread across the school is key to developing a powerful learning culture. Most head teachers nowadays visit classrooms regularly and involve themselves in what used to be called 'management by wandering about.' Learning walks are immensely popular, although in many cases they are more like monitoring walks. Heads also insist that middle leaders observe members of their departments or year teams to make sure they are on track, and of course, classroom observation has become a key feature of performance management.

There is often a disparity between the theory of open classrooms and the practice. In many schools where open classrooms are said to exist, they are open only for monitoring visits, whether from senior leaders or middle managers. In how many are classrooms genuinely open so that teachers are not only free to visit other classrooms but positively encouraged to do so?

In schools where sharing pedagogical approaches to learning is given high priority, the focus on classroom observation is rarely simply about monitoring. It is about learning, sharing and celebrating. This is a key feature of the gradual improvement agenda because for this level of trust and openness to take hold across the school it takes time and a relentless commitment to making it happen. It cannot be imposed overnight.

The first step is to ensure that performance management and the monitoring of the quality of teaching is kept separate from sharing good practice. Admittedly, this is not easy to do. There are times when the quality of teaching needs to be the sole focus of the leadership team and inadequacies in this area must be dealt with urgently and boldly. In other words, the quality of teaching needs to be brought up to a certain standard across the school before a less threatening atmosphere can be developed. There is no getting away from the fact that weaknesses in teaching have to be dealt with and weak teachers either improved or, to put it bluntly, moved on. This does not necessarily result in the whole staff feeling threatened; indeed, most teachers agree that weaker staff reflect badly on the school and should not be in the classroom. In my experience, I have often found that taking on underachieving staff has had a positive effect and not the negative one I was expecting. Teachers don't like the idea that they are 'carrying' their colleagues, and the majority are aware of the simple fact that weak teachers let children down.

While weaknesses in teaching are being addressed, there is no reason not to celebrate and share excellent teaching. Addressing weak teaching should be a confidential matter, although in practice everyone in the school quickly becomes aware that something is going on, but as the quality of teaching in the school improves, staff are less likely to feel threatened by classroom visits.

There is no room for complacency, however. It is too easy to assume that the quality of teaching is good and therefore now needs only light-touch monitoring to ensure that it stays good. It will only stay good if it continues to develop. Teaching is never learnt; it demands continual improvement. So, how can we create genuinely open classrooms?

First, the head's door is always open – a phrase that usually refers to the office door. In this case, it should be the door of the classroom. Head teachers should encourage colleagues to come and visit their lessons, to comment on them and to advise them how they should improve. It is important for heads to show that they are open to improving their own teaching, admitting weaknesses and showing others that they are still developing their classroom skills. A head who is not threatened by colleagues' observations presents a powerful model to other staff. If I can criticize the head, then his or her criticisms of me are likely to be seen as constructive rather than punitive.

Second, keep all doors open if possible. Obviously, there are times when noise needs either to be shut out or contained but an open door is a sign of welcome. Teachers in departments which work well together are always wandering in and out of each other's rooms, and they often pick up on the good practice they catch a glimpse of as they walk through. Traditionally, this happens most often in creative areas like art or design where teachers move about looking for materials or extra space, but there is no reason why it shouldn't happen everywhere. This kind of interaction is positive and non-threatening, but it needs to be taken a step further if real development is to take place. Simply visiting each other's lessons, while useful, is not enough. Time must be put aside to ensure that lessons are observed for a purpose – to learn something. And once the lesson has been observed, this should lead not to feedback but to a discussion about the nature of the learning that took place and the effectiveness of the teaching techniques. This involves a great deal of trust, and trust takes time to develop, but once it is established, real learning can begin, longer discussions of pedagogy become possible, and the quality of the teaching and learning experience begins to improve much more quickly.

There are practical steps to be taken and teachers need to be given not only the encouragement to observe others but the time to do it. There is only so much sharing that can be done in non-teaching periods and, nowadays, teachers are usually so overwhelmed with planning, preparation and marking that they can rarely make time. The solution is to provide cover. This sounds expensive, but, in practice, it isn't, especially when compared to the costs of CPD generally. If heads put aside a proportion of the CPD budget for classroom observation, the learning gains are likely to be far stronger than spending the money sending colleagues on commercial courses. A good first step is to ask, or in some cases require, teachers to observe at least three lessons a year, two of which will be paid for from the staff development budget. Small-scale research projects are also very effective in encouraging this kind of interaction and these are discussed later in the book.

Once classroom visits become part of the pattern of everyday life for teachers they become less and less threatening and much more about sharing. In schools where teachers regularly watch each other teach, genuine pedagogical discussion becomes much more common. The real gauge of a school's commitment to teaching and learning is the nature of the discussions which take place in the staffroom. In genuinely outstanding schools, teachers talk about teaching all the time. They share their experiences; they lament their disasters and celebrate their successes while others join in not to criticize but to learn.

A shared enthusiasm for improving teaching is therefore at the heart of a good school's learning culture.

At the start of this chapter, I began by exploring the complexities of defining and then creating a powerful learning culture in a school but, ultimately and inevitably, it comes down to a genuine, wholehearted, undiluted focus on teaching and learning. In an age of acceleration, it is easy to lose sight of the destination, it is easy to lose concentration as distractions multiply, it is easy to forget the wider curriculum, it is tempting to see yourself as a system leader rather than a classroom teacher, the quick fix can seem like the line of least resistance and the politics of it all can at times be absolutely infuriating. And yet, whatever the complexities, there is really only one thing that really matters: learning. A head who teaches, who shares ideas, who encourages staff to share their teaching skills, who avoids distractions and who thinks more about the classroom than the system is well on the way to creating a genuine learning culture. It won't happen immediately, it takes time. But it will happen.

Key points

- Rapid change does not always result in long-term improvements.
- The current focus on system leadership is in danger of diverting attention away from the classroom.
- What works in one school does not necessarily work in another.
- School cultures are complex and hard to define, but effective cultures always have an intense focus on teaching and learning.
- Extra-curricular activities are a key part of a school's culture.
- Political concerns sometimes divert school leaders away from the more fundamental aspects of their roles.
- School leaders cannot be expected to respond to the relentless demands made of schools by politicians, the media and society in general.
- The head of teaching and learning role may not be as effective as it sounds; all leaders and, indeed, all teachers should see teaching and learning as their prime directives.
- Head teachers should always teach; they should be head teachers.
- Good behaviour is dependent on good teaching.
- Genuinely open classrooms facilitate pedagogical discussions and mutual support, both of which lead to long-term improvement.
- Genuine school improvement takes time.

> **Practical ideas**
>
> - Create a list of all the extra-curricular activities undertaken in your school, and then evaluate their impact on children's lives, on teaching and learning and on the curriculum. Are there any which could be seen as detrimental to learning either because they take too much time out of school or because they distract teachers from their teaching?
>
> - In a senior leadership meeting, consider the extent to which the STEM agenda and/or the EBacc impacts negatively or positively on the work of the school.
>
> - Look again at the roles and responsibilities of the senior leadership team. To what extent is an intense focus on teaching and learning built into every role?
>
> - Consider how open your classrooms really are. How often do colleagues watch each other's lessons outside of performance management and other monitoring visits? How much co-teaching takes place? How often are senior leaders observed teaching?

Notes

1 S. J. Ball. 2003. The Teacher's Soul and the Terrors of Performativity. *Journal of Education Policy*, 18:2, 215–228.
2 B. Levin. 1998. An Epidemic of Education Policy: (What) Can We Learn from Each Other? *Comparative Education*, 34:2, 131–141.
3 I. Stronach & B. Morris. 1994. Polemical Notes on Educational Evaluation in the Age of 'Policy Hysteria.' *Evaluation & Research in Education*, 8:1–2, 5–19.
4 R. Williams. 1981. *Keywords: A Vocabulary of Culture and Society*, London: Fourth Estate Ltd.
5 J. Thomsett. 2015. *This Much I Know About Love Over Fear*, Carmarthen: Crown House Publishing, p. 57.
6 J. Dunford. 2016. *The School Leadership Journey*, Woodbridge: John Catt Publishing, p. 121.

Leadership for learning

The myth of the hero head

The concept of the hero head is paradoxically both outdated and increasingly fashionable. When the idea first gained traction, it was used to describe the charismatic swashbuckler who strode fearlessly into failing schools and turned them round in a matter of months. They were masters of the quick fix described in Chapter 1, and they generally made discipline their mantra. They were incredibly ambitious, often for themselves rather than the schools they led. As a result, most tended to move on to other schools within a couple of years, and many moved out of the profession into more lucrative consultancy roles. Some gained considerable kudos by turning around a series of schools, using a combination of compelling magnetism and the quick-fix toolbox. And they became the darlings of politicians and the media. How many of their interventions led to lasting change is highly questionable, and there are dozens of examples where the departure of a charismatic head has led to a sudden sharp decline in standards.

The cult of the hero head quickly became closely aligned with football manager syndrome: if results were not obvious immediately, the head could be dismissed, and a new hero sought. The idea of gradual improvement over time was disregarded. As in sport or, indeed, business, results were expected straight away.

Fortunately, there have been so many accounts of disastrous hero heads that the world seems to have woken up to the idea that charisma and confidence may not be enough. The idea that the most important person in the school is the head still lingers, however. At a recent open day, a parent asked me directly, 'If a school is as good as its head, how long do you plan to stay here?' Parents have learned to regard the head as the key to a school's success, but, as we shall see, the reality is much more complicated than that, and the success of a school cannot be put down to the actions of one man or woman.

The hero head may have faded from view – although television programmes like *Educating Essex* have hung on to the idea – but the new executive head teacher role can, in many ways, be regarded as the same idea repackaged. Now the head does not have to be charismatic, only highly successful. As a successful head in one school, it is naturally assumed that he or she will be equally successful anywhere. So, it then becomes a 'moral imperative' for him or her to take control of other schools. The hero head has been replaced by the super executive who will lead a group of schools to success, and as this is essentially a business model, they can expect to be highly paid and highly regarded. Cynically, this could be described as a progression from charisma to cash. So much for the moral imperative.

The executive head teacher moves not only out of the classroom but, more often than not, out of the school as well. His or her role becomes absorbed into the management of the trust and it is the new business-like status which provides the approbation once craved by the hero head.

But is the head really that influential? The most effective head teachers realize that what influence they have may not last, and it is incumbent upon them to ensure that the school continues to improve after they have left. Mary Myatt, in *High Challenge, Low Threat*, addresses the issue of the 'hero leader' directly and astutely: 'There is a fundamental flaw with the idea of a hero leader and it is this: when they are gone, they are gone.'[1] She goes on to point out that sensible leaders 'regularly ask themselves, "If I wasn't here to do this work, what would happen? How would the organisation continue to thrive?"'

Succession planning is a key task of any leader, and acknowledging this makes the obvious point that schools cannot rely on one person. Others are important too. The logical next step is therefore to recognize that the leader's role may not be as important as he or she would like to think or as fundamental to the success of the school as much of the management training suggests. Certainly, anyone who has taken part in a National Professional Qualification for Headship course cannot fail to have come away with the idea that the visionary leader is the key driver of a school's success. In reality, it is a team of people who create success.

John Hattie's classic and comprehensive meta-analysis of research relating to achievement, *Visible Learning*, makes an interesting distinction between two major forms of leadership, instructional and transformational:

> Instructional leadership refers to those principals who have their major focus on creating a learning climate free of disruption, a system of clear teaching objectives, and high teacher expectations for teachers and students. Transformational leadership refers to those principals who engage with their teaching staff in ways that inspire them to new levels of energy, commitment and moral purpose. . .[2]

Unsurprisingly, accordingly to the meta-analysis, it is the former style which has the greater impact on student outcomes. It would be too simplistic to suggest that transformational leadership equates directly to the style of the charismatic head teacher or principal, but it is clear that the most effective means of school improvement will be led by an instructional leader who takes the time to put things in place to establish a sustainable climate for learning.

According to Hattie's impact scale, leaders may be disappointed to learn that they fall neatly into the low to medium category with a score of 0.36. The instructional leader has a higher score than the transformational leader but below the high impact scores for the quality of teaching (0.44), micro-teaching (0.88) and student–teacher relationships (0.72). The professional development of teachers scores highly (0.62), and it here that leaders can perhaps have the most impact. The point is obvious, however: leaders have an impact, but they are part of a complex web of influences which lead to a school's success. The most effective leaders acknowledge this and act accordingly; they don't see themselves as heroes but as collaborators.

Structural changes in the teaching profession are undoubtedly having an impact on the way leaders lead. Many executive leaders have left the classroom behind to concentrate on management and strategy. Both common sense and research suggest, however, that it is those who stay behind to concentrate on what goes on in the classroom who are likely to have the biggest impact on the achievement of the students in their care.

Leaders as teachers

In the previous chapter, I emphasized the importance of heads or principals as teachers. I would now like to develop this idea in order to explore the ways in which leaders who teach influence teaching across the school. We have seen how staff value teaching heads and the credibility it gives them when discussing pedagogy, but the influence of regular classroom experience impacts more powerfully on a leader's approach to his or her role than many appreciate.

First, there is the appreciation of the mechanics of classroom management. A head who does not, for example, wrestle with the latest registration software or attempt to input data into the various tracking systems used by the school rarely has an accurate understanding of just how frustrating it can be for staff who have to use these systems every day and in every lesson. A leader who doesn't have to engage with them can easily be convinced by the information and communications technology (ICT) manager, or whoever is responsible for setting the things up, that they work perfectly and that it's only the inadequacies of the staff that cause problems. In my own experience, I have frequently found myself pointing out that software systems simply do not work for busy teachers, even if on paper they offer glorious time-saving opportunities. Sharing the frustrations of day-to-day life with colleagues is vital if leaders are to gain a true understanding of how the school works.

Second, there is the question of empathy. A good example is the results analysis meeting conducted in all good schools nowadays. As a new head teacher, it took me a long time to ensure that when the time came to evaluate a class's results, teachers focused on the teaching rather than the failings of the pupils in their classes. The rigorous management approach to examination analysis suggests that you should look coldly at the data and then explore ways in which to ensure performance improves. If a class underperforms, it is down to the teaching. There is a lot of truth in this, and my line management meetings adopt this position as the starting point in every discussion about pupil progress. However, there are times when you must acknowledge that sometimes, no matter how good the teaching and how comprehensive the support, some pupils simply do not respond. A leader who does not have his or her own class in mind when involved in such discussions is less likely to empathize with excellent teachers who have failed to have an impact on one or two key pupils in their classes. I have often found myself asking challenging questions of the teachers in my school, fully aware that I have encountered exactly the same problems in my own teaching. I used to rationalize this by insisting to myself that I must focus on the quality of teaching in the school to drive up standards – and that's certainly true. However, a genuine understanding of the complex pedagogy of classroom management is essential if senior leaders are to develop a real understanding of how progress works in their schools.

Heads who simply cover the occasional lesson when a colleague is absent rarely get that vital sense of ownership fundamental to good teaching. The thought of a regular commitment to a Year 7 class may sound daunting to a head with a thousand things to do, but there are huge benefits. One of the most obvious is that you get to know 30 children in your school really well. You know their names, the way they work, something about their backgrounds and a lot about their progress. This gives you a deep and lasting insight into the culture of the school – and you can see the culture change as improvements you make take effect. Heads who stay put – those committed to gradual school improvement – add to their relationship store every year: by the fifth year, they will know 150 pupils really well.

Heads who teach also get the chance to see parents in a completely different light. It is sadly the case that the majority of parents with whom senior leaders spend time are the difficult ones, the ones who get to you after they have worked their way through class teachers, tutors, year heads and so on. One of the most dispiriting aspects of the job is the fact that most of the time you meet parents who are dissatisfied with some aspect of the school, and if you only meet those parents, you are in danger of paranoid thinking. Is this how parents really see the school? The vast majority of sane, well-balanced and supportive parents never come near you. If you have your own class, however, you meet them all, and you get to talk about teaching.

Regular contact with your own class means regular contact with the boundless enthusiasm of young people. One of the real pleasures of teaching is spending time with young people who are full of hope for the future and buzzing with energy. This kind of stimulus is available in very few other professions, and it offers senior leaders a regular means of recharging their batteries, reminding them what the job is all about.

The classroom is also the laboratory where you can try out new ideas. Heads who are genuinely interested in the practicalities of teaching and learning do this as a matter of course. A head who continues to work hard at becoming a first-rate classroom teacher is also a much better teacher of teachers. I am sure that many of you are familiar with senior leaders who have lost touch with the classroom long ago and lead staff meetings and training sessions in a manner which is decidedly dry. A lecture featuring a PowerPoint is hardly the way to inspire others. A good classroom practitioner is able to use his or her skills to lead highly effective training sessions, especially if the examples used are from his or her own classes. And, as we shall see, leading teaching through carefully thought out training is a key skill for leaders of highly effective schools.

Heads who work with a genuine spirit of enquiry not only enjoy visiting other classes to learn rather than to monitor; they are also keen to explore best practice in other schools. The notion of a head teacher as a lead explorer is a pleasing one. This can easily be arranged. Heads love showing people around their schools, and it is easy to contact colleagues to ask if you can arrange a visit and observe a few lessons. Personally, as a secondary head, I have found my visits to primary schools the most enlightening, and I have always brought back good ideas and new ways of thinking as a result. Heads are encouraged nowadays to work as part-time inspectors, and this, too, is an excellent way of getting into other schools and having a really good look at what is going on. The benefits to your own school are immeasurable. I don't think I have ever visited another school without bringing something back to use at home.

Working with the system

The difference between a classical musician and a jazz musician is a matter of precision. Classical musicians are taught to read music with incredible accuracy; they play with expression, but it is expression within strict boundaries. Jazz musicians have much greater freedom. Many of them nowadays are highly accomplished performers capable of playing at the very highest level in any genre, but when they are playing jazz, they delight in the freedom to depart from strict notation. A jazz musician can bend the notes, sustain them, shorten them; he or she can play the melody off the beat or on the beat or leave it behind entirely. And yet, the structure is always there: they follow the patterns of the songs which form the basis of their improvisations; they follow the chords underlying the melodies, and they sing the lyrics in their heads. This is how head teachers should work within the system.

New head teachers often feel constrained by the demands placed upon them by the dozens of authorities which govern their existence. They find themselves accountable not just to pupils, staff and parents but to a wide range of other bodies: the governors or the academy trust, the local authority, the Regional Schools Commissioner (RSC), the DfE, the English Funding Authority, the Health and Safety Executive, the Office for Standards in Education, Children's Services and Skills (Ofsted), the Food Standards Agency, social services and the local community, among others. With so many authorities each issuing regular demands for information, it is easy to allow this aspect of the job to dominate your day.

On top of this is the demand for policies. The DfE has lists of the policies which should be displayed on the school website, but most schools have dozens of others reflecting all aspects of school life. A head who embarks on a review of policies could spend a year doing it.

There are also daily emails which seem not to ask but demand instant replies, and, if you let them get to you, daily emails from parents asking questions which often take hours of your time to answer. On top of all this, as every school leader knows but rarely acknowledges in public, are the constant demands for information from governors (see Chapter 6).

Nor should we forget the tyranny of data. Some schools are awash with data and leaders feel duty bound to pore over it at every opportunity. Commercial software packages are now common in most schools, and they provide so much data that its pursuit can lead head teachers mad with despair. At the time, however, it feels like your duty to deal with it all, to stay on top of it and to ensure that your understanding is better than anyone else's on the staff – just in case.

There is simply too much to do and too much stuff to absorb. The trick, as always, is to recognize that you can't do it all. Much of it can be delegated, and although it sounds dreadfully unprofessional to say so, much of it can be quietly ignored. After a while, you learn what's important and what isn't: the surveys you are told must be completed can usually be avoided, the documents the DfE insists must be read are usually summarized and the fantastic commercial learning tools you are offered daily can simply be binned. Personally, I have always found emails from the Learning and Skills Council (LSC) particularly helpful as they were clearly labelled LSC; this meant I could quickly discard them safe in the knowledge that they probably wouldn't be relevant to me and, if they were, they were written in such suffocating jargon I probably wouldn't have understood them anyway.

Knowing what to spend time on and what to skip is a vital leadership skill, as is delegation. The heads who go under are those who try to do it all and doing it all is impossible. We can all understand why this happens: they feel responsible, they feel the heavy burden of duty pressing on them all the time, they feel guilty that they are paid more than their colleagues and they feel personally accountable for everything that goes on in the school. Some, however, and this reminds us of the hero head model, attempt to do everything because of a misguided belief that they are the only ones who can do things properly.

Delegation is essential for every school leader not only for their own sanity but also in order to develop other staff. The most effective school leaders recognize the fact that there will be lots of people in their school who are much better at certain tasks than they are. The trick is to find them – and this can take time. This is another feature of the gradual art of school improvement: it takes time to get to know your colleagues and to understand their strengths and weaknesses. When you know your colleagues well, you can begin to think about what they might be really good at and allocate duties accordingly. Sometimes, you'll get it wrong, but if you know them well you are far more likely to get it right than if you make instant decisions based on hastily put together job descriptions and a day-long interview.

Perfection is simply not possible. The most effective school leaders are skilled in the art of letting things go. I once knew a head teacher who had three trays on his desk labelled 'today,' 'tomorrow' and 'too difficult.' He argued – fairly convincingly, I might add – that most of the things in the 'too difficult' tray disappeared if left there long enough. While I wouldn't necessarily advocate this approach to a new head teacher, the point is obvious. For leaders to be truly effective, they need to cut themselves some slack. They need to work out what is important and deal with it. They also need not be afraid of letting things go. This isn't a failing or a dereliction of duty; it is an assertion of character and confidence – and it can be done with style. It is a skill beautifully summed up by the great Australian poet, Les Murray, in his poem 'The Quality of Sprawl.' Sprawl is all about having the confidence to do things which are not necessarily the obvious things to do. It involves never worrying about your image and never being ostentatious. It includes imagination and flair but not self-aggrandizement or favour seeking. In essence, it sums up the relaxed confidence of a genuine leader.

All school leaders should learn the quality of sprawl, and they should never be afraid to depart from strict notation.

Innovation

The pace of change in society means that innovation is always essential. It is fundamental to the development of a good school. Schools that don't change sink into the mire. Doing it as we've always done it is dangerous, and the idea that once the school is working well it is time to slacken off can lead only to a decline in standards. Complacency is the key feature of schools which require improvement.

However, innovation for the sake of it is equally damaging. Changes need to be considered carefully and the implications of those changes thoroughly discussed. Successful innovation is a slow process; making things new takes time.

Schools leaders are often seduced by the glamour of innovation, and this can lead them into serious difficulties. There are too many examples of innovation for the sake of innovation which have proved disastrous in schools. We are all probably familiar with some of the experiments that used to appear regularly in the journals of the Specialist Schools and Academies Trust: Year 7 curriculums based on primary models, with one teacher for most of the day; learning passports, with pupils choosing what to study and when; topic-based programmes involving extended cross-curricular projects; entire programmes of study taught in a foreign language; and skills-based curriculums involving intensive vocational work and very little academic study; among others. There were, of course, some highly innovative and very successful curriculum plans, the best of which tended to focus on literacy and/or numeracy, but these were outweighed by those which were supported enthusiastically for a time and then hastily withdrawn when the positive impact planned tended, in reality, to be largely illusory.

The current culture of rapid change has, to some extent, curtailed the vogue for radical experimentation as schools struggle to cope with new performance measures, new Key Stage 2 assessment tests, new General Certificates of Second Education (GCSEs) and new A-Levels, but it is also worth remembering that the Free School movement is predicated on the notion of new ideas and different ways of working.

The key point to make about innovation is that is must be thoroughly thought through and very carefully planned. It also takes time: time to get right, time to embed and time to evaluate.

The rise of multi-academy trusts has introduced a new form of experimentation: imposed innovation. I once attended a briefing led by Anders Hultins, co-founder of the chain of 30 Kunskapsskolan schools, who, at the time, had just joined the Pearson school improvement team. He was advocating a complete school improvement package for schools which was to include a curriculum plan, policies, staffing structures, development planning systems and all the software and hardware necessary to implement it successfully. On the face of it, for struggling schools, this sounds like an excellent idea: a prepackaged system which can be imposed within a few days, which has been proved to work elsewhere and which allows teachers to get on with their teaching. However, such an extreme level of imposed organization, which totally ignores the complexity of each individual school's culture and context, is doomed to failure. Innovation must come from within and be tailored to the individual needs of each particular school. It cannot be imposed.

Multi-academy trusts have, almost inevitably, begun to create school development packages which they impose on the schools that join them. A successful school will be keen to share its success with a less successful school, and it is therefore tempting to impose its own structures and values based on the principle that what works here must work there. In some cases, it does; in many it is destabilizing and self-defeating. For a good or outstanding school to reach out to another local school, offering advice, guidance and support, as well as sharing both teaching and leadership expertise, the multi-academy model can be very effective, especially if the leadership team of the lead school is sensitive to the needs and context of the school it is helping to improve. Once the numbers increase, however, this kind of support becomes more and more difficult.

RSCs are very keen for successful trusts to take on more schools and this stretches the leadership team of the lead school to the limit. The solution, therefore, lies in a uniform approach. The larger trusts now impose their own particular way of working on the schools they adopt, and although these systems may not be as detailed as those advocated by Anders Hultan, they nevertheless tend toward homogeneity and, to some extent, blandness. In some contexts, these systems are effective, but that strikes me as more a matter of chance than design; in others they stultify and anaesthetize, a process which often leads to falling standards and widespread disaffection.

It can be argued, of course, that the government already imposes a fairly extreme level of uniformity on schools thanks to the national curriculum, progress measures, the inspection framework and the examination system. Certainly, in an international context, the UK is often identified as one of the countries where the government interferes most strongly in the day-to-day running of its schools. However, there is still room for innovation, albeit with constraints, and great opportunities for head teachers with a real sense of pedagogical vision to shape the curriculum to meet the needs of the pupils in their schools. It is ironic, however, that some of the most regressive, least innovative curriculums are seen in the Free Schools set up to allow greater freedom.

Despite the constraints, the ability to innovate is one of the most attractive and inspiring activities leaders can undertake. It is vital for an effective leader to keep looking ahead, to keep adapting the curriculum to meet the needs of pupils and to keep improving the quality of teaching and learning as society changes at an ever-increasing pace. It is also vital for personal job satisfaction as it is both intellectually stimulating, and a great way to avoid complacency and boredom. It must, however, be driven by a genuine need to improve the quality of teaching and learning, and never by motives of self-aggrandizement or self-promotion.

The steps which enable successful innovation are simple:

1 Establish the need for change.

2 Explore as wide a range of alternatives as possible.

3 Consider the consequences of each proposal thoroughly.

4 Cost it. I hate to include this, especially if you know you are on to a good thing, but it has to be done.

5 Consult as widely as possible: staff, parents and, above all, the pupils who will be affected.

6 Plan its implementation thoroughly, always thinking of the pitfalls.

7 Implement.

8 Evaluate it early on. Don't wait until the end of the year, do it straight away. Within the first few weeks look at how its working, what needs to be tweaked and what needs to be ditched.

9 Change things if necessary.

10 Fully evaluate at the end of the year and then revise, replan or, if necessary, abandon it completely. There is no shame in recognizing that some good ideas simply don't work.

Innovation also sends a powerful message to everyone in the school. It says that this is a school that is moving ahead, that this is a school that keeps up, that understands the zeitgeist, that puts the needs of pupils first and that never rests on its laurels.

Two examples

Here are two examples from my own experience which serve to illustrate the power and importance of innovation to the leadership of learning.

The first focused on reading. As an English teacher, I have long been concerned about the great primary/secondary reading divide. Once children move up to secondary school, and this is the case with boys in particular, far too many of them stop reading. They read only what they need to read for homework and the only fiction they encounter is in their English lessons. Those who do read tend to read the same kind of things they have always read – and sometimes that means Harry Potter, over and over again, or ghastly teen fiction where the main characters are horses. There is also the problem that, in too many schools, the books that feature in class at Key Stage 3 are often years out of date and simply not challenging enough for those who enjoy reading.

English teachers bear some of the responsibility for this. It is a bugbear of mine that so few English teachers read children's literature, preferring to stick to a drag through *Goodnight Mr Tom* for the umpteenth time. This is particularly disappointing given the quality of writing for children today.

I set out, therefore, to address a series of genuine needs: to ensure that children keep reading when they move up to secondary school and to ensure that boys, in particular, are encouraged to read, that pupils are presented with the most up to date and exciting books and that all pupils are challenged. I was also conscious of a more pressing need: far too many Year 7 pupils start secondary schools with levels of literacy which do not allow them to access the rest of the curriculum. The need for innovation was therefore obvious.

Most schools attempt to address this problem through their English departments or via a whole-school approach to literacy. I wanted to take a more radical approach. The solution I began to explore involved the creation of a whole new subject. Initially it was called Literacy to link up with the primary curriculum, but in the end, it simply changed to Reading because that what it's all about. Reading was to be an additional subject – additional to English and not necessarily taught by English teachers.

The starting point was therefore six periods a fortnight of English and four additional periods of Reading. Then came the really interesting part: the schemes of work. This proved to be quite straightforward. The weakest readers needed intensive support, and this was to be achieved by small classes where the pupils simply read, supported by a teacher, a teaching assistant and sixth-form volunteers. The next decision was to create a pair of top sets, either side of the timetable, where pupils would read some of the most demanding books around. Here I envisaged a combination of classic texts – why on earth shouldn't Year 7 pupils read *Great Expectations*? – and those which were bang up to date. Pupils prize the latest things: they watch the latest films, play the latest computer games and listen to the latest music. They should also read the latest books. The sets between the top and the bottom were to be equally challenged but with a greater emphasis on the latest books and less emphasis on demanding classic literature.

As in Robert Frost's 'The Road not Taken,' where 'way leads on to way,' curriculum change leads to curriculum change. In order to accommodate four extra periods of Reading, adjustments had to be made elsewhere, and it was at this point that the real challenges of innovation were encountered. The creation of Reading as a separate subject more than fulfilled the original aims of the change, but great care was needed to avoid making changes in other areas simply to make things fit. It was therefore necessary at this point to stand back and consider what other pupil needs were evident in the existing curriculum structure.

The first step was to consult staff – not only to sell the Reading idea but also to get them to think about other ways of improving the Year 7 curriculum. This was a demanding leadership exercise in itself because subject teachers are always anxious to protect their own subjects. To get them to think more broadly was challenging to say the least. We began, therefore, by exploring the weaknesses in the Key Stage 2 curriculum. This led to strong calls for numeracy to become a separate subject like Reading, but in the end, it was very difficult to disentangle numeracy from Maths, and ultimately, it had to be acknowledged that only Reading was key to all other subjects. Once this was out of the way – although, to be honest, it has never really quite gone away – we looked at the humanities and science. It quickly became clear that we had a strong and effective science curriculum, but our humanities curriculum bore no relationship to the sparse offering of our feeder primary schools.

We therefore decided to take a good look at needs in this area. We wanted to ensure a smooth transition from Key Stage 2 to 3, but above all, we wanted to give students a rich experience of all aspects of the humanities. If we could link it to the Reading programme, even better. The solution, after a great deal of discussion, was to create another new subject called People and Places, which covered all three humanities (History, Geography and Religious Education) but tied in tightly to the Reading curriculum, thus creating genuine cross-curricular opportunities. For example, pupils might be reading Eva Ibbotsen's *Journey to the River Sea* at the same time they are studying rivers.

This gave us some of the time we needed on the timetable to introduce Reading but more was required – and more innovative thinking was required. This time we looked at physical education (PE). We were not only conscious of the need to ensure that pupils got enough exercise but also aware that, for many, the traditional games and PE programmes were not suitable. The need, therefore, was to come up with a plan which would encourage even the most reluctant child to see the value of physical exercise. The breakthrough came when we started to think not about games but about healthy lifestyles. We were then able to look at Food Technology, a subject which often sits within the Design Department. We quickly recognized that its links with PE were much stronger than those with Design. A new subject quickly emerged: Food and Fitness. This gave us the final period we needed to introduce Reading and, at the same time, allowed us to revolutionize our approach to physical well-being.

At every step of the way, genuine need led us and at no point did we seek to change things just for the sake of it or simply to make things fit. The result was a highly innovative curriculum that seemed to fulfil the needs of our pupils much more precisely than the existing one.

The next stage was planning – and we spent almost a year planning its introduction. This involved intensive professional development for staff but, above all, planning time so that well-thought-out and imaginative schemes of work were put in place. We, of course, had to create a substantial budget for new books and resources, but this turned out to be money well spent. Money spent on books and staff time is rarely wasted.

The new curriculum was duly introduced and monitored very carefully – in the first few weeks, every month and at the end of the year. We even paid the University of Exeter to come into school and evaluate the programme from a completely objective standpoint. Again, an expense but a necessary one to ensure that we were genuinely fulfilling the aims of the original innovative plan. Changes were made as we went along, but the overall structure proved to be remarkably sound. Nearly a decade later, the school still follows a modified version of the Reading curriculum, so effective is it in meeting the needs of its pupils.

The second example is less comprehensive in its impact but equally compelling as an exercise in innovation. This time, we were concerned that the Year 9 syllabuses and timetable structures were not fulfilling pupil needs. This is a debate continually being rehearsed in schools across the country but usually from the standpoint of a choice between a standard three-year Key Stage 3 curriculum or a truncated two-year one. When we looked at what pupils were doing in class some obvious findings emerged: by Year 9, pupils were getting bored with the same old subjects and needed a change, far too many subjects were drifting along as if they were waiting for the serious business of GCSE study to begin, too many classes lack challenge and too many pupils were becoming disaffected. We looked in detail at three-year GCSE courses, but ultimately, we felt that pupils were not really mature enough for examination classes, and we didn't want to push them on to the examination treadmill too soon. An innovative solution was required.

Once again, the needs of the pupils led the way: we wanted to create a curriculum that would engage and inspire them, we wanted to prepare them for Key Stage 4 without necessarily starting GCSE courses and we wanted to really challenge them. The solution was arrived at after hours of discussion, lots of visits to other schools and detailed discussions with pupils.

In the end we created a series of Year 9 pathways. The core subjects remained as they were, but in addition, we created a simplified option system which allowed pupils to choose one of seven pathways. Each pathway has three subjects, and each is designed to appeal to a particular type of pupil. There are pathways for academic high fliers, pathways for creative types, pathways for those of a practical inclination and so on. It was the element of choice which proved to be most powerful as not only could pupils choose which set of subjects they would most likely enjoy but they could also drop some of the subjects they liked least. So, for example, drama could be dropped in favour of another less active subject. We also introduced new subjects into Year 9 – business studies, media studies, Spanish from scratch and so on – and these proved very popular for pupils wanting a change.

The key difference between the Year 9 Pathways programme and the more common three-year Key Stage 4 was that the Year 9 choices weren't final. At the end of Year 9, pupils could opt again for new subjects at GCSE and start afresh. The only subject where this wasn't possible was Spanish, for obvious reasons.

As with the Reading curriculum, innovation was driven by the needs of the pupils. It was discussed at length and well planned – and, of course, evaluated fully. This, too, survives in the school to this day. Its impact was, in fact, quite remarkable. By offering a simple element of choice, pupils felt that they had control of their learning, attitudes to learning improved dramatically and attainment rose because option choices which proved to be inappropriate were rethought at the start of Year 10. The best example of this is Business Studies: this is a subject that always has great appeal as a GCSE choice. It has the glamour of big business, of future earnings, and *The Apprentice*. In reality, for many pupils, it turns out to be very dull indeed. Those who genuinely enjoy the subject continue to GCSE; others get it out of their system in Year 9 and make better choices in Year 10.

Effective and long-lasting innovation demands sophisticated leadership skills, but above all, it requires an intensive focus on the purpose of innovation – the development of learning. It is also a slow process. The very word innovation seems to demand swift action whereas, in reality, genuine innovation may take years.

The leadership team

The hero head rarely values his or her team; effective heads rely on their teams. Truly effective heads create teams capable of running and improving the school long after they are gone. They also ensure that all members of the leadership team put teaching and learning first, and they encourage them to work in and around the system. They are key collaborators and the engines of change when innovation is required. Getting the team right is one of the most fundamental aspects of strong leadership and a real skill in itself.

The dubious nature of the head of teaching and learning role has already been explored in Chapter 1, where the point was made that all leaders should take responsibility for teaching and learning. What does this mean, therefore, in terms of leadership team roles?

The first point to make is the importance of delegation. Strong leadership does not mean that you have to hang on to everything. Micromanagement is rarely effective, and head teachers who attempt to control every aspect of the school inevitably sink under the weight of responsibility. The key, as always, is trust. You must have confidence in your staff, and they must feel empowered to take ownership of their duties without feeling the need constantly to check back in to seek reassurance. This level of trust is built up over time – another important plank in the art of gradual school improvement – but it starts with the appointment process discussed later. Trusted staff get on with things, make decisions and innovate; they also tend to work much harder on behalf of the school because they feel that their contribution is not only important but valued.

The second point is the obvious one: all senior leaders should have responsibilities directly related to teaching and learning. They will, of course, have their fair share of administrative duties and oversight of the nuts and bolts of day management, but they should all be in no doubt about their key responsibilities with regard to learning. To support this, leadership team meetings have to be carefully thought out. If agendas become dominated by administrative activities, the obvious solution is to schedule a separate meeting which focuses solely on teaching and learning. In my own school, the Wednesday morning meeting deals with administration and management, and the agenda always looks something like this:

1 Matters arising

2 Staff development

3 Weekly/day-to-day items

4 Health and safety

5 Trips and visits

6 Assemblies

7 Items and requests from staff

8 Thursday's discussion

9 Any other business (AOB)

The most important meeting, however, is the Thursday meeting which has no agenda and covers one topic only each week. The only rule is that this is a discussion about learning, and it is here where the real work of the school gets done.

Senior leaders are then encouraged to ensure that the primacy of learning is evident in every meeting they conduct so that middle managers and classroom teachers are in no doubt about what the school is all about. Line management meetings, therefore, must also focus on teaching and learning. Time constraints mean that the two-meeting approach of the leadership team cannot be replicated at middle management level, but it is important nevertheless to ensure that the bulk of the meeting focuses on what goes on in the classroom. To achieve this, a common agenda is useful (see the Line Management meeting template in the Appendix). A series of simple headings help ensure that pupils are always at the heart of the discussion:

1 Progress and standards

2 Intervention – vulnerable and disadvantaged pupils

3 CPD/developing teaching and learning

4 Curriculum/assessment developments

5 Day-to-day management

6 AOB

Leadership teams, of course, require specific roles but these too should focus on teaching and learning. The most common pattern has individuals responsible for the oversight of a Key Stage (Key Stage 3 or Key Stage 4 in secondary schools), the sixth form, disadvantaged pupils and inclusion. In some, a colleague takes responsibility for transition; in others, there is more of a focus on classroom-based student welfare. It is important to remember, however, that these roles are by no means discrete: one member of the leadership team may have oversight, but he or she is the responsibility of everyone on the team.

The piece of advice I find myself offering most often when I visit other schools is 'You need to get out more,' and this is particularly relevant to members of the leadership team who often only venture out to go on 'leadership courses.' Senior leaders should be 'outwards facing,' making sure that they regularly visit other schools to share ideas and observe good practice. Observing classes in other schools is undoubtedly the most powerful form of CPD available: not only do you always come back with an idea to try out in your own school; you also get to spend time free from the pressures of day-to-day management simply focusing on classroom practice. And the perceived standing of the school in the local league tables is irrelevant: schools in challenging circumstances often have some of the best teaching, the most innovative ideas and the most interesting examples of classroom pedagogy.

Senior colleagues should also be encouraged to continue to improve their own subject teaching. It goes without saying that I am a strong advocate of senior leaders as teachers, and I think, where possible, they should all have a substantial teaching commitment, including examination classes at all levels. They should play a significant role in their departments in school, and their CPD should still retain an element of subject enhancement. Too many senior leaders think that now they have been promoted to the leadership team, they can say farewell to subject-based training courses. This is daft: the best senior leaders are subject experts as well as expert classroom practitioners. They attend subject network meetings and are always keen to get involved in pedagogy-based research projects. One of the most effective means of doing this, Trios or Triads, is explored in a later chapter.

A collaborative approach to teaching and learning ensures that the leadership team operates as a team. In too many schools, duties and responsibilities become separated out and the sense of teamwork is diminished. Regular discussions based solely on teaching and learning help draw the team together to give a real sense of purpose and direction.

The whole team

So far, we have looked at the roles of those members of the senior leadership who teach but what about the finance manager or the administration manager. Virtually every leadership team nowadays includes at least one member of the non-teaching staff, so how can we ensure that they are integral to the teaching and learning agenda?

The finance manager occupies a unique position in a school. He or she is undoubtedly one of the most important members of staff but often one of the most isolated. In too many schools, the finance team is hidden away in administrative offices, separated from the main school where very few teachers and pupils ever venture. A quick survey of staff would reveal that finance managers are there to deal with the budget, look after the accounts, tell the head teacher it can't be afforded, obsess about health and safety and answer the occasional question about payslips.

In the best schools where all staff are regarded as key to the development of teaching and learning, care is taken to ensure that finance managers become involved in as many aspects of the day-to-day functions of the schools as possible. This means direct involvement with pupils and teachers in relation not only to basic administrative activities but also to what goes on in the classroom. The purpose of a school is after all education not administration, and it makes sense for one of the most significant roles in the school to be shaped with this fundamental principle in mind.

But how is this to be achieved? Finance managers already have a great deal of knowledge about what goes on in a school thanks to their understanding of the school itself, staff salaries, building issues, catering, cleaning and so on. The trick is to bring this knowledge to bear on what goes on in the classroom and to ensure that opportunities are created which enable administrative staff to work with pupils and teachers, to get into classrooms and to take part in discussions about teaching and learning.

Finance managers are not teachers so how can they become involved more directly in the essential business of a school, teaching and learning? There are some simple steps and some that are perhaps a bit more radical.

First, it is common practice for finance managers to attend the leadership team's business meetings. They should, of course, be encouraged to attend all meetings and especially those where the discussion is to focus solely on matters of pedagogy. Only then will he or she begin to appreciate the real concerns of school leaders. The budget is important, management of the buildings is important, but nothing is as important to the leadership team as the development of learning. It is vital that finance managers discuss not only the costing of a proposed programme of study but its impact and effect as well. This is particularly relevant when it comes to the consideration of CPD. This is often a cost heading with a significant expenditure attached; it is therefore vital for the finance manager to understand not just a basic outline of the proposed training but its purpose and value. And the value can only be measured by evaluating its impact in the classroom.

Finance managers should also be encouraged to play a more visible role around the school and be seen as part of the teaching team, even though they are not teachers themselves. Simple things help: administrative staff should be part of the 'tuck your shirt in, don't run in the corridors' chorus; they should eat in the dining hall, take their breaks in the staffroom and be part of the duty rota overseeing pupils in the playgrounds or dining halls. Greater visibility means greater participation in the school and not just its administration.

Visits to classrooms to check on maintenance issues are often left until late in the day when the children have gone home, but classrooms should not be sacrosanct during the day. A finance manager who is seen out and about in classrooms is regarded as part of the furniture by pupils, just as teachers are. More important, such visits allow managers to get a real understanding of what it's like when lessons are taking place or what it's like to be surrounded by children. Just being aware of what is going on will have an impact on decisions made in the finance office. In some places, administrative staff take prospective parents and pupils on tours around the school. This isn't done simply to save the head some time; it is done to show that the school is a community where everyone is focused on learning. Leading a tour is a great way to get to know what goes on in a school because in order to explain it you have to understand it. The best way to learn something is, of course, to teach it. Answering parents' questions encourages a thorough understanding of all aspects of the school's culture, ethos and classroom practices.

It should not be forgotten that administrators have skills which are likely to be valuable to teachers across the school. There is no reason why finance managers should not occasionally help out in maths lessons, or in business studies, for example. They could also take part in Careers activities, bearing in mind that, most of the time, pupils have contact only with people who have experience of one career – teaching.

A more radical way of involving administrative staff in the classroom is the co-tutor role. Most schools operate a tutor group system, and each tutor group is led and managed by a teacher. In some schools, teaching assistants take on this role. However, a really good way of ensuring that administrative staff break out of their offices and interact with children on a daily basis is to appoint them as co-tutors. Working alongside the teacher, they can really help during tutor time. They get to know the class, and they take part in the learning. In some schools, co-tutors can work with small groups of children during tutor time to help them with their reading or their homework; sometimes a one-to-one chat helps with anxiety or other health issues.

Such a system need not be expensive. For example, it can be done on a voluntary basis. Not surprisingly, lots of staff welcome the chance to get out into the classroom, if only for 20 minutes a day, and appreciate the new visibility it gives. They also enjoy the fact that it makes them feel much more a part of the school. In most secondary schools, there will be sufficient volunteers to create co-tutors in most, if not all Key Stage 3 classes.

It is simple tweaks like those described earlier that draw finance managers into the real work of the school, allowing them to develop a much great understanding of what schools are really all about. They then feel part of a learning community and not just back office functionaries.

A finance manager who is involved in the day-to-day business of the classroom is a much more valuable member of the senior leadership team than one who focuses solely on business administration. With this kind of colleague in place, the leadership team focus on teaching and learning, so often diluted during the management discussions which often dominated school leadership team (SLT) agendas, is not only sustained but also strengthened. With a senior administrator fully cognizant of the importance of teaching and learning, and a key part of all the discussions which help to shape it in the school, the improvement agenda is much more likely to be shared by everyone, not just the teaching staff. As a result, it will be much more powerful and is likely to result in a genuine learning community, a condition so many schools aspire to but far too few achieve in practice.

Appointing leaders

A head teacher's ability to appoint his or her own leadership team is one of the key privileges of the role and one of the most important. More often than not, when you take over as the head, you inherit a leadership team which you then have to mould to your vision and adapt to your perceptions of the needs of the school. This can be incredibly difficult: deputies who have been in post for decades see no reason to change and often resent the bright ideas of the newcomer. This can be especially fraught if the deputy applied for the post of head teacher and didn't get it. Over time, however, opportunities will arise which allow you to develop the team. Once again, this is a gradual process.

Dealing with colleagues who are set in their ways can be difficult but there are ways to make sure that they are working with you, not against you. Before explaining how you think it should be done, it is important to listen to how they have been doing it. Don't forget that they know the school far better than you, and even if they have some attitudes which make your teeth itch, they will nevertheless have a huge bank of knowledge on which you can draw. Once you understand where they are coming from, you are in a position to explain your thoughts about the school. With their views in mind, you will be able to present your ideas in ways which they can accommodate, and you are much more likely to be sensitive to their work patterns and opinions. If they think you are on their side, and if they think your ideas are not really new but simply an extension of their own thinking, then you will be able to move ahead much more quickly. A head teacher who arrives in a school and starts laying down the law is much more likely to meet sustained resistance.

A useful way forward often involves a review of existing responsibilities. More often than not, for example, you will find excellent people in the wrong jobs. In my school for example, I inherited a team of colleagues who had worked together for years. I spent time getting to know them, exploring their strengths and weaknesses and really thinking about what the school needed to move forward. It dawned on me one day, however, that the person leading the sixth form was in the wrong job. I therefore moved her to take charge of inclusion and asked another member of the team to lead the sixth form. The result was quite remarkable. Both colleagues relished the opportunity of a change, after fairly static senior leadership team careers, and both rose quickly to the challenge. It was the right move, but it was done with care and considerable thought, an instant change which took time to enact.

Sometimes, of course, there will be senior leaders who do not wish to change, and these leaders have to be dealt with. If you can't persuade them to join the team, then you will have no option but to move them on or sideline them. The work of the school is too important to be held up by one individual, and although it may strike you as kinder to let them carry on as before, in the end you will be letting your pupils down. It is when dealing with issues such as this that heads really earn their money.

As you spend more time in school, you will have more opportunities to appoint new members of the team, and this must be done with great care.

First, you need to make it clear to staff that time-serving does not secure a leadership position. You will encounter colleagues who see themselves as next in line for promotion and the obvious candidate for the job. You also need to explain that the right person for the job may be someone in the school much younger than they might expect or, more to the point, not even in the school at all. Some posts lend themselves to internal promotions but for many an external appointment is essential. Good human resources (HR) practice insists that all posts should be externally advertised but internal appointments are sometimes much more appropriate, and the HR spanner can usually be disentangled from the works if you can offer a good enough reason to appoint internally.

I am personally a great advocate of internal appointments if a suitable candidate is available. The adage "never advertise until you know who you are going to appoint" may be totally unprofessional, but it is often the most effective way of securing the best appointment. Certainly, someone who has spent time in a school where learning is at the heart of things will fit into the leadership agenda much more successfully.

The appointment process itself is both challenging and fascinating. It starts, of course, with the advertisement and the job description. It is very tempting to rattle off a standard template and see who applies, but, if you want to attract the best candidates, a great deal of thought needs to go into the details you send out to prospective applicants. There you can make it clear that what you are looking for is someone who is fascinated by teaching and learning, an expert teacher and a real team player. The exact duties of the role do not have to be specified at this level, unless it is for a very particular role like head of sixth, as these will need to be shaped to the colleague you eventually appoint.

The application itself is also important, and it is good practice to specify how you would like candidates to apply. A simple task such as 'Outline the ways in which you would improve teaching and learning in the school' tells you much more than a letter of self-promotion. This kind of task is an excellent discriminator: applicants who apply for job after job will have a set reply which they will lever into place. It will be full of platitudes and say all the right things about self-improving schools and system leadership. A candidate who has really thought about the job will have done the research: he or she will demonstrate an excellent knowledge of the school (not any school, this particular school), will have analysed the results to identify areas of weakness, will have looked in detail at the website and will therefore offer an application that genuinely seeks to address the question you have asked. These are the people to interview.

If you have enough applications, this is a great time to air your prejudices. Most heads will throw out applications which feature spelling errors – and they are right to do so: an applicant who cannot be bothered to check his or application thoroughly is not going to cut the mustard at the senior leadership level. I like to discard those whose moral outlook strikes me as deeply unsound – folk singers, for example. This may sound dreadful – and I am sure it amounts to unlawful discrimination – but you will have to work with these people on a day-to-day basis, and if you can't bear the thought of planning curriculum change with someone likely to burst into a rousing rendition of his or her favourite sea shanty, you shouldn't interview the person.

The interviews themselves are the real testing ground. They should be much more than a friendly chat, and the level of challenge must be high. These are people who will be expected to lead at the highest level: they will need to be smart, resilient and completely committed. They also need to be in tune with your thinking and able to feel comfortable with the plans, aspirations and drive not only of the senior leadership team but of the whole staff as well. In other words, are they the right fit for the school?

For a senior leadership position, I like to stretch and challenge the candidates as much as possible but it also important to allow time to really get to know them.

You will get a feel for who they are from their references and from their appearance and demeanour as soon as they walk through the door. What you really need to test are their attitude, their skills and their ability to think like the rest of the team.

A typical interview day might look like this:

- 8.30 The candidates arrive and are met by the senior team. The head briefs them on the school and the nature of the role.

- 9.00 A tour of the school, led by pupils

- 9.45 Preparation time (during which the pupils on the tour offer feedback on the candidates)

- 10.0 Candidates teach a whole lesson observed by two senior colleagues.

- 11.00 Break – in the staffroom

- 11.30 Candidates discuss their lesson with a senior leader.

- 12.0 A series of tasks – a sophisticated in-tray exercise to test their ability to prioritize, synthesize and, above all, their skill at writing. One element of the task will be an angry letter from a parent, whose complaint is justified, demanding a response.

- 12.30 The candidate is informed that the parent who wrote the angry letter has turned up at reception demanding to see a senior leader and you will have to see them now. The role of the parent can be played by a parent or a suitably outgoing member of the staff (we were lucky enough to be able to draw on the services of a professional actor).

- 1.00 Lunch

- 2.00 A meeting with the school council or a group of pupils from all years. Pupils use their own questions, with some basic guidance, and the meeting is observed by a governor.

- 3.00 Formal interviews with the head, a deputy and a governor

The timings will need to be re-arranged, and for deputy appointments this process might spread over two days, but the level of demand and the nature of the activities is clear. At every stage feedback is gathered – from pupils, from staff and from governors. The lesson is the most important activity because it is always a mistake to employ a weak teacher, even if as a senior leader he or she will be doing less teaching than main-scale teachers. A senior leader should be an excellent teacher, ready to lead others towards excellence. I never have any qualms about sending candidates home at this stage: if their teaching is not up to snuff, there is no point in going any further with them. Some heads argue that it is important to allow them to continue as it is excellent CPD for them and that we should be gracious enough to allow them the full experience to help them further their careers. My view is that it is unfair to waste their time if you have no intention of appointing them – and a weak teacher should not be appointed.

The acting scenario may sound like an unnecessary charade, but it is an excellent test of a candidate's ability to cope with demanding situations – something which is inevitably a key part of any senior leader's role – and it is often the part of the day which candidates find most enjoyable. Enjoyable in hindsight, that is.

As always, feedback from pupils is essential. They rarely get it wrong. They are able to sniff out a phony with fantastic ease, and they are experts at identifying the candidates who are most likely to fit in and who really get what the school is all about. They rarely go for the ones who want to make friends; they choose the professionals, those who seem fair and those who are interested in them and what goes on in the classroom.

The irony of the full interview process is the fact that the formal interview at the end of the day is the activity which tells you least about the candidate. It should be seen as an opportunity to confirm, to finalize and negotiate rather than as the climax of the day. Another irony is the power of the feedback interview with the unsuccessful candidates as it is here that they often show their true colours. The candidate who you came close to appointing may well turn out to be gracious in defeat, utterly charming and grateful for your time; the ones you had your doubts about often argue, sulk or simply walk off.

Getting the leadership team right is fundamental to the school improvement process. It has to be done with great care, and it takes time. Building a team is a gradual process and learning to work as a team is one of the most difficult aspects of strong leadership. Really good leaders are rarely at the front, but they are always in the vanguard. Eventually, you will realize just how effective the team has become. You will be delegating more and more and worrying less and less about the things you have delegated, you will be confident that everyone is moving in the same direction and the impact of this carefully nurtured synergy will be evident in the steady improvements taking hold across the school.

The digital leader

Much of what has been discussed so far may smack of conservatism: a traditional focus on teaching and learning and a strong leadership team in a school resisting the urge to academize or chase the chief executive officer salary. It is time, therefore, to consider the role of the head teacher in the digital world where digital immigrants struggle to keep up with the expertise of digital natives and technology advances with a rapidity both dazzling and overwhelming.

There are two aspects to digital leadership: the use of technology in the classroom and its use as part of the leader's toolkit for doing the day job. A huge amount has been written about the role of computers in the classroom, so I won't go into it here. Suffice it to say that much of the research suggests that the panic of the 1990s and early 2000s, when we were all terrified that pupils were missing out if we didn't fill every class with the latest equipment, seems to have abated. Unsurprisingly, it seems that good teaching has the most impact, and computer technology has limited impact on student progress.

The use of technology in leadership roles is more interesting and there is no doubt that the age of the email has contributed dramatically to the sense of acceleration in the world of education. Most head teachers receive at least 100 emails a day – some of us many more than that – and this is something that has to be managed. The daily inbox avalanche undoubtedly contributes to the stress of the role and is more than capable of diverting and distracting even the sanest and most balanced individuals. As with any in-tray exercise, it's all about selection. Good leaders can run through their inboxes with remarkable rapidity, deleting and deleting so that what's left can easily be dealt with. Personally, I like to keep a near-empty inbox, and once I have deleted the spam or the congratulatory letters from the DfE, I try to deal with each email there and then. Heads who go under tend to let their in-boxes fill up until the very thought of dealing with them becomes overwhelming.

It is important to establish some rules for emails – both personal and for the whole staff. Some heads make their email addresses freely available to parents, for example. That's a personal choice, but it can lead to dozens of parents contacting you directly about the most trivial of issues. A sensible protocol is to ensure that there is a filtering system so that emails get to you only when they need to. This can be as simple as an email address that begins head@ or principal@ which can be filtered by your administration team or your personal assistant (PA), if you have one.

The delete rule is also important. Don't be afraid of deleting things. You may think something could be of use one day – or might be important in the future – but if you don't delete it, you'll be looking at it again and again over the next few weeks, wasting huge amounts of time. If it's really important, you'll be contacted again. Or if you realize it's important later, you can always dig it out of the trash.

The hardest rule to stick to is the one that insists on a pause before replying. It can be very enjoyable rattling off a semi-abusive email to a parent or colleague who has upset you in some way, but this is something you may well regret a few hours later. The send button is far too accessible. Similarly, the reply-all button is dangerous, as is the forwarded email which includes something abusive about the recipient buried in the email chain you omitted to reread. The use of emails is something that has to be done with great care.

Staff need to be encouraged to delete and to handle parental contact equally carefully. They should also feel comfortable not to answer emails after hours at home. One of the most insidious aspects of email communication is the always-on nature of mobile technology. It is far too easy to check emails throughout the evening and then decide to answer one or two to get them out of the way. It is up to school leaders to model sensible behaviour here and avoid replying to emails, whether from parents or staff, after about seven o'clock at night. This then allows staff to do the same. It is the only sensible way to achieve a work–life balance. This is, of course, obvious, but how many heads make this kind of behaviour explicit?

The use of social media throws up even more issues. As a head teacher, I have always avoided a social media presence as it is too easy to get caught up in endless arguments about trivial things which eventually involve dozens of people. Staff need to be warned regularly about their social media use, both from a safeguarding point of view and in terms of their professional behaviour. Younger staff who inhabit social media with considerable skill are often incredibly naïve when it comes to communicating with pupils, sixth formers especially, or indeed with parents.

More positively, digital technology offers fantastic opportunities for senior leaders to develop teaching and learning in the school. First, technology has allowed a huge number of tasks to be done quickly, thus allowing more time to devote to things that really matter. It is much quicker to write an email than to send a letter; a text reaches a colleague instantly whereas to connect via a phone call is often extremely difficult to arrange across two busy schedules. Modern technology has also allowed schools to create fabulous online prospectuses, and every school now has a website which can be kept up to date and fully interactive. Marketing has never been easier – provided, of course, you remember to update regularly.

Technologies such as Twitter allow leaders and teachers to exchange a huge amount of information quickly, and for many, there is no better way of keeping abreast of the latest educational research. The blog is also an incredibly useful tool for keeping up with the world, whether you are writing one yourself or reading the work of others. Never before have heads been able to have direct contact with leading international researchers so easily and so quickly.

The key thing about technology is, of course, that it offers a set of tools, and these tools have to be used wisely. Very little thought often goes into equipping computer suites because the orthodox view is that these are 'good things' which children must have. They are certainly useful to have, but when you look closely at their impact on learning, the results are often surprising. The use of ICT is another of those subjects which must be discussed regularly if leadership teams are to continue to improve their schools. Technology must not be allowed to distract from the focus on teaching and learning which must be at the heart of every school's improvement strategy. The digital leader should be technologically well informed yet suspicious enough to evaluate the impact of every innovation that new technology seems to offer. In other words, a digital native but also a digital sceptic.

Improvising

Many of the leadership skills described in this chapter have involved risk-taking, innovating, adapting, selecting and the ability to work in and around systems. I have already touched on the idea of head teachers as improvisers, but the more you look into both the demands of the role and the traits of successful leaders the more you realize that the ability to improvise is a fundamental leadership skill.

Heads who do things by the book run perfectly adequate schools. They are great administrators, they introduce highly effective systems, and they follow policies to the letter. Heads of truly great schools have all these skills but use them as a starting point. They are not afraid to bend the rules if it is in the best interest of pupils and they are not afraid to risk innovating if a better way is in sight. The important point to note, however, is that you cannot start out like that. You have to learn the systems, follow set patterns, internalize the policies and then move on. You have to know the rules before you can break them. A head who takes over a school and then sets about changing it with wild improvisatory abandon is heading for disaster; improvising is a skill acquired gradually after hundreds of hours of practice.

The great Victorian poet Gerard Manley Hopkins said, 'The effect of studying masterpieces is to make me admire and do otherwise.' This is a principle every senior leader should bear in mind. You need to study how it's done before doing otherwise. So, good heads are always aware of the latest innovations; they keep up with contemporary pedagogy; they question it, test it and debate it. Above all, they seek to understand it fully before incorporating it into their own philosophies. A jazz musician learns the chords of every song before improvising a new melody. Charlie Parker, the master of bebop, put it more bluntly: 'You've got to learn your instrument. Then, you practice, practice, practice. And then, when you finally get up there on the bandstand, forget all that and just wail.' The idea of my more sober head teacher colleagues just wailing always makes me smile.

In a fascinating article on improvisation as a mind-set, Karl E. Weick discusses 'organisational improvisation' using 'the vehicle of jazz improvisation as the source of orienting ideas.'[3] He emphasizes the importance of spontaneity and intuition yet stresses the need not to overlook 'the major investment in practice, listening and study that precedes a stunning performance. A jazz musician is more accurately described as a highly discipline "practicer" [sic] than as a practitioner.'[4] Not a bad description of an expert leader.

Leadership is stressful, difficult and demanding. It involves a set of skills that need to learned, developed and honed. The best leaders practise and then improvise, and they do so with a thorough understanding of the real world of the classroom. And yet they always have a touch of sprawl.

Key points

- The 'hero head' model may have disappeared, but the new 'executive principal' role may have become its contemporary replacement.
- The head or principal may not be as important as system leadership models lead us to believe.
- Succession planning is vital to the long-term success of a school.

- Leaders need to teach in order to empathize with their colleagues, to understand day-to-day classroom mechanisms and to model good practice.
- Heads should not be hidebound by rules and regulations; improvisation is a key skill.
- Delegation is essential if leaders are to be free to innovate.
- Innovation should be done with care, but it is the key to avoiding complacency.
- Leadership meetings should always focus on teaching and learning.
- All staff should be encouraged to visit other schools to develop and enrich their practice.
- It is important to include all members of the leadership team in teaching and learning, including the finance manager.
- Interviewing new staff is one of the most important aspects of leadership. Promotion should never be based on time served but the ability to do the job.
- Getting the right leaders in the right place is fundamental to effective school improvement.
- Learning how to live and thrive in the digital world is now a key leadership skill.
- Great leaders improvise.

Practical ideas

- Review the amount of teaching done by members of the leadership team. Do they really make it a priority? How often are their lessons covered, and how necessary were these cover periods really?
- Create a succession plan for every role in the school. Can you?
- Heads and principals should take time to review the extent to which they genuinely delegate.
- Arrange an in-service day during which all members of staff visit other schools.

- Review your leadership team agendas. How often do you really talk about teaching and learning?

- Make sure you include your finance manager in all SLT meetings.

- Review your interviewing schedules in the light of the outline in this chapter. How effective are they, and to what extent do they focus on teaching and learning?

- Learn to improvise. Miles Davis will show you the way!

Notes

1 M. Myatt. 2016. *High Challenge, Low Threat*, Woodbridge: John Catt Educational Ltd, p. 45.
2 J. Hattie. 2009. *Visible Learning*, Oxon: Routledge, p. 83.
3 K. E. Weick. 1998. Improvisation as a Mindset for Organizational Analysis. *Organization Science*, 9:5, 543.
4 Ibid., p. 544.

Real improvement planning

The vision

Every school has to have a vision, and there are now so many of them the word is in danger of becoming totally devalued. More often than not, leadership courses use *vision* as their starting point, and all aspiring leaders are tasked with dreaming up a vision for their school. The first step is a short paragraph; the next stage is to boil it down to one pithy, memorable sentence. Inevitably, the result is to strip it of its meaning entirely. A brief trawl of school websites produces a long list of vision statements. Here are some examples:

- Inspiring learning, achieving excellence
- Knowledge and truth
- Inspire and achieve
- Our mission is to inspire the community to embrace the fullness of life
- Working together, creating opportunities
- Respect, aspiration, perseverance, achieving excellence together
- Learning at the heart of the community
- Achievement for all
- Believe, inspire, succeed

These are all very worthy but, ultimately, meaningless. They rarely, if ever, relate to what goes on in the school, and they all sound roughly the same. At best they are lofty ambitions which seek to sum up one or two aspects of school culture. When my governors asked me to come up with a new vision statement for the school, I found it incredibly difficult to avoid the standard set of platitudes. In the end, '[a] caring community where learning is prized' seemed to capture what we were all about, but when you add it to the list of visions listed above it quickly loses its meaning. The longer vision statement was more satisfying (see the Appendix) and came closer to capturing the culture and ambitions of the school but, even in 450 words, it is really impossible to encapsulate the philosophy and vision of such a complex institution.

The only sensible vision is an intense focus on teaching and learning. This is where improvement planning should begin and end.

The school's headline vision is different from the head teacher's vision. He or she may not be able to express a vision in one or two words, but there should be one. The word *vision* itself is off-putting and something of a misnomer; it has faintly religious connotations or even echoes of prophecy. One of the *Oxford Dictionary*'s many definitions is, however, appropriate for school leaders: 'A mental image of what the future will or could be like.'[1]

A vision of the future of teaching and learning in a school does not drop out of the sky, it is based upon a hard-headed analysis of the school's strengths and weaknesses. It must be anchored in reality and start with an honest appraisal. Too many visions fail to recognize the real issues, focusing, like the worthy straplines described earlier, on vague plans for educational excellence. A vision must be robust, realistic and, above all, workable. Suddenly, the word *vision* doesn't sound quite so prophetic.

The leadership team's vision of what the school should be like is the basis for improvement, and this gives the direction needed to plan. How these plans are expressed is another matter. Through detailed analysis of a school's strengths and weaknesses, and careful discussion of the way forward, the leadership team should be able to develop a clear sense of what needs to be done. In other words, even before they sit down to write an improvement plan, they should be clear about exactly what needs to be improved and how they are going to go about making those improvements.

The name of the document itself needs some thought. When such things were first introduced into schools, they tended to be labelled school development plans, only later moving to the term *school improvement plans*. In many ways, a better title is the school learning plan, if only because it puts learning front and centre from the outset.

The self-evaluation form (SEF)

The SEF is one of those documents that used to be demanded by inspection teams but which is no longer requested. Any school leader should have one, however, and it would be daft not to offer it to inspectors for their scrutiny. There is no point in attempting to finesse its contents: the only useful SEF is one which offers a rigorous and thoroughly honest evaluation of the school's strengths and weaknesses. A head teacher who prepares an overly positive evaluation of the school merely demonstrates that he or she does not know the school, has something to hide and is not really capable of effective self-evaluation. Effective heads are realistic and often hypercritical. They know what needs to be put right and are not afraid to acknowledge it.

It is not, of course, just a document for inspectors. It is much more important than that. It offers a fixed point in the year when leaders are obliged to do a full evaluation of the progress of the school. Having a set format is also important as it ensures that all aspects of the school are considered, not just the headline figures. It also prompts detailed consideration of improvement over time, and in that sense, it is an excellent way of avoiding complacency, one of the great dangers of operating as a good or outstanding school.

The SEF is a good starting point for the learning plan as it really forces you to think about what needs improving. Some leadership teams spend hours and hours slaving over hot keyboards in order to come up with comprehensive documents that cover school life in fantastic detail. The most effective SEFs, however, are often short, precise and analytical. The best ones are a few pages long. Indeed, for several years now, I have attempted to produce an SEF in as few pages as possible (see Appendix) – a short document which indicates precisely the strengths and weaknesses of the school.

What should an SEF include?

There is no getting away from the fact that the easiest way to put together a comprehensive analysis of the school's current performance is to use the inspection framework. I agree entirely that school improvement should not be focused solely on preparing for an inspection (this is a topic I shall explore later in more depth), but the framework is a useful tool which is easy to adapt to your own particular circumstances. I would therefore suggest building the SEF around the key framework areas: quality of education (including the old overall effectiveness), behaviour and attitudes, personal development and leadership and management. It is also important to come up with a judgement for each area based on hard evidence. Far too often, leadership teams will happily declare, for example, that the quality of teaching in the school is at least good and often outstanding based on very little evidence.

The judgement discussion is often the most important part of the school improvement process – and it takes time. A judgement of the quality of teaching will involve careful analysis not only of the evidence but of the systems providing that evidence. Most schools have instituted some kind of system of regular lesson observations, but how often are these tested and evaluated? Leadership team members may feel confident that their judgements are accurate, but how do they know? How often do they observe lessons jointly in order to compare findings? How often do they invite visitors from outside to validate their judgements? In the same way that examination boards moderate coursework or oral activities, leaders should moderate their teaching and learning judgements. It is too easy to assume that your standards are accurate when, in fact, they could be far too generous, leaving the door open for a view of the school that is both rose-tinted and complacent.

An honest discussion of the judgements to be put into the SEF will highlight areas of weakness and indicate where improvements should be made. At first it may seem as if the areas of weakness are fairly random: pockets of weakness in various parts of the school that need sorting out independently. However, a thorough analysis of every aspect of the school's performance is likely to identify common themes. These should form the basis of the learning plan.

What to include in a learning plan

Let us begin by discussing what not to include in a learning plan. Commercial development planning software usually demands the inclusion of a great deal of information which is not directly relevant to school improvement. Hours of time can be wasted by senior staff fulfilling the unnecessary requirements of these sorts of planning packages. It is important to identify from the outset what can be left out.

The most controversial aspect of what not to include is surely budgetary information. Most school finance handbooks, and nearly all advice given to governors, suggest that every improvement must be fully costed. Of course, schools must operate within a budget, but it is easy for a potentially highly effective learning plan to be destroyed by an obsessive focus on costs. The Department for Education (DfE) leads the way in this kind of thinking: anyone who has had to prepare an action plan for the DfE will understand perfectly. DfE forms usually demand absurdly detailed finance data based on proposals and plans for the future which cannot possibly be costed accurately in advance. It is as if by merely writing them down, the figures will therefore be accurate.

Attempting to cost an improvement plan is a dangerous undertaking. A carefully worked-out programme of staff development may be exactly what the school needs to help improve areas identified in the SEF which are key to student outcomes. An outline figure can perhaps be proposed, but the actual costs are unlikely to be known until the work is well underway. Too many deputy heads bury themselves in their offices attempting to add figures to perfectly good plans before finally deciding simply to make up numbers which look convincing. It would obviously be foolish to plan an ambitious programme of improvement for a school which could not possibly be delivered within a sensible budget; it is equally foolish to spend hours trying to apply a cost to every proposal. As always with this kind of planning, attention drifts away from teaching and learning towards completing the document itself. I would be very interested to see how many of the DfE action plans bear any relation to what actually takes place in schools. Similarly, far too many schools have impressive looking improvement plans which are rarely looked at again once they have been completed. Things move on too quickly for plans such as these to be of any practical use.

It may be difficult to convince governors of the validity of this approach, but I would advise leaving out financial information entirely. Focus on what needs to be done to improve the school and then do as much as you can afford. When I first removed budgetary information from the learning plan, I created a second document relating to more general aspects of the development of the school. It included financial projections (i.e. how we were going to balance the budget), capital works, maintenance, staffing issues, work with the parent–teacher association and so on. It was detailed and comprehensive, and no one ever read it. I now produce one document based entirely on teaching and learning. The costs come later.

There is also the issue of the sort of distractions identified in Chapter 1. It is tempting to include in the plan some of the key issues which are likely to feature prominently in the work of the leadership team in the coming months. Leaders can be tied up for days exploring issues such as conversion to academy status, joining a trust, managing a building project or dealing with a serious community matter, among others. These are all vital activities which cannot be ignored, but put them in the learning plan, and they take over.

The only effective way ahead is therefore to focus entirely on what the school needs to do to improve teaching and learning.

An example plan

As with the SEF, the learning plan should begin with a brief outline of where the school is now. This will include a description of starting points and outcomes. How much progress have pupils made, in other words, attainment on entry, followed by an analysis of examination results?

This will lead to the identification of strengths and weaknesses (based on the SEF) and a clear indication of the priority areas for the school. It is important to include basic performance information at the start of the plan, if only as a reminder of where the school is now. This doesn't have to be detailed, but it should clearly signal the areas in need of improvement. It is also useful to include examination targets early on in the plan to indicate a clear sense of direction.

The next step is to outline the key issues in broad terms; these will be refined and explored in detail later as they make their way into departmental plans. Unsurprisingly, the three broad areas are likely to stay the same year on year and can be easily summarized:

Key Issue 1 – Improve the quality of learning

Key Issue 2 – Raise attainment and secure sustained progress

Key Issue 3 – Sustain improvement across the school

Key Issue 1 relates directly to classroom practice and generates a common thread to be explored across the school in the coming year; Key Issue 2 looks more closely at assessment and progress, focusing on particular groups and the actions needed to help improve their learning; Key Issue 3 is more generic, highlighting the need for the school to keep innovating, researching and responding to national developments.

Under each key issue, you can then focus on the specific areas for improvement identified by the SEF. For example, the areas identified for the plan could be summarized thus:

Key Issue 1 – Improve the Quality of Learning

To achieve this, we will need to do the following:

A **Ensure lessons make learning relevant to students**, foster curiosity and build a love of learning

B **Refine questioning skills that secure more rapid progress in lessons**, for example, by using strategies that improve student retrieval or recall of facts or that check comprehension

C **Narrow the word gap that exists between our most and least successful students** by explicitly teaching 'tier 2' as well as 'tier 3' words

D **Improve student skills when applying (or transferring) knowledge** by including a greater range of decision-making or problem-solving activities in lessons

E **Make progress more visible** in lessons by explicitly teaching students, particularly in Key Stage 5, metacognitive and memory recall skills as well as supporting their note-taking and organizational skills

F **Further refine teachers' use of instructional language** so that it both recognizes mistakes as a positive learning tool and lessens the stress associated with constant reference to examinations

G **Continue to adapt, renew and, in light of intense budgetary pressures, protect our curriculum** so all students are engaged by their lessons and better prepared for the ongoing changes to assessment systems in all key stages[2]

All this is shared with staff early on in the process (see the following discussion) so that they can respond to each of the key issues in their departments or year/house teams. Each head of department or year team leader is asked not only to consider every aspect of the whole school plan in his or her work for the year but also to choose at least one specific objective from those listed under Key Issues 1 and 2 on which to concentrate. Which ones they choose will obviously depend on their departmental priorities. This then allows them to create their own departmental or year team plans, which usually comprise two whole school priorities and one specific to their own subject or year area. An example of a department plan is included in the Appendix.

The departmental/year team plans thus become the drivers of school improvement. Each one begins with examination targets for the year ahead at both Key Stage 4 and A-Level (these are based on Fischer Family Trust estimates but modified using the professional judgement of the heads of department). These are followed by detailed plans aimed at addressing the chosen Key Issues set out simply in two columns headed 'Action' and 'Impact.' Each department or year plan fits on one side of A4: it is simple, precisely targeted and, above all, achievable. The actions identified in departments can then be used in the construction of performance management targets, thus creating a clear line of sight from whole-school issues to individual classroom practice.

There is also a detailed whole school plan, set out in the same way as the department plans, and this is devised by the leadership team to support the delivery of the various objectives. This is a detailed table which includes training (continuing professional development [CPD]) plans, whole school work with pupils, descriptions of the various proposed department or thematic reviews, monitoring work, line management discussions and so on.

Evaluation is a vital component of every learning plan, and every new plan is prefaced by a detailed evaluation of the previous year's plan. Work done to achieve each objective is outlined and its impact discussed. Each plan also includes an analysis of results compared to targets. An example of a departmental self-evaluation document is included in the Appendix.[3] It is also important to note that everyone has access to everyone else's plans and evaluations. This means that those heads of department or heads of year who are less confident in their planning can use the work of more experienced colleagues as exemplars to help them produce much more effective plans of their own. Shared evaluations also inject a degree of healthy competition into the process; no one wants their results to be out of line with those of their colleagues.

Most school improvement plans cover three or four years; this one covers one academic year. As a consequence, it is able to be much more specific in terms of actions to be taken in the months ahead. It has to be put together quickly (the complete plan is published to staff and governors before the end of September) so that work can begin immediately. It is a live document which teachers refer to throughout the year. Staff are encouraged to make their plans very precise, often focusing on one or two actions. The impact of this very detailed, carefully targeted work in departments may seem like 'marginal gains,' but the accumulated impact is often profound. Instead of worthy but vague long-term ambitions, the most effective school improvement planning focuses on small but significant steps.

This is not to disregard long-term planning, however. After all, genuine school improvement is a slow process. The introduction to the whole-school plan always includes a list of more general, longer-term objectives. The key point, of course, is that the short-term, precise targets of the individual department or year team plans point towards the longer-term targets.

The learning plan should be a one-stop shop: a reference guide and a genuine working document. By keeping the plans short and focused, they are much more likely to be used on a daily basis. The final learning plan is actually a lengthy document, but its heft belies its simplicity: it essentially comprises an outline plan for the whole school followed by each individual department and year team's plan. The table of contents gives a sense of its structure:

1 Introduction

    a Context/where are we now?

    b Curriculum

    c Inclusion and challenge

    d Examination performance

    e Examination targets

    f Evaluation of last year's Whole School Plan

    g Key issues for this year

    h Longer-term targets

    i Sources for key issues

2 Year team self-evaluation and learning plans

3 Department self-evaluation and learning plans

4 Learning support/inclusion plans

5 Appendices

    a The SEF

    b Data sources

    c Assessment and marking policy

    d Lesson observation form

    e What does an outstanding lesson look like?

    f The training programme

The inclusion of key documents in the Appendix is deliberate. It turns the learning plan into a reference document, giving staff another reason to look at it regularly. It also becomes a useful handbook for line managers who can refer to it in their meetings to check progress against objectives, and it gives governors a much greater understanding of the departments they visit.

    This kind of document has a real sense of coherence and common purpose. Everyone in the school is working towards the same goals, using the same plan. Staff therefore have a clear sense of direction and specific actions on which to focus. This means that the learning plan is built into the day-to-day work of the school rather than being a plan produced for governors which is left to gather dust on the shelf.

The learning plan cycle

The learning plan should be woven into the school calendar; it is a live document that helps drive many of the regular activities of leaders at all levels in the school. A plan which covers three or four years can easily be forgotten; an annual plan is much more likely to be referred to regularly throughout the year.[4]

Improvement planning is an ongoing process. Leadership teams should regularly be exploring issues likely to contribute to next year's plan. A continual focus on teaching and learning is essential. Discussions are likely to include regular updates on data, national developments, recently identified issues for the school, CPD, research, the views of the school council, departmental reviews, feedback from middle leaders and other key staff and so on.

A first-rate leadership team rarely lets teaching and learning take a back seat.

Planning for the next academic year needs to begin in the spring. In April or May, it's a good idea to convene a special leadership team meeting to bring together the various concerns and innovations which are to underpin the new plan. A detailed discussion should aim to draw up an initial list of key issues to present to staff, and reference should be made to the school's long-term issues to ensure that the ultimate direction is still clear.

The new key issues need to be explored by staff for two reasons: first, to ensure that they are familiar with them; second, to give them a sense of ownership. A good way of doing this is to make the key issues the subject of a training day or a series of twilight training sessions.

A very successful model used for many years now involves whole-staff training over four days in a local hotel. We are fortunate in that we have managed to broker a good, out-of-season deal with a parent who allows us to use his hotel's conference room for the training. We take three or four departments out each day, and each day is led by two members of the senior team. Training takes place during school time, but the cover costs are minimal because the event is timetabled during Year 10 work experience week which takes place after Years 11 and 13 have left. We can therefore train the whole teaching staff for the cost of two or three commercial courses, which must surely be something of a bargain. Staff also enjoy a day out, with a good lunch, which ensures that they adopt a positive approach to the day's work. The off-site location is essential if distractions are to be avoided, of course. The same meeting in school would involve constant interruptions, and far less work would get done. We evaluate every session and the responses always suggest that the training is one of the highlights of the year. It is also incredibly important in terms of generating enthusiasm for the construction of a new learning plan.

The training is designed to allow staff to learn about the key issues and to discuss them in the context of their own departments. By the end of the day, the whole school key issues are fixed, teachers are aware of them having worked with them all day, and they are ready to go away to write their own departmental plans. These are drafted by the end of the summer term, but they are always revised in the light of the examinations in the summer. Plans are submitted in the first two weeks of the autumn term so that the full document can be put together by the end of September. Every head of department and year head has a meeting with school leadership team in the first two or three weeks of term to review examination performance and the learning plans are discussed as a key part of these meetings. It is at this stage that the departmental/year team plans are 'signed off' ready for publication.

The construction of the SEF follows the same pattern. It is drafted in the summer term in order to underpin initial discussions of the new key issues and then revised after the exams. If the school is confident in its predictions and skilled at self-evaluation, there are likely to be few surprises. This makes early planning much more straightforward.

Once the full plan is published, it becomes a working document. A full CPD programme is constructed, based, of course, on the key issues, and staff are encouraged to get involved in small-scale research activities relating to the plan. From this point onwards, the focus is on implementation and review.

Performance management discussions remind staff of the key issues and progress against them is monitored at the six-month review meetings. Governors are asked to take the learning plan with them when they attend department meetings, and this ensures that they, too, are aware of the school's priorities. It also reminds them that these priorities relate directly to teaching and learning and not the more mundane topics which usually occupy governors' thoughts. Learning walks and leaders' observations always consider the learning plan key issues, and some of the CPD sessions are devoted to sharing good practices arising from the various activities taking place across the school. It is also important to refer to the learning plan on a regular basis in department meetings and full staff meetings. Implementation and review therefore run across the year until the time comes to evaluate and move on to the next year's plan.

Line management

Line management systems are often neglected in schools and many leaders simply pay lip service to the process. Too many leaders see these meetings as a chance to catch-up, to have a friendly chat and, perhaps, to touch on one or two topics the head is keen to talk about. When conducted regularly and with rigour, however, they form a key part of the school improvement agenda.[5] In order to ensure that line management is effective, the purpose of the meetings should be made clear:

- To build successful departments and outstanding leadership
- To monitor student progress in subjects and in year groups
- To identify approaches that would address where progress is not being made
- To revisit and assess the extent planned actions in classrooms are improving student progress

- To develop consistent approaches to key teaching priorities
- To share best practice (two-way process)
- To discuss management issues and agree on next steps
- To listen to the challenges of leadership and offer help

It is also important to follow a common format and to record the outcomes of the meeting in order to keep the rest of the leadership team informed. A useful agenda might look like this:

1. Progress and standards
2. Progress of disadvantaged groups
3. Development of teaching and learning, including key issues from the learning plan
4. Lesson drop-ins
5. Leadership of the team
6. Management- weekly/day-to-day issues
7. Any other business (AOB)

Effective line management keeps everyone informed. It focuses the head of department or year team leader on improvement issues; it ensures that the line manager is fully aware of what is happening in the department; it guarantees a continual focus on progress and standards, encouraging everyone to think about the progress of particular groups, the disadvantaged especially; and it ensures that everyone on the leadership team has a good grasp of the teaching and learning issues affecting all parts of the school.

Embedding the plan

The most effective improvement plans are embedded in the day-to-day functioning of the school. The aim should always be to ensure that the plans become real; too many plans are written because schools are expected to have them. The approach outlined earlier ensures that everyone in the school is not only aware of the plan but also fundamental to its success. Weaknesses must be identified and acknowledged, and the culture should allow admission of failure or weakness. An exam review meeting will be pointless if all that happens is that the head of department concerned merely attempts to justify poor results. We have all heard the excuses. What can you expect with a class like that? How do you expect me to get the top grades with so little curriculum time? The exams have changed again, and we weren't given enough time to adapt and so on.

Effective leaders openly acknowledge weaknesses, and indeed errors, and then focus on what they are going to do to improve. Effective improvement planning needs this level of honesty to make it work. Once weaknesses have been identified, planning can begin.

It is also vital to ensure that the plan is shared. If, as described previously, the whole teaching staff is involved in identifying the key issues and then given the time to work on them, then the chances of success will be much higher. If the key issues become the staff's issues, they won't be forgotten, and the work will proceed. The annual plan is the most effective way of keeping the key issues alive, but it needs to be supported by carefully designed structures to check its progress along the way. These include governor visits, departmental reviews, line management meetings and performance reviews.

And if everyone is on board, and all the systems are in place, you never know, you might just fulfil that aspirational vision emblazoned across the school prospectus.

Key points

- Most schools' one-line vision statements are fairly meaningless.
- Genuine visions are based on a hard-headed analysis of strengths and weaknesses.
- The SEF is a key part of the improvement cycle and not just a document for inspectors.
- The SEF should be intensely focused on teaching and learning first; budgetary and administrative information can be recorded elsewhere.
- The learning plan should focus intensively on teaching and learning.
- There should be a clear improvement calendar driven by the learning plan.
- Effective line management systems help drive the learning plan.
- The learning plan should be embedded in the day-to-day activities of all staff.

Practical ideas

- Consider whether your school's vision statement is designed to build on the strengths and weaknesses of the school or is it merely window dressing.

- Review your SEF. How honest and accurate is it really?

- Compare your learning plan to the example in this chapter. Does it have the same intense focus on teaching and learning?

- Do you have a robust line management system? Do you have an agreed-on agenda which focuses on teaching and learning? Review the notes of recent meetings and consider how effective they are and how much time was spent discussing pedagogy.

- Invite a governor into school as an objective observer to question staff about the learning plan. Is it embedded in their day-to-day work?

Notes

1 Oxford Living Dictionaries online: https://en.oxforddictionaries.com/definition/vision
2 For the complete key issue list, see the Appendix.
3 Self-evaluation and departmental learning plan guides are also included in the Appendix.
4 See the Appendix for an example of the learning plan cycle.
5 Line management templates are included in the Appendix.

# Staff development

The importance of staff development cannot be underestimated. Often regarded as something confined to training days, it is seen by many as a necessary evil: something senior staff struggle to arrange and the rest of the staff are forced to endure. If leaders don't value it, then the staff won't value it, and that constitutes a huge missed opportunity. It is easy to fill training days with expensive speakers bought in for the occasion, demonstrations of new software, compulsory updates covering special needs, health and safety, safeguarding and so on. But if that is all it is, the school is unlikely to move forward. Continuing professional development (CPD) is vital to the health of the profession and the future of education.

Most school leaders believe in lifelong learning, and this is a mantra to be heard recited again and again during training sessions, but how many school leaders actively promote lifelong learning amongst their staff? And what does it really mean in the context of schooling? Teachers are busy people, and most of the time they are teaching, planning or marking. Finding time for training is incredibly difficult; finding time to continue your own personal learning can seem like a step too far. In an ideal world, teachers would be allocated personal learning time when they would be free to develop their teaching skills and increase their subject knowledge. This is unlikely ever to happen in a country whose politicians treat teaching staff at best with disdain, at worst with contempt. It is the job of the school leader, therefore, to make time, to convince staff of the value of professional development, and to incorporate it seamlessly into the life of the school. Nor is CPD simply a matter of training. It is a highly complex area which covers a lot more than safeguarding updates and tips on classroom practice.

It is helpful to consider three distinct aspects of a teacher's role: teachers enter the profession as subject experts, they learn to become pedagogical experts (though many don't realize how skilled they actually are at this) and, even if they never take on any kind of leadership role, they develop considerable leadership expertise as part of their day-to-day management of the classroom. Thinking about professional development in each of these three areas helps us broaden our thinking about the type of training we should be offering staff in our schools.

A significant element of a school's CPD programme should be devoted to developing and refining a teacher's pedagogical skills. This can be done in a variety of ways. I shall explore the importance of research later on, but it is important to stress from the outset that teachers must be involved in exploring new ideas, keeping up with the latest educational thinking, and sharing good practice. Effective CPD makes this possible. Some staff will be keen to study for postgraduate degrees, and they should be encouraged to do so, although helping them financially is getting harder and harder to do in these straitened times. Others will be content with reading; it is therefore essential to ensure that there is a good staff library on-site which is regularly added to with the latest books on educational theory and practice. In some schools, leaders provide useful summaries of educational theories and use them as the basis for after-school update sessions, or simply introduce them in staff meetings.

Collaborative learning is a powerful way of enhancing a teacher's skills. Working in pairs or trios allows the rapid exchange of information and skills, and the opportunity simply to visit a colleague's classroom can be an education in itself, particularly if that classroom is in another school. Mentoring a younger colleague on an initial teacher training (ITT) programme is also an excellent way of ensuring that a teacher's skills remain up to date. Trainee teachers nowadays experience increasingly sophisticated training programmes in schools or in universities where they learn the latest theories and the most up-to-date techniques. While supporting their first forays into the classroom, the opportunity to learn from their training programmes should not be overlooked.

Developing teachers' leadership expertise is the second strand of a good-quality CPD regime. The most obvious way of doing this is to appoint them to a promoted post and support them into it. However, this is not always possible in schools where very little movement is available. The obvious way around the problem is to create shadowing opportunities so that ambitious staff can work with more experienced colleagues in order to see what leadership roles actually entail. Much of this can be done as part of the day-to-day routine – a second in the department effectively shadows the head of department all the time anyway – but it is important to offer other opportunities in school to make this kind of thing happen. This may involve a small time allocation or simply the construction of sympathetic timetables, but it is important to encourage this sort of sharing. It is also valuable CPD for the person being shadowed, first, because they tend to up their game to impress their colleagues but, second, because it makes them think about their own practice in ways they may not have done before.

As we all know, the best way to learn something is to teach it, and a very powerful form of CPD is to get teachers, whether new to the school or very experienced, to lead CPD sessions themselves. This can be difficult to set up in the first place but once established it is the sort of activity teachers find they really benefit from. This is the basis of the challenge coordinator role as described later. ITT mentoring is another obvious way of developing leadership, and we should not overlook the usefulness of some of the more established leadership qualifications such as the National Professional Training qualifications or the Outstanding Teacher Programme. These are expensive, but when delivered well, they can be highly effective.

Heads should also look to facilitate training for staff beyond the school. The chance to become a marker for an examination board is an obvious example – teachers can learn a huge amount by marking the papers they are preparing their students for – but there are other part-time roles in specialist bodies which some heads discourage their staff from undertaking but which, in fact, bring a great deal into the school. This includes union representation which, as awkward as meetings with union officials can sometimes be, offers staff opportunities to develop a wide range of professional skills beyond the classroom. There are also some greatly stimulating roles connected with teaching schools – some require part-time help with teaching school management, but all offer the chance to become Specialist Leaders in Education (SLEs). How SLEs are deployed is variable but in the best teaching schools they enable teachers to support colleagues in other schools and thus develop both their own leadership and classroom skills. Nor should we forget in-house opportunities such as working with the Parents and Teachers Association or becoming a staff governor.

Perhaps the most neglected aspect of staff training is the subject specialism. Most teachers come into the classroom because they love their subject and the majority have spent three or four years at university learning it in considerable detail. In schools we tend to take subject expertise as a given and assume teachers will keep up with their own specialist areas. In reality, this is often not the case. I mentioned in Chapter 2 my particular bugbear, the fact that so many teachers of English don't read teenage fiction, not to mention contemporary adult fiction, but I am sure this kind of thing is not confined to English departments. If anything, English teachers are more likely to continue to develop their subject expertise beyond university because it is a lot easier to keep up with the literary world than, say, the worlds of science or engineering. The point here, however, is that we should be encouraging staff to develop their subject knowledge. Heads are usually keen to encourage their staff to study for postgraduate degrees in education, but how many are brave enough to suggest that a more traditional academic subject-based degree might be a better option? Maybe not a better option but certainly as good and equally as likely to benefit pupils in the classroom.

Teachers as researchers

The problem with teachers as researchers is the word *research*. For teachers who enjoy working in the classroom, the idea of spending time gathering data and testing hypotheses is distinctly off-putting. To be honest, a great deal of educational research seems to be more concerned with the gathering of data rather than exploring new ideas. Anyone who has taken part in any kind of postgraduate research in education will have been scarred by the need to come up with a proposal, work out how to test it, do the background reading, think about triangulating the evidence, devising questionnaires, creating effective methods of evaluation and so on. The thought of undertaking this level of activity while keeping up the day job is likely to alarm even the most ambitious members of staff.

Of course, it doesn't have to be like this. To make research effective in schools, and to build it into the improvement process, a much more straightforward approach should be adopted. After all, the fundamental purpose of research is simply to come up with an idea and then to test it out to see if it works. If teachers are asked to do this, then the word *research* becomes much less threatening.

One of the most effective ways of building research into day-to-day practice is the use of Trios or, as they are more threateningly known in some schools, Triads. There is something about a Trio which makes it work. Teachers working in pairs can become too relaxed, postponing meetings, letting things slip, not taking things too seriously. A quartet allows one member of the group to take a back seat: 'Nobody will miss me this week.' A group of three, however, seems to ensure that everyone takes part as no one wants to let the other two down.

Trios

The Trio project began by chance when I agreed to spend time with two primary colleagues visiting lessons from Reception to Year 13. What we observed was fascinating. Unsurprisingly, the most striking thing we saw was the way in which independent learning, so strong in Reception, was steadily beaten out of children as they moved up through the system.

The outcome of this first, tentative Trio, was a training day which involved every member of staff visiting a primary school and then hosting a visit from a primary colleague. The next step was to create cross-phase Trios where one secondary colleague worked with two primary colleagues to observe lessons, plan together and then deliver a lesson observed by the other two. Outcomes were always recorded and shared at staff meetings. This generated a huge amount of interest and led us to revise our CPD programme in order to focus on Trios.

Since then, we have explored the idea in lots of ways. In larger departments, three staff have worked together to examine a particular problem, for example, differentiation in middle-ability sets, what makes an A* student and how to use teaching assistants more effectively. Cross-curricular Trios have tended to focus on a wider range of non-subject-based matters: pupil engagement, literacy and numeracy, teacher talk, gender, pupil premium students and so on.

When we became a teaching school, it seemed obvious that the way to ensure that schools in the alliance really began working together was to make sure that classroom teachers had the chance to work together. As a result, the focus of the alliance became bottom up, not top down. Obviously, the logistics of setting up Trios across wide geographical distances and with very different school cultures were a challenge, but once in motion the results were the same: a high degree of engagement, an intense focus on pedagogy and, for some, a renewed interest in classroom practice.

The Trios we run now are more focused and always result in a written outcome shared with other staff. Teachers have explored topics as diverse as questioning, the use of keywords, curiosity in the classroom, 'grey students' (those who sit quietly and hide themselves away), the use of iPads and so on.

The outcomes of the research benefit the whole school and generate a great deal of discussion, but the biggest effect is on each teacher's classroom practice. A renewed interest in pedagogy encourages a much more reflective approach to planning and teaching. Moreover, the nature of discussion across the school has changed, with staff eager to discuss their experiences in other classrooms and, more recently, in other schools. In other words, the involvement of teachers in research has helped to change the culture of the school.

Teachers who engage in research see themselves both as subject experts and specialists in pedagogy, and the result is better teaching. The use of Trios is a simple and effective way of encouraging a renewed emphasis on teaching skills and a shift in focus from accountability structures to classroom practice.

Challenge coordinators

The challenge coordinator role was initially devised as a response to a particular school development need. I had become acutely conscious of the fact that our approach to what were then known as gifted and talented pupils simply wasn't working. What is now blindingly obvious, but was less obvious to us at the time, was that isolating brighter pupils in this way is impossible. If you are going to challenge the brightest, you need to challenge everyone.

While it is useful to be aware of the various groups so that their progress can be tracked, and those falling behind identified and supported with carefully considered intervention strategies, the most important factor in ensuring strong progress is the quality of the teaching. This is true for all groups of pupils. A good teacher is aware of the needs of the pupils in his or her class, planning and adapting lessons accordingly.

Of course, the quality of teaching is inconsistent in every school, but the most successful schools develop ways of ensuring that good practice is shared so that standards keep rising.

The key to this is, of course, challenge but not challenge only for the most able but challenge at all levels. Every child needs to be challenged, and every teacher needs to think about how to challenge everyone in their classes as effectively as possible.

Senior leaders usually know exactly where they will find the best practice in their schools, and they know which teachers are able both to engage and challenge the pupils in their classes. The trick is to ensure that the best practice is shared and disseminated across the school. A complete shift in our approach was therefore needed, and this led to the creation of the challenge coordinator role.

The idea developed out of a series of lesson observations where a great deal of excellent teaching was observed. The common factor, on this occasion, was that some of the best teaching was being delivered by our youngest staff. It is easy to overlook the fact that teachers joining the profession nowadays are much better trained than they were in the past and, of course, much more up to date in their understanding of pedagogy and engaging teaching techniques. The accepted notion that good teaching depends upon experience is no longer the case; experienced teachers, though effective in the classroom, often depend upon tried and tested methods which they have used for years. In other words, they become stale.

As a result of discussions around who was offering the most effective teaching in the school, we decided to abandon the gifted and talent approach and move to a much sharper focus on challenge. In order to do so, we made the decision to appoint four Challenge Coordinators whose role would be to seek out best practice and share it across the school.

Although we didn't rule out more experienced colleagues, we aimed to target those who were early in their careers and, more importantly, those who were already delivering high-quality lessons on a regular basis. And we weren't short of applicants. We offered a Teaching and Learning Responsibility (TLR) point plus one period a week for planning. We also agreed that we would cover their lessons so that they could observe good practice around the school. Dissemination was to be via staff meetings, staff training sessions and small-scale research projects to be published on the school website.

Of course, colleagues who had been in the school some time were deeply suspicious of the plan, but it was remarkable how quickly the four young teachers who were appointed managed to turn things around. There is clearly some deep psychology at work here: experienced colleagues who had perhaps been somewhat resistant to new ideas were quickly seen to be responding to the training delivered by our new challenge team. If the training had been delivered by the school leadership team (SLT) or an external consultant, they would have undoubtedly been less than committed. The big surprise was how willing they were to pay attention to much younger colleagues talking about teaching. A cynical view could be that they felt some kind of maternal or paternal prompting to give the youngsters a chance, but even if that was the case, that feeling clearly disappeared very quickly as they realized how much they had to contribute. Consequently, the pace of improvement began to develop rapidly, and more and more conversations about pedagogy were to be heard in the staffroom and around the school.

In addition to the whole school benefit of this kind of approach, the Challenge Coordinator role has proved to be an excellent staff development opportunity in itself. There is now a clear progression for some colleagues from newly qualified teacher (NQT) to recently qualified teacher (RQT) to challenge coordinator. The role is an excellent way of not only encouraging them to continue to develop their own teaching – you've got to be good if you are going to tell others what to do – but also as an insight in leadership and whole school issues. Consequently, our first cohort of challenge coordinators quickly moved on to senior positions in the school.

Since the creation of the programme, the challenge team has been involved in a wide range of school improvement activities. They regularly lead staff in-service training sessions (INSET), they have visited other schools to share good practice, they have presented break-out sessions at our teaching school conference and they have observed hundreds of lessons. They are regularly invited into classrooms to discuss teaching strategies, and they frequently welcome colleagues into their classrooms to demonstrate specific techniques. One member of the team has focused on preparing students for Oxbridge/Medical school, and as a result, the number of students receiving university offers has improved significantly. Others have concentrated on research, with recent topics covering, for example, 'Recall of Key Subject Specific Terminology,' 'Using Piaget's "Staged Questions" to Encourage Independent Thinking in Lower Ability Groups' and 'Using Abstract Questioning to Encourage Thinking about Ethical Issues in Year 8 RE.'

The challenge coordinators now form a key strand of our whole school improvement strategy and their work is closely woven into each new school learning plan. We have also found that by engaging them so fully in the development of teaching and learning, and by giving them whole school experience early on in their careers, we are much more likely to retain first-class teachers in the school. The programme is also very attractive to new staff considering whether to work here or not. Most surprising of all, it is highly valued by our more experienced staff to whom it has given a new lease of life.

Classroom to classroom

Collaborative work in schools tends to be a top-down exercise. Senior leaders get together to plan some kind of joint activity, or more often than not commission an external visitor to review a department or offer support in some other way. Most CPD is therefore devised by the people least likely to benefit from it. A much better approach is to think classroom to classroom, connecting teachers both in-school and across schools.

Senior leaders can easily forget how isolated classroom teachers can become, especially if they work in small or one-person departments like religious education, music or drama. Teaching five lessons a day with very little interaction with other teachers, it is easy for colleagues to retreat into their own worlds and familiar routines. Getting them out into other classrooms is one of the most powerful forms of training available – and usually the most appreciated by those involved.

CPD should not be confined to training days; it should continue across the year. Creating time for teachers to visit other classrooms does involve expense – usually lessons have to be covered – but it is always money well spent and the costs can be kept to a minimum if staff agree to use gained time or give up the occasional free. It does have to be planned, however. There is much for be said for a flexible approach to start with: colleagues unused to observing other people's lessons may feel less self-conscious if they are invited into a classroom by someone they know well, usually in their own subject area. However, the most successful programmes require staff to step outside their comfort zones and begin to explore a wider range of lessons. This can be a gradual process: the first observation of a colleague in the same department; the second could be a similar subject area (e.g. a history class for an English teacher); the third should be something very different (a science specialist observing a drama lesson). Ideally, the next step should be observations in other schools, and this can most easily be arranged using the Trio format described earlier.

It should be stressed from the outset that these observations are solely for professional development. There should be no judgements, and any notes should be for the observer's personal reflections. They should not be used to critique the lesson. It is important to make time for the lesson to be discussed after the observation, but this should be from the standpoint of shared learning rather than a critical appraisal of the lesson. This approach means that colleagues will be far more likely to welcome colleagues into their classrooms and then feel encouraged to return the visit.

The benefits of this kind of observations are significant, especially when you consider how easy they are to arrange:

- Lesson observations become more about learning and less about monitoring.

- Everyone who visits someone else's classroom learns something.

- Once out of teacher training, there are very few chances for teachers to learn new techniques. A visit to another lesson may provide an opportunity to undertake an activity they may never have thought of doing in their own classroom.

- Shared learning is highly stimulating: most teachers return to their own classrooms with a new sense of purpose.

- Teachers also get the chance to observe pupils they teach in a different context:

    - How is your colleague managing the behaviour of the child who is disruptive in your lesson so successfully?

    - What kinds of activities engage and challenge the brightest?

    - How are they accommodating the needs of pupils with special education needs and disabilities (SEND)?

    - Are they aware of the pupil premium pupils in the class?

    - Are they linking anything they are learning in this subject area with what they are learning in your lessons?

Above all, classrooms open up and CPD becomes a shared activity. In the best schools, there is a strong pedagogical culture where teachers talk about teaching all the time; if they are observing other people's lessons on a regular basis, they will always have something to talk about.

Lesson monitoring can often become oppressive; lesson sharing is liberating. It also has the effect of raising the bar in terms of teaching quality. Teachers who observe other teachers quickly realize how good many of them are, and they are therefore prompted to ensure that their own lessons reach the same high standards. Most teachers are capable of teaching good or outstanding lessons on a regular basis, but isolated and comfortable in their own rooms, they fall back on tried-and-trusted methods. When classroom doors are open to colleagues, they are much more likely to think about updating and improving. When the excitement of teaching returns to those who have settled into old, familiar ways, the quality of their teaching improves dramatically.

Successful CPD is all about helping teachers to become reflective practitioners so that they are able to evaluate their own teaching and thus work out how to improve. Successful leaders of CPD are able to create a culture of sharing in the school which is seen as supportive and never punitive. They can then use this culture subtly to manage change: this involves moving from the introductory lesson observation phase described previously to a system of guided observations. Weaker colleagues can be encouraged to observe more effective classroom practitioners, and the very best teachers persuaded to offer demonstration lessons involving advanced pedagogical skills. In a culture of open classrooms and professional sharing, this kind of prompting will seem natural and supportive, thus helping to drive up standards across the school.

Schools where lesson observations are commonplace soon find that the line between observations by colleagues and monitoring visits by senior staff begins to blur. Monitoring becomes part of the lesson sharing culture and is much more likely to be welcomed. Senior leaders must monitor the quality of teaching and learning, but when it is seen as part of a general discussion of pedagogy, it becomes much less threatening. The aim should be to work towards a culture in which a monitoring visit is indistinguishable from a learning visit. Nor should we forget that senior leaders should be just as concerned about improving their own teaching as everyone else in the school.

A planned programme

The most effective CPD programmes in school comprise a number of key strands and therefore need to be carefully planned. They should cover the following:

- Departmental activities
- Trio/collaborative work
- Lesson observations

- Work on achieving performance management objectives

- Opportunities to engage in research

- Personal skills-based development.

In schools where CPD is given high priority, a structured programme is put in place before the start of term, with regular events locked into the calendar alongside department and staff meetings. It is usually possible to timetable a series of regular after-school training sessions without breaching directed time constraints. It may be better, in fact, to have fewer staff meetings and more training sessions, especially since most of the information delivered in staff meetings could easily be done by email. These regular sessions should be based on the key issues identified in the learning plan, but there should be sufficient flexibility built into the system to accommodate new issues which crop up mid-year or changes of direction based on the effectiveness of the training delivered so far. It is a good idea, too, to give staff a choice of training activities so that they feel they are involved rather than instructed.

Planned training events are often delivered in schools by the leadership team. This can be effective, but I think it is important to include as many other members of staff as possible so that training become collegiate rather than authoritarian. The 'all in it together' ethos is important here: staff need to feel that they are working together towards a shared goal rather than simply attending compulsory training. The challenge coordinator model described earlier is an excellent way of involving younger staff in the delivery of training, and it has the added advantage of being based directly on the findings from work done recently in the classroom.

Training sessions are not one-off events; they should build on each other. Care must be taken during the planning stage to ensure that there is a coherent pathway through the training and across the year. Colleagues should then be encouraged to develop what they have learned in the training sessions in their own departments or year teams so that these become CPD opportunities too. The role of the line manager is key here as he or she needs to be able to discuss with colleagues the relationship between the work they are doing in departments and the whole-school training. If the departmental learning plan aligns with the whole school learning plan, as described in the previous chapter, this should be fairly straightforward. It is then possible to extend the learning further by suggesting Trio or research activities or other forms of collaborative work. Line managers should also be regularly discussion feedback from lesson observations, and these, of course, can be related directly to both the learning plan and the CPD sessions. The aim is the seamless transference of learning.

An example CPD plan is included in the Appendix. It follows the learning plan pattern outline previously: the starting point is the whole school training where the key issues for the coming year were identified and explored, coupled with the evaluative work done by departments and year teams at the end of the summer.

Topics are then suggested for the various training opportunities taking place across the year, including department meetings and activities, Trio and collaborative work, performance management meetings and after-school research sessions.

The aim is coherence. If the key issues for the school have been identified correctly and agreed by staff, then the training programme becomes much more credible and relevant to the day-to-day activities of staff, especially if it is focused, as it must be, on teaching and learning. If staff understand the relevance of the training programme, they are much more likely to engage with it and then take it beyond the timetabled training sessions. In schools where this kind of system operates effectively, you often find that other CPD activities – individual research, master's studies, requests to go on external courses – begin to tie in neatly with the whole school priorities.

Departmental reviews

More and more schools have adopted what can only be described as 'mini-inspections' to ensure that everyone is ready for an inspection when the call to arms eventually arrives. These can take a variety of forms, from full inspections led by external advisors which attempt to mirror the current national format as closely as possible to short reviews targeted on particular departments. While these can be seen as a form of CPD in themselves, it is important to distinguish once again between activities aimed at monitoring and those focused on developing the staff taking part. Any activity which involves some kind of review will inevitably include an element of monitoring, but there is no reason why such reviews cannot be focused on development first and monitoring second. In schools where the culture of sharing is strong, departmental reviews are seen both as supportive and a key part of the whole school improvement agenda. As with all aspects of long-lasting school improvement, it takes time to get to this point, but genuinely collaborative reviews are a sure sign that the improvement agenda is embedded in the day-to-day practices of the school. A department keen on sharing will be a department happy to accept criticism. Defensiveness tends to close down improvement; acceptance of positive criticism leads to rapid improvement.

Leadership teams need to work hard to ensure that department reviews are seen as collaborative. It is therefore vital that the head of department, if not the whole department, is involved in the planning process. It is also worth thinking about the review programme itself to ensure that all areas of the school are treated equally. It is very tempting for the head to target the underperforming departments, but this immediately sends the message that the reviews are for monitoring purposes only. They will therefore be seen as punitive rather than supportive. Of course, any competent leadership team will want to look closely at underperforming departments, but this can be done outside the review process. A scheme which has long-term school improvement at its heart is much more likely to review departments in order, on a rolling basis, rather than according to last year's results.

This also ensures that all departments are reviewed, and none become complacent. It also allows leaders to celebrate the work of those under review on a regular basis.

The school learning plan is a good place to start when devising a review. Members of the department will hopefully have been involved in choosing which aspects of the school's key issues on which to focus and will therefore already have a sense of ownership of their department's improvement plan. If, for example, the area for development chosen this year relates to improving the progress of the disadvantaged pupils, this could become the focus for the department review. It could be, however, that the head of department feels that good progress has already been made here and would prefer a slightly different approach. The main thing is to ensure that everyone involved is clear about the focus for the reviews and equally clear that the aim is to help improve the quality of teaching and learning. It is not to identify weak teaching, although inevitably this may turn out to be a by-product of the process.

Alongside the identification of the review focus, it is important to explore the context of the department and, of course, its strengths and weaknesses. This not only involves an analysis of the data but consideration of the whole range of activities in which members of the department are involved as well.

What follows is an example of a department review scheme which has been tried and tested over a number of years in several schools. It is by no means definitive, but it offers schools insight into effective review processes which can easily be adapted to suit their own contexts.

Department reviews – an example method

First, it is important to define the purpose of the review process. Department reviews allow us to do the following:

1 **Know our strengths and our gaps.** In order to drive improvement, it is essential we know our students well so we can better meet their needs. So, the first advantage of any department review is that it provides teams leaders with a means of knowing more about what we do well and what gaps we need to close. It allows us both to identify areas for improvement and celebrate outstanding practice.

2 **Further enhance the skills of our middle leaders.** We have outstanding staff working at the school, but one of our challenges is avoiding complacency. Middle leaders play a prominent part in shaping the conclusions of the review report and supply, in the majority of cases, key evidence to inform the learning points arising from it.

3 **Clarify our CPD needs.** CPD is one of the key aspects of our practice. By having a review system, we continue to make sure that the most appropriate next steps are identified and supported with time and training.

4 **Build greater consistency in teaching and learning across the school and within departments.** With a relentless focus on classroom practice, we can all build a clear sense of what outstanding looks like as well as enabling leaders to know where the very best practice is so that that expertise can be shared. Evidence of progress should be observed during lessons and in books.

5 **Make sure every student fulfils his/her potential.** Particular attention needs to be given to the progress made by different groups of students, for example, SEND, Pupil Premium (PP), most able. The support given to these groups needs to be evident

6 **Develop strength in the leadership of departments.** It is vital for team leaders to be able to identify areas of development and build improvement into their day-to-day activities.

The department review process should be common to all reviews and understood by everyone involved. Key points include the following:

- Reviews should be completed for all departments over a three-year cycle with reviews set out on an annual basis on the calendar.
- Reviews can be requested by departments.
- Themed reviews may be included as one of the reviews carried out each year. For example, we may want to look at the progress of pupils with special educational needs, or we may focus on a cross-curricular theme such as literacy or numeracy.
- Where requested, subject leaders in one subject will be able to shadow a review undertaken in another subject, provided all parties agree.

Review reports should be short, well written and provide clear next steps. Each will comprise an account describing the following:

- **The department context:** a summary of the current position of the department, to include current performance in Key Stages 4 and 5, outcomes from the previous review (strengths, gaps that needed closing) and consideration of the extent to which these issues have been addressed
- **Achievements:** current strengths and best practice within the department
- **Next steps:** recommended priorities which, when addressed, will enable gaps to be closed
- **The evidence underpinning the review:** In some cases, an appendix of additional evidence will be supplied where further information has been gathered in advance of the publication of the review report – this is typically where student interviews are included.

The process should be outlined clearly and understood by everyone involved. There are several important stages.

Before the review, line managers should meet with subject leaders to identify any evidence needed to support the process. This is likely to include the following:

- An analysis of how well students make progress from Key Stage 2 to Key Stage 4 and from Key Stage 4 to Key Stage 5
- Recent lesson observation findings for all members of the department identifying strengths and areas for development
- Copies of findings from any work scrutiny or pupil interviews undertaken
- A request for students to be interviewed on the day of the review

This meeting could be done more formally, with a presentation by the head of department to the leadership team outlining the strengths and weaknesses of the department and identifying key focus areas. The SLT member leading the review will then meet to agree the timetable, activities and lines of enquiry/focus points that will take place during the review week (normally with the line manager joining the subject leader).

During the review, the following activities will be included:

1 **Paired 30-minute drop-ins.** Classes will be visited by the subject leader (or second in charge) with a senior leader to observe pupil progress in lessons and books. The head of department should provide feedback to the teacher after the lesson. No written lesson plan is required, but it is expected that staff will be able to demonstrate a good understanding of individuals and identified groups in the class. Feedback should be in line the school and departmental policies.

2 **Student interviews.** Senior leaders with or without subject leaders will meet students to discuss their attitudes to learning in the subject.

3 **Work scrutiny.** Senior leaders with subject leaders and teams (as agreed) will sample student work to determine how feedback can support students to make progress.

4 **Lesson 'snaphots.'** On occasion, the senior leader and the subject leader may forego some 30-minute drop-ins to make short lesson visits to all members of the team over an hour.

5 **Student questionnaires.** To augment findings from student interviews, it may be necessary to use online questionnaires (using the school's virtual learning environment or other providers like SurveyMonkey) to gauge the impact teachers have on the progress being made in their subject.

6 **Constructing the report** – Working alongside the senior leader charged with writing the final report, the subject leader will help to construct the headlines for the review. Subject leaders will also review and, where appropriate, amend the draft review prior to publication.

The review should be completed quickly and made available to all those involved as soon as possible. Throughout, it should be stressed that this is a formative process: the aim is to support improvement. It should be regarded as a professional development activity, not an inspection activity.

An interesting approach to this stage of the review is to share the findings over lunch with the whole department so that the details can be discussed openly and honestly. Some leadership teams may also consider adding an element of '360 degree' review by asking members of the department to comment on the nature and effectiveness of the review process itself.

What happens to the final report will vary depending on the culture and ethos of the school. In most schools, the report will be shared with members of the department and the leadership team. Headlines may be shared with governors. In truly confident schools, however, departmental reviews can be made available to all staff so that good practice is shared and celebrated, and improvements can be supported by colleagues across the school. In those schools where staff are under huge pressure to improve outcomes in order to climb out of a category this may seem like an overly optimistic dream, but school improvement is a gradual process, and to achieve this kind of openness must surely be the goal of every head teacher and senior leader.

However, through the review, there is, of course, the danger that it will be forgotten as soon as it is over. It is therefore important to build in some kind of mechanism to check that any recommendations have been followed up on and any action points put into practice. This can be done in a variety of ways. For example, the head of department may wish to construct a series of learning walks, accompanied by senior leaders, where changes can be pointed out and the impact on pupils observed. In the same way as we expect to be able to identify progress in pupils' work, we should expect to see progress in the work of our departments. We may not be able to identify huge leaps forward, but the gradual art of school improvement is all about incremental change.

Reluctant staff

Every school leader will be familiar with staff who at best can be described as reluctant but who sometimes appear downright obstructive. They cannot, of course, be ignored, and they need to be catered for in any effective CPD structure. The trick is, of course, to get them on board, but this can take time. There is undoubtedly a group of staff in every school who will be less amenable than the majority. Unfortunately, these colleagues are rarely acknowledged in serious discussions of school improvement. The tendency is to work around them or, in the worst-case scenarios, to move them on. The solution, as always, is to adopt a gradual approach, allowing time for them to see the value of the training you have planned and to appreciate its relevance both to their own teaching and the overall improvement of the school.

I have sat through too many farewell speeches in which colleagues speak in glowing terms about the school as it used to be, not to be aware of the powerful influence of nostalgia. I much prefer to think about what the school could be, not what it once was, but not everyone thinks like that. For colleagues new to leadership, to hear about the glories of the past can be a seriously depressing experience, the implication being that the school was once great and now it isn't. The plain fact is, of course, that the Arcadian times lingered over in the staffroom probably didn't actually exist. It is up to school leaders to create a new Arcadia or, at least, a compelling vision for school improvement to which everyone can subscribe.

In many ways, colleagues who have become set in their ways often prove to be a key issue when it comes to establishing a new direction for the school. Ironically, we all know about this problem, and we all know that these people exist in schools, but how often do we acknowledge them as a problem? How often do we see commercial CPD courses aimed at colleagues who have become tired and dispirited? Admittedly, it is difficult to imagine exactly how such courses could be advertised without causing offence – 'a refresher course for the terminally jaded' or 'revivifying tired and obstructive staff'? – but there is a problem here which we shouldn't shy away from addressing. Senior leaders are often offered courses based on dealing with 'difficult conversations,' but where are the courses aimed at breathing new life into colleagues who have been teaching for 30 years and now dream only of retirement and a quiet life?

There are ways forward, of course, and with patience, it is possible to ensure that everyone becomes actively committed to the school improvement agenda. First, never trash the past. A new head teacher who systematically criticizes everything done by his or her predecessors will inevitably upset large numbers of staff, no matter how ineffective the previous incumbents proved to be. Staff were all, of course, involved in what went on in the school before and are likely to take criticisms of the previous regime as criticisms of themselves. This is especially true of staff who have been in the school for some time. No matter how much is wrong in a school, sudden change is rarely as effective as gradual improvement. Reluctant colleagues are especially vulnerable to the shock of the new.

In a recent television series, James May – who has incidentally turned out to be an intelligent and witty commentator now that he has escaped the dreadful shadow of Jeremy Clarkson – compared the design histories of German and British cars. In particular, he compared the revolutionary thinking of TVR with the incremental approach adopted by Porsche. While TVR created some strikingly radical designs and turned out model after model, many of which were highly innovative, their cars were plagued by mechanical problems, and the production systems they employed always failed to make a profit. Porsche, on the other hand, kept the same design for decades gradually refining and improving it – the Porsche 911 on sale today is not dramatically different from the original model first sold in the sixties. The same is true of school improvement. Dramatic changes may be innovative and, sometimes, necessary, but it is the gradual refinement of existing practice which brings about genuine school improvement. Reluctant colleagues are much more likely to acquiesce in gradual improvement and much more likely to feel valued if the work they have done in the past is both appreciated and used as a platform on which to build.

It is also important not to confuse reluctant staff with incompetent staff. Many are highly skilled and keen to continue to produce outstanding outcomes for the pupils they teach. The problem is that they have seen it all before and they need persuading that the programmes you are suggesting will genuinely have an impact and are different to all the other things they have been forced to try out over the years. So, make sure they are regularly consulted and, above all, involved. We have seen how younger teachers new to the profession, in roles like those of the challenge coordinators described earlier, are able to engage and inspire senior colleagues, but it is also true to say that giving reluctant staff new responsibilities can be equally stimulating. Leaders need, therefore, actively to identify outstanding aspects of their practice and then encourage them to share their expertise. Who isn't flattered by being asked to share their knowledge and experience?

There is also a degree of patience involved. As improvements in the school take hold and more and more staff align with the vision of improved teaching and learning as set out in the Learning plan, even the most reluctant staff have to recognize that something is working. It may take time but gradual persuasion, even if it is tacit, is likely to be much more effective than authoritarian ultimata.

Staff forum

Of course, valuing the input of staff in the school improvement process should not be restricted to those who are reluctant to engage. It is important to give all staff a voice in the school. This is not as straightforward as it sounds, however. Head teachers are often proud of their open-door policies and talk confidently about how easy they are to speak to and how actively they encourage staff to talk to them about all aspects of the school's policies and practices. How often this actually happens is highly questionable, however.

No matter how approachable leaders regard themselves to be and how confident they are that colleagues speak to them all the time, they have a tendency to overlook the fact that holding a senior position in the school is in itself intimidating. A head teacher is necessarily distanced from his or her staff. It is part of the job. Simply because colleagues join in conversations with you in the staffroom or are happy to talk to you about an issue you have raised doesn't mean that they have the confidence to come and talk to you directly about their concerns. They are particularly wary of criticizing the leadership team in case it could present them in a poor light and potentially damage their standing in the school.

This is something it took me a while to appreciate. I have never considered myself to resemble anything remotely close to a figure of authority, but it turned out that, in accepting the role of head teacher, this is what I had become. I may have been naïve, but I suspect there are lots equally naïve senior leaders out there who have yet to appreciate how intimidating they are to the staff in their schools. For a while, I tried to convince my colleagues that I was genuinely approachable and that the distance between us meant nothing. However, it eventually dawned on me that I am the head and that a certain distance is inevitable. I therefore sought other ways to encourage staff to say what they genuinely thought about the school and the decisions being made by the leadership team.

The solution was the creation of what became known as the Staff Forum, and although it has proved to be an excellent way of gauging staff views on a whole range of matters, it is a solution which regularly causes me great anxiety. It is undoubtedly a good thing and a great idea; it does mean, however, that I am often forced to hear things which make me feel somewhat uncomfortable and which cause me to question closely some of the decisions I have made. I know, however, that this questioning process is incredibly important and is now a key part of my approach to whole-school improvement.

The idea is simple. All staff are invited to a meeting once a month to discuss anything they like. The important point to note, however, is that members of the leadership team are not invited. Staff choose one of their colleagues to chair the meeting, and he or she then feeds back to the head the next day. The agenda is decided by those attending, with topics for discussion submitted to the chair in the week before the meeting. There are no restrictions regarding what can be discussed. The feedback is given entirely anonymously: the chair goes through the various points made without naming the member of staff who raised a particular issue or any of those involved in the discussion. It is then up to the head to take on board the ideas discussed and respond at the next full staff meeting.

This can seem like a threatening process for a head teacher and yet its value is hard to over-estimate. Staff feel that they have a genuine voice in the improvement of the school and really appreciate the head teacher's attempts to address any concerns raised. Often, this is easily done; sometimes, however, the topics discussed relate to complex issues which take time to explore fully. I can't say I enjoy the feedback meetings, and some have given me sleepless nights, but I now cannot imagine running a school without them.

Teaching schools

Any consideration of professional development should consider the valuable role teaching schools were designed to fulfil. Many of the activities outlined above can easily be facilitated by working with a local teaching school. Most have sophisticated CPD programmes, many host research networks and nearly all of them offer colleagues the chance to visit other schools, either through trio work or shadowing schemes. They make 'getting out more' much easier, and they offer great opportunities for teachers and leaders to work with their counterparts in other schools. They also make sharing good practice much easier. All things considered, they offer school leaders a range of services which complement perfectly the kinds of things they are doing in their own schools – at least they should do.

A summary of the work of teaching schools should therefore offer a fitting finale to a chapter on professional development. Unfortunately, however, the original vision of the teaching school has been degraded and its usefulness to school improvement compromised. It is nevertheless worthwhile to take a few moments to consider the potential effectiveness of a system set up to share good practice, provide outstanding teacher training and provide support for other schools.

In November 2010, the Schools White Paper proposed a new national network of teaching schools, modelled on the concept of teaching hospitals. The National College, working closely with the Training and Development Agency for schools was asked to lead on developing the teaching school model and to implement methods of designation and quality assurance. Just over 100 teaching schools were designated in the first cohort, with a further 100 added in April 2012. The intention was to build up to about 500, but the project proved so popular with schools that there are currently more than 800 listed on the Department of Education (DfE) website.

The initial vision was a powerful one and gave outstanding schools the chance to develop and share their expertise across a wide area. It promised to allow schools to work with each other to drive up standards both locally and nationally. The teaching school network was therefore a first step towards the creation of the now common ambition, 'a school-led system.'

And it worked. Schools grouped together in local alliances and really seemed to relish the opportunity to work together and not in competition. They were able to fill the gaps left by the withdrawal of local authority support, and in the most effective alliances, a strong culture of mutual support and encouragement took hold.

Things have changed, however, and many teaching school leaders are now concerned that the movement – and it was a movement – has lost its way.

Originally, the focus was on 'the big six': initial teacher training, continuing professional development and leadership development, succession planning and talent management, school-to-school support, SLEs and research and development. A glance at the latest guidance, however, reveals that the ambitions of the 'big six' have been trimmed to 'a more focused role' which now consists of three priorities: ITT, school-to-school support and professional and leadership development. This means that key activities such as succession planning, SLEs and research have seemingly been abandoned.

For many senior leaders, the opportunity to engage in genuine school-based research was one of the most attractive aspects of the entire programme, and some really impressive work was done in this area. Teachers at all levels worked together to explore the effectiveness of pedagogy in the classroom, and they grasped the opportunity with a real sense of excitement. For many, it resulted in a renewed interest in classroom practice, but it also helped to enhance their view

- Teachers at all levels should lead CPD sessions; teaching a new skill is one of the most powerful ways to learn.

- Teachers should be encouraged to visit other schools and other classrooms as often as they can.

- Teachers are often put off by the word *research*; remove the word and research in schools becomes much more likely.

- Trios or Triads offer a highly effective and relatively cheap means of professional development.

- Younger staff make excellent leaders of CPD.

- Collaborative work should always be classroom to classroom, not boardroom to boardroom.

- A planned CPD programme linked to the learning plan is key to effective and long-lasting school improvement.

- Departmental/year team reviews offer an excellent way of ensuring that there is a continuing conversation in the school about pedagogy; they should be more about sharing good practice than about monitoring the quality of provision.

- Reluctant staff can be motivated by working with young colleagues and by having their expertise openly acknowledged.

- The creation of a Staff Forum is an effective way of finding out what staff really think about what's going on in the school and its current direction.

- Although the teaching school movement has lost its way in recent years, it is still a powerful and useful means of collaborating with colleagues in other schools.

Practical ideas

- Review the range of CPD experiences of your staff. How many focused on subject development, how many on leadership and how many on pedagogy? Do you have the balance right?

- Insist that all teachers make regular visits to other schools. This could be built into their performance management objectives.

- Organize staff into Trios or Triads both in school and across schools. Your local teaching school may be able to help with this.
- Consider creating challenge coordinator roles for young staff as described in this chapter.
- Do you have a planned CPD programme which stretches across the year and is it linked directly to your learning plan?
- Do you have a regular, planned departmental review programme? Is it about shared learning, or is it a monitoring mechanism? What changes would you need to make to allow departmental reviews to drive the whole-school discussion of pedagogy?
- Consider setting up a Staff Forum to ensure that you get genuine feedback regarding your leadership of the school.

The curriculum

The school curriculum is constantly under discussion, whether in the media or in political discourse. We have already seen how frequently articles in the media call on schools to build new subjects into the curriculum in order to address society's ills and how often politicians look to schools to solve political problems. The curriculum is, of course, also a key element of educational discourse, emerging again and again as a topic for debate, the most recent example being Amanda Spielman's review of the inspection framework. Shortly after her appointment as Her Majesty's Chief Inspector of Schools, she initiated a discussion of the relationship between the curriculum and performance tables which will no doubt place her at odds with the Department for Education's (DfE's) policy division.

Although constantly in the news, it has to be acknowledged that the curriculum on offer in most schools has changed very little over the years, despite huge changes in society. The conclusion of Raymond Williams's *The Long Revolution*, though written over 50 years ago, makes the point: 'The fact about our present curriculum is that it was essentially created by the 19th century, following some 18th century models and retaining elements of the medieval curriculum near its centre.'[1]

Despite the arrival of the new national curriculum in 1988, for many school leaders this statement holds true, and as the world develops more and more rapidly outside of school, the pressure to reform becomes increasingly urgent.

John White's study of the aims of the national curriculum, *Rethinking the School Curriculum*, reinforces the view that, despite revisions to the 1988 blueprint, schools are growing increasingly out of touch with the world beyond the classroom.[2] He describes schools as being 'in the grip of custom' and ends by suggesting a number of 'general lessons for the curriculum as a whole.' In particular, he mentions the need to 'reverse introspection' and encourages individual subjects to look beyond themselves; he advocates 'interconnectedness,' suggesting that subjects need to be aware of connections across the curriculum; the 'primacy of the practical' is also important, in the sense that students need to be active and independent learners; and the notion of greater student choice, beginning at Key Stage 3, is felt to be vital in order to make education more interesting and more enjoyable for all students.

All of this still holds true and it has held true for some time. It is difficult, however, to envisage any really radical changes to the curriculum in the near future. Changes are likely to continue to be minor and incremental. No other aspect of educational reform illustrates more effectively the importance of school improvement as a gradual art.

What do we mean by the curriculum?

A school curriculum is more than a list of subjects. There are a number of key elements. First, there is the statutory national curriculum which the majority of schools still follow, despite the freedoms given to academies and free schools. Second, there are those subjects which are prescribed by law but which, for many, sit outside the academic curriculum: religious education, sex education, careers advice and guidance and work-related learning. Finally, there is all the other stuff: extra- or co-curricular activities which, though rarely included in school prospectuses as part of the curriculum, are often vital to the life and culture of the school.

The definition can then be broadened still further if we draw back from the subject list to examine the philosophy underpinning the curriculum. Sean Harford, Office for Standards in Education's, Children's Services and Skills (Ofsted's) director of education, used the following working definition in a recent speech:

> The curriculum is a framework for setting out the aims of a programme of education, including the knowledge and understanding to be gained at each stage (intent); for translating that framework over time into a structure and a narrative, within an institutional context (implementation) and for evaluating what knowledge and understanding pupils have gained against expectations (impact/achievement).[3]

In other words, the curriculum is a framework involving both skills and knowledge which schools deliver as a coherent narrative to their pupils. As this is a definition prepared for Ofsted, it perhaps inevitably moves on to include impact and achievement. This strikes me as more about evaluating the curriculum rather than the curriculum itself. However, the only way to check that a curriculum is doing what you want it to do is to evaluate it, though not necessarily in terms simply of achievement in examinations but the wider achievements of pupils who have been through the system. This is where we move from what subjects they should be studying to much more fundamental questions about why they are studying in the first place. Is it all about success in exams, paths to employment, or more about developing a love of learning to sustain them in later life? These are questions we could spend hundreds of hours debating. Let's assume, therefore, that we all understand what we mean when we talk about the curriculum and move on to more practical considerations.

Despite the constraints of the national curriculum, the inspection framework and the government's performance tables, there is still room for innovation, and good school leadership must involve regular scrutiny of the curriculum. For many school leaders, working with the curriculum is one of the most interesting and rewarding aspects of the role, as it is here they can often make a significant impact on the culture of the school, its day-to-day operation and, of course, the lives and prospects of its pupils.

A head teacher new to a school would be strongly advised to take a careful look at the curriculum to see if it was really meeting the needs of the pupils in the school, as well as making the most effective use of teaching staff. A full-scale curriculum review should be undertaken regularly by leadership teams in any case and not only in response to national curriculum change. This has to be done with care, however, because once the various constraints are considered – these include the requirements of the national curriculum, performance measures and legal duties – there often seems very little room to manoeuvre. However, with imagination and genuine concern for what pupils actually need, there is more flexibility than would initially seem to be the case.

The core curriculum cannot be avoided but it can be delivered in a variety of ways. Of course, the amount of time given to each subject is the key to greater flexibility. A school that devotes 12 hours a week to English and maths, as many do, will find that scope for additional subjects is limited. There are also government 'recommendations' to be considered: the time allocated to physical education (PE) and games is a good example. Although it is possible to reduce the time pupils spend involved in PE, it is rarely a good idea. Not only will there be a need to justify the reduction to governors, parents, inspectors and local authority (LA) reviewers; it also will not go down well with pupils. There are some battles not worth fighting. It is therefore better to accept that substantial amounts of time will need to be allocated for English and maths, and the recommended hours for PE, Religious Education, and Personal, Social and Health Education (PSHE) should be accepted.

Once the core is in place, there is room for innovation. However, as we saw in Chapter 2, curriculum innovation must be carefully thought out, thoroughly planned and, above all, fit for purpose. There is no point in creating a dazzlingly original curriculum if it does not meet the needs of pupils. A discussion of what pupils' need is therefore essential and, as we have seen, this relates very closely to the leadership team's vision for the development of the school. At Key Stage 3, for example, once the core is in place, there is room for considerable imagination in terms of subject choices. With strong foundations in English and maths, and more particularly literacy and numeracy, it is possible to build a fairly unique curriculum by simply allocating more time to particular subjects or by introducing subjects which are perhaps less common in other schools. If it is apparent, for example, that pupils in the school would benefit from an enhanced scientific offer – perhaps because the school is located in an area surrounded by firms specializing in science and technology – it would be fairly easy to create a much more extensive science curriculum compared to those commonly available in most mainstream schools.

This is the flexibility that the Free School movement is supposed to offer. It is ironic, therefore, that most Free Schools adopt very traditional curriculum models eschewing innovation for tried and tested methods more likely to appeal to their parents. Mainstream schools and academies are, in fact, much more likely to construct innovative curriculums, and despite the constraints, they already have the ability to do so.

With a modicum of imagination, it is easy to see how minor adjustments can make school curriculums much more appropriate for the pupils that follow them and the communities they serve. Here are some examples:

- A school based on the coast or in an area of outstanding natural beauty may well wish to build a greater emphasis on geography, geology or environmental studies into Key Stage 3, before offering all three subjects at General Certificate of Secondary Education (GCSE) and A-level.

- A school serving a deprived catchment area with high numbers of pupils who enter the school with low prior attainment may well wish to introduce a wider range of practical subjects lower down the school, leading to a range of vocational opportunities at Key Stage 4. This flies in the face of Michael Gove's insistence that all children deserve a truly academic education, but it recognizes the real-world issues faced by pupils in these schools.

- Schools in areas of the country serving highly educated, middle-class populations are able to adapt their curriculums accordingly. The English Baccalaureate (Ebacc) may be very appropriate for the majority of pupils in these schools but, as always, adaptations are possible. There is no reason why Latin shouldn't be on the curriculum from Year 7, and it may be relevant to include much greater emphasis on the humanities and the arts.

- Although becoming less and less popular nationally, there is a great scope to distinguish the curriculum by placing much greater emphasis on languages. This could well be appropriate for schools serving communities where lots of different languages are spoken, but it could equally be important for those in areas with easy links to the continent and beyond or those closely connected with the tourist industry.

- In schools serving troubled populations, strong emphasis on PSHE and personal support may best suit the needs of pupils.

- Faith schools are frequently under scrutiny in the media, but schools based in strong faith communities are able to adapt their curriculums appropriately provided they pay attention to laws covering equalities and freedoms.

- Rural schools often have unique challenges and it is essential to bear these in mind when constructing curriculums in these schools. Adaptations which focus on jobs in the rural economy are obvious, but it is also important for leaders to address issues such as isolation and a lack of access to the kind of opportunities those who live in towns and cities take for granted. The best rural schools, for example, make sure that their pupils have the chance to experience multicultural Britain, the chance to see plays and exhibitions, and the chance to travel widely. These are aspects of the curriculum that perhaps sit outside the normal subject choice discussion, but they are key to making sure that the curriculum is fit for purpose and matches the needs of its pupils.

- Similarly, for schools in inner-city areas, it is vital that the curriculum takes into account its pupils' lack of access to, and experience of, the countryside.

It is this kind of thinking which makes curriculum planning exciting, despite the constraints.

Playing the game

Much has been made recently of what has been described as 'game-playing' in schools; in other words, schools choosing examination courses in order to boost their standings in the performance tables. This kind of thing was, of course, inevitable. School leaders now work in a very competitive environment. No matter how collaborative schools become, they are always aware that their status in the community must be maintained, often simply to attract enough pupils to make the school financially viable. If schools are measured so publicly, then performance tables become impossible to ignore. School leaders risk seeing their schools vilified if they appear at the bottom of the tables. Nor is it simply about parental dissatisfaction and parental choice. A school with poor performance data is more likely to be inspected, more likely to be put into a category and more likely to be forced to join an academy chain. It then becomes more difficult to attract high-quality staff – remember that schools in special measures are not allowed to employ newly qualified teachers – and the best teachers already on the staff often leave to find better prospects elsewhere.

Is it surprising, therefore, that head teachers look to find ways to bolster the position of their schools in the league tables? It is here that the quick-fix culture appears at its most damaging and virulent. Leaders often panic, opting for courses that offer easily attainable progress points without really considering either their quality or whether they match the needs of the pupils who end up taking them. In the past few years a whole industry has sprung up to provide advice for panicking head teachers. One of the most successful was PixL, an organization which seemed to combine the revivalist zeal of American evangelists with the data skills of Russian internet hackers. Of course, PixL has always denied its role in promoting quick-fix solutions, and it is fair to say that, as the organization has grown and evolved, it has become much more interested in promoting long-term improvement strategies. The rush to points-scoring courses was nevertheless something of a phenomenon when performance tables began to take hold of the nation's psyche.

More recently, the move from attainment measures to progress measures, and the DfE's list of approved courses, has made it much more difficult to game the system, but the temptation is still there. Fewer schools are now entering entire year groups for courses such as the European Computer Driving Licence (ECDL) but many are still looking closely at the courses where their pupils are likely to gain the most points. The drop-off in entries for modern languages is a good example. Although the Ebacc attempted to ensure that schools would increase the numbers of pupils taking languages, as the significance of the qualification has faded from public consciousness, more and more school leaders are looking at their pupils and deciding that languages are not for them. Higher points-scoring subjects are more appropriate. Languages have always been a 'difficult sell' in some schools: they are difficult, and many see little point in learning another language. However, in terms of offering a fully rounded education, and in order to prepare pupils for global markets, language learning is surely one of the most important skills a child can learn.

Senior leaders now spend hours poring over the various 'buckets' in the Progress 8 calculation in order to maximize each pupil's point score. ECDL may not offer the quick fix it used to, but by substituting GCSE PE for French or Spanish, for example, a pupil is more likely to achieve a higher progress score. If this is done for every pupil, the school can substantially improve its overall score. This may look initially like skilful management, and the school may well be judged to have improved substantially, but it raises very awkward questions. First, and most important, are pupils now studying the courses that suit their needs or are they studying the courses that suit the school's needs? Second, how long lasting are these 'improvements'? It doesn't take much of a cynic to regard this kind of curriculum management as an educational version of the king's new clothes.

Ofsted's interest in the curriculum and its effectiveness is aimed to some extent at countering the pressures of performance tables, but as long as the tables exist, they will act as a constraint on genuine curriculum development. The curriculum, therefore, is an aspect of school improvement where heads need to tread carefully. The importance of performance data cannot be denied and yet a head truly interested in school improvement and, more to the point, doing the right thing for pupils, needs to have the courage to hold firm and avoid the quick fix. Game playing may produce the results needed to secure an acceptable position in the tables, but it is unlikely to secure improvements which will see the school flourishing in the long term. Of course, for ambitious leaders, the temptation will always be to apply the quick fix and then move on to promoted posts thanks to their evident successes in turning things around. A leader who sees the moral imperative in terms of long-lasting improvement is much more likely to take a graduated approach.

With the system as it is, there will always be a tension between playing the game and genuine progress. It is the system that is wrong, not the heads who struggle with it. One can only hope that a more realistic view of student progress emerges at some time in the future which will allow school leaders the time they need to bring about genuine improvement without obsessing over performance points. I am sorry to say that the gradual art of school improvement may not be a method fully endorsed by the secretary of state for education.

Broad and balanced

It is the aim of every school to offer a broad and balanced curriculum, but what does that mean for schools today? It would be good to think that it meant offering pupils a wide range of subjects covering the things they really need to know to make their way in society plus a choice of subjects enabling them to follow their interests, develop as individuals, prepare for stimulating careers or simply expand their minds. I think this is what we all aim for, knowing, however, that such are the constraints on the curriculum that this level of perfection can never be achieved.

In reality, a broad and balanced curriculum today is one which seeks to satisfy the needs of pupils in a heavily circumscribed environment. A school curriculum today has to attempt to do the following:

i   Meet the needs of pupils

ii Fulfil the requirements of the law and the national curriculum

iii Be mindful of the performance tables

iv Take into account the local context

v   Offer challenge at all levels

vi Consider both the academic and the vocational

vii Prepare pupils for future careers

viii Inculcate a love of learning

ix Reflect the vision of the school

It is no mean feat to get this right: the curriculum is an answer to a very complex series of questions which must nevertheless be asked.

Matching the curriculum to the needs of pupils is about much more than analysing data relating to attainment on entry. This is a good starting point, of course, but there is no simple equation linking attainment on entry and the subjects to be studied. Obviously, with a weaker cohort, more time will necessarily have to be spent on literacy because, without reading skills, pupils will not have access to the rest of the curriculum, but low attainment does not necessarily imply either a restricted offer or a particular set of subjects. It is too simplistic to assume that weaker students will be better suited to more practical courses like PE and Technology, with lots of vocational choices at Key Stage 4. Nor should we endorse the notion that languages, for example, or separate sciences are for the brightest. It could well be that low attainment on entry is a symptom of poor teaching at Key

Stage 2 rather than an innate inability to learn challenging subjects. As always, the most important consideration here is the needs of pupils, and to get this right, schools really have to know their pupils. This may seem like putting the cart before the horse – you can't wait to construct the curriculum until after pupils have arrived in school – but you can adapt it for future years, assuming that your intake remains relatively stable year on year.

Getting to know pupils takes time: it takes a while for school leaders to build an accurate picture of what each cohort is capable of, what its limitations are and what are its real challenges. Leaders need to heed the advice of their teachers and listen carefully to what their colleagues are saying about the school. Above all, they need to see them in the classroom. This is where the importance of the head teacher as head teacher comes in again. A head who spends time in the classroom is likely to have a much greater understanding of his or her pupils' requirements than one who doesn't teach at all.

Knowing pupils in the classroom should then be complemented by a consideration of the school in the community. It is also important to think about relationships with other schools. For example, a comprehensive surrounded by selective schools will have a complex relationship with parents. For many, no matter how poor the grammar school, the comprehensive will always be second best. It will therefore be tempting for the comprehensive to attempt to behave like a grammar school in order to mollify disappointed parents whose children didn't pass the entrance tests. This may be a good marketing tool, allaying parents' fears and convincing them that their children will nevertheless be receiving a proper academic education, but it may not be right for the school at all. In attempting to out grammar the grammar, it may well end up offering a completely inappropriate curriculum.

I have personal experience of exactly this dilemma, working in a comprehensive school a few miles away from one of the most selective grammar schools in the country. When I arrived here, it was clear that the previous head had decided to adopt as much of the grammar school paraphernalia as possible to convince parents that his school was by no means a second-best choice. Consequently, there were gowns in assemblies, a school song, strict setting, rigid uniform rules and so on. The irony was that all this simply reminded everyone of the existence of the grammar school down the road. I therefore had to work hard to create a new image of the school based on an entirely different vision of education. This took a while, it has to be said, but gradually the school became recognized as an alternative to the grammar rather than as a substitute.

It is still the case, however, such is the ingrained view that grammar schools are perforce better than comprehensives, I still have encounters with parents who will forever be disappointed with what we offer simply because we are not the grammar school. I remember one conversation with a parent in particular. She was the mother of an exceptionally bright girl who eventually achieved a solid set of A grades at GCSE and A*s at A-level. She was constantly critical of the school, however, because we are not the grammar school. When I eventually said to her, 'Isn't it true that however good the quality of education here, because of your disappointment at not getting your daughter into the grammar school you will always regard us a second best?' she thought for a moment and agreed that it was true. The complex relationships between schools and between parents and schools are therefore key aspects of the educational contexts underpinning curriculum planning.

The degree of challenge is also an important consideration. You may have decided that a certain combination of subjects is a perfect match for the pupils in your school, but do they offer sufficient challenge? There will always be a dilemma here. You may get the subject areas right, but it would be wrong to assume they will therefore meet the needs of every pupil. A good example of this is a school which acknowledges a genuinely low-ability intake might be better served by intensive literacy support, coupled with access to a range of practical or vocational subjects, but which then fails to ensure that these subjects are sufficiently demanding. Just because a subject is vocational doesn't mean that it shouldn't be demanding. Indeed, one of the main reasons the DfE has had so much trouble introducing vocational options in schools (and there is a sad record of failed attempts to do so stretching from Technical and Vocational Education Initiative (TVEI) to T Levels) is that vocational is, for many, synonymous with easy. Consequently, schools channel their weakest students into vocational courses, and the various examining boards lower their standards accordingly to ensure that their pass rate remains high. School leaders need to be highly attuned to the needs of pupils if they are to ensure that courses which may appear perfectly suited to the school's intake offer genuine challenge.

Planning should therefore involve close attention to attainment on entry, a realistic understanding of pupils in the classroom and an awareness of the complex relationships between schools and parents. The next step is to adopt and then adapt the core curriculum to ensure that it provides firm foundations on which to build the rest. Understanding pupils' needs will help delineate the nature and structure of the core: if literacy is an issue, then more time must be devoted to bringing pupils up to the required standards. If numeracy is poor, the same will also be true. The needs of pupils will dictate the time allocations for each core subject area, and of course, there will need to be at least some regard to the demands of the performance tables. Next, those subjects prescribed by statute must be considered, but these too can be delivered flexibly enough to ensure that they relate to need rather than convention. Faith schools will want to devote more time to RE; others may afford it less emphasis. In both cases, there will be an impact on the rest of the curriculum in terms of time.

The other areas of the curriculum will similarly be dictated by the needs of pupils. Schools may choose to focus on the Ebacc, or on a vocational offer, or a set of subjects more appropriate to the school's local context. Whatever route is chosen, every aspect of the curriculum plan should be examined to ensure it offers a good fit. A clear sense of progression is also essential: Do the subjects offered at

Key Stage 3 build on those delivered at Key Stage 2, and do they move on naturally to Key Stage 4 and the sixth form? Does every pupil have access to a route through the system which is appropriate to their particular needs?

Those schools which focus on preparing pupils for GCSE examinations early on in Key Stage 3 particularly need to think about progress. There may be a perfectly sensible route through the system which leads directly to GCSEs but the danger here is that pupils' learning will be limited, especially if it is tied too closely to examination specifications too far down the school. As Amanda Spielman said at the launch of Ofsted's annual report 2017/18, '[i]f [children's] entire school experience has been designed to push them through mark-scheme hoops, rather than developing a deep body of knowledge, they will struggle in later study.'[4] More to the point, they may be put off learning for good.

The effectiveness of the curriculum should be rigorously tested. A good way of doing this is to choose a selection of pupils as case studies. Who is chosen will, of course, depend on the composition of the school's intake, but a basic sample group might include a low prior attainer, a student with special needs, a speaker of English as a second language, a higher prior attainer and one with emotional difficulties. For each student, plan a route through the curriculum. If a route is not possible, or not ideal, then questions should be asked, and the plans reconsidered. This can be a demanding and frustrating exercise, but it is worth it: not only does it demonstrate the inclusiveness of the school, but it will also ensure greater engagement, fewer discipline problems and, ultimately, higher performance at all levels.

Above all, leaders must ensure that the curriculum is stimulating and engaging in order to help pupils develop a lifelong love of learning. It must therefore be much more than simply fit for purpose. Schools with utilitarian curriculum plans which simply offer the core curriculum plus one or two additional choices are unlikely to inspire their pupils. Once all the building blocks are in place, this should therefore be the key question: Is this a truly inspiring curriculum?

Choice

The importance of choice should never be underestimated as it is choice that is likely to ensure the highest levels of pupil engagement. Choice also means variety, and this is something which pupils desperately need if they are to make their way through five years of study. I am convinced that my shabby language skills are due largely to the mind-numbing lack of variety offered by the French course I had to endure at school. In the first year we were each given a copy of *Cours Illustré* which we worked through in exactly the same way in every lesson. We read a passage, we answered the questions around the class and we wrote something. We rarely spoke (French people didn't apparently feel the need to speak in those days). In the second year we were given *Cours Illustré 2*, which was exactly the same as the first book but a different colour (blue instead of orange, I think). The colour changed every year, but neither the book nor the teaching changed a bit. It was fantastically boring. The only thing I learned was that every French family had a pet monkey (and, when meeting visitors from France, I still ask hopefully, 'Ou est le singe?').

Choice is difficult to engineer in the first couple of years of the secondary curriculum, and to some extent, choice at this stage could prove to be overwhelming for pupils moving up from primary school. Most secondary schools follow a fairly traditional national curriculum-based pattern, and even though some schools have experimented with topic-based plans or primary-style teaching with one class teacher for most of the time, there is undoubtedly a standard Key Stage 3 curriculum being delivered in the majority of schools in the UK. There may be some slight adjustments with regard to languages or design technology rotations, but for the most part pupils in Years 7 and 8 tend to follow standard curriculum patterns quite happily. After two years, however, change is required.

Schools are increasingly opting for three-year Key Stage 3 programmes in order better to prepare their pupils for their GCSEs. There has been considerable debate about the effectiveness of this kind of arrangement, with strong support on both sides. Its advocates point to the extra time it allows teachers to deliver much more demanding and content heavy GCSE courses; its detractors say that teachers are missing an opportunity to provide a rich and fulfilling Key Stage 3 curriculum before pushing children back on to the examination treadmill. The question of maturity is also a key consideration: some argue that pupils are too immature to begin GCSEs in Year 9, and they haven't acquired the skills they will need to tackle such demanding courses; others are adamant that by Year 9 their pupils are certainly mature enough and itching to get on with examination preparation. The key considerations here are, of course, the nature and the needs of the pupils in the school.

In Chapter 2, I outlined the approach adopted in my own school which, in many ways, was an attempt to achieve a kind of halfway house between the key stages. After much debate and discussion, we ended up creating a pathway system: all pupils follow the core subjects, but in addition, they get to choose one of seven pathways, each of which contains three subjects, and a few will be new to them (business, media, Latin, etc.). The pathways are constructed after asking pupils what their ideal three subjects would be and therefore modified each year.

There is not, in fact, a huge amount of choice for pupils in this system, but it feels as if there is. We have a pathways evening, where the system is explained to parents, and a step-by-step options process, where we help pupils make the right choices. Of course, one key feature of the plan is that pupils can often drop a subject they really don't enjoy. In a way, we offer the illusion of choice rather than comprehensive choice, but it has an impact nevertheless. Commitment to learning and general enthusiasm in the classroom has improved dramatically since adopting the new system. Pupils are then given the chance to opt again for their GCSE courses beginning in Year 10, having tried out a few subjects already. This means that they can choose GCSE courses with more knowledge and more confidence, and they are therefore more likely both to enjoy them and succeed in them.

Choice at Key Stage 4 is essential. The Ebacc may have narrowed the choices available but the Ebacc isn't for everyone. It is true to say that if pupils have to take maths, English language and English literature, double or triple science, a humanity and a language, there isn't a great deal of room for optional subjects. Most schools now offer three options or four at the most. For pupils following separate sciences, a two-option choice is not uncommon. There is some choice here – history or geography, French or Spanish or both – but it is by no means comprehensive. The Ebacc does suit some students, however, and it is important that is available to those who would benefit from it. What its status will be in a few years' time (the plan for 75% of pupils to be studying the Ebacc by 2022 is still in place) is uncertain, but there is no doubt that this kind of academic approach will continue to benefit large numbers of pupils in mainstream schools.

That said, more and more schools are moving away from the Ebacc and concentrating on Progress 8. This is, of course, simply another way of allowing government strictures to dictate the curriculum but there is greater flexibility here and more opportunities to tailor subject choices to the needs of pupils. All pupils still need to study the core subjects, with maths and English double counted, but there is scope in the 'open buckets' to introduce a wide range of subjects, ranging from the highly academic to the vocational. Of course, there is now a DfE list of approved Level 2 courses which count in the performance tables but, nevertheless, the choice is there. Head teachers are thus able to design systems which go a long way towards catering for the needs of their pupils while keeping an eye on the Progress 8 requirements which will help them stay the right side of zero when the league tables are published.

The real issue with choice is, of course, guidance. Comprehensive independent advice and guidance (IAG) is vital at both Key Stages 4 and 5, and in many ways, it is true to say that it is IAG which locks curriculum subjects into their places in the puzzle. IAG is therefore a key element of curriculum design, not something that is bolted on as an afterthought. The Gatsby standards (which disappointingly have nothing to do with *The Great Gatsby*) rightly recognize the importance of IAG in curriculum design and, if implemented fully, will go a long way towards ensuring that pupils make better choices in the future.

Research tells us that pupils start thinking about the sixth form in Year 9 and university courses as they choose their A-levels or Level 3 courses in Year 11. It is vital, therefore, that progression routes are discussed regularly and mapped through the curriculum. An effective curriculum will offer a variety of routes up through the system for all pupils both for those who know exactly what they want to do when they leave school as well as those who have no idea.

Standing up for the arts

The decline in the take-up of arts subjects over the past few years should be a matter of national shame; the fall in the number of examination entries in the arts is unforgivable in a nation with such strong creative industries. It was to some extent unavoidable, however, once the government began panicking about international competitiveness as a result of the rise of China, and then inevitable when it began to take the deeply flawed Programme for International Student Assessment tests to heart. Changes to the examination system over the past decade could almost have been designed to diminish the status of arts in schools. The Ebacc focused attention on core academic subjects, English, maths, science, languages and humanities, and ignored subjects like art, music and drama almost completely. The introduction of league tables based on performance in English and maths ensured that schools began to allocate much more time to these subjects, largely at the expense of the arts which then came to be considered expendable. Next came Progress 8, with its double counting of maths and English, and its privileging of science, leaving only three out of the eight buckets (but, in reality, three out of ten with the double counting) for 'other' subjects.

At the same time, we saw the rise of the STEM (science, technology, engineering and mathematics) movement, with huge amounts of time and significant sums of money pumped into schools to promote the take-up of examinations in science and technology. The university sector then waded in with its list of 'facilitating subjects' which effectively added another nail in the coffin. Although Russell Group universities made it clear that they wanted only two facilitating subjects, the result was that subjects not on the list were avoided as a matter of course.

Parents, aware of the government's concerns over the UK's lack of international competitiveness and worried about the employment prospects of their sons and daughters, not surprisingly began to advise against taking arts subjects in favour of STEM. This meant that schools still determined to offer arts subjects, despite the government's lack of support for them, found themselves with ever diminishing numbers opting for courses at both GCSE and A-Level until they became financially unviable.

We now have a situation where more and more schools, despite being strong advocates of the arts, are simply not able to offer the full range of arts subjects. Far too many schools no longer offer music GCSE, and those that still manage to attract an A-level cohort are few and far between. The same is true of drama and increasingly true of art and graphics. Equally worrying is that the culture has become so toxic that students who would have excelled in an arts subject are now opting for safer choices in order to secure university places. I recently had a very sad discussion with an amazingly talented artist in Year 12 who opted for biology instead of art because she felt that art would not be considered academic enough for her to secure a good university place or, indeed, future employment. An A* in art would almost have been guaranteed; instead, she ended up with a C grade in biology.

In its 2016 report on social mobility and the skills gap, the Creative Industries Federation outlined the importance of the arts to the UK economy:

> The creative industries are one of Britain's biggest success stories, worth £87.4bn in GVA. The creative economy (which includes those in creative jobs outside the sector) employs one in every 11 working people. It has been the fastest growing sector of the economy since the 2008 financial crash. It has highly attractive jobs and ones that are also at low risk of being replaced by robots in the future. In her keynote speech at the Conservative Party Conference, Prime Minister Theresa May named the creative industries as a key strategic sector for the economy at large.[5]

The report went on to discuss the growing skills shortages, the likely impact of Brexit, calls from the Confederation of British Industries to support arts industries and the lack of opportunities available to young people keen to enter the arts. In the conclusion of the report it recommended the dropping of the Ebacc target (now reduced from 90% to 75%), for 'outstanding' status to be dependent on offering at least one creative subject in lesson time, an audit of the skills gap in schools and much better career advice.

There is also the compelling argument which points out that children in schools now are preparing for jobs that don't yet exist. In order to ensure that they can take on new roles and new job opportunities, they will need to be highly creative, flexible and able to draw on a much wider range of skills than workers in previous generations had. Arts subjects teach these vital skills.

It is also worth pointing out that even in the most conservative industries, in fact, especially in the most conservative industries, employers are likely to prefer traditional subjects like art, literature, classics and music rather than subjects like business studies which parents think have industry appeal.

As discussed in Chapter 1, arts in the curriculum is not just a matter of employability, it is a matter of culture. Creative subjects are vital to the emotional as well as intellectual development of all pupils in schools, not just those with particular talents in the arts. It is time that politicians recognized the fact that we don't need to focus all our attention on competing with Chinese mathematicians and realized the importance of the arts in creating fully rounded individuals able to take on the world. It may sound ludicrously pompous to say it, but we are a creative nation, a literary and musical nation. Our writers, artists and musicians have shaped, and continue to shape, the cultures of nations around the world. We should not be encouraging our most creative thinkers to abandon their paint brushes in favour of pocket calculators and Petri dishes. We should, of course, equip students with the skills they need to succeed in maths and science, and we should be encouraging those with scientific interests, of both genders, to pursue careers in science, but this should be done side by side with encouragement for the arts. For the UK to succeed internationally we need mathematicians, scientists and artists. Perhaps it is time to revive the old-fashioned concept of

Renaissance men and women who are highly skilled in many areas rather than masters of one limited field.

This brings us back to that unanswerable question, What is education for? It is a question which underpins every aspect of school improvement but one which is especially relevant to the curriculum discussion. Head teachers and senior leaders really need to have an understanding of what they think education is for before even beginning to think about redesigning the curriculum. They will inevitably find that their view of the curriculum sits uneasily with the government's view, but the art of curriculum design is all about finding the space between, the shaded area of the Venn diagram where vision and governmental constraints overlap.

Senior leaders must create curriculum plans with due regard to the Ebacc, Progress 8 and the other performance indicators, but if they don't do their best to retain and promote creative subjects, they will really be letting their pupils down. The financial implications of small groups in arts subjects may make it difficult to offer a comprehensive range, but every pupil is entitled to an education in the arts. Creative thinking will make it possible and will help develop the next generation's creative thinkers.

Vocational education

If the arts have suffered as a result of the imposition of the Ebacc and the performance tables, it could be argued that the impact on vocational subjects has been even more profound. There are numerous examples of schools with highly developed vocational offers, which genuinely met the needs of pupils, forced into adopting much more academic curriculums. A well-known example in the West Country saw a very successful school, which had won awards for its innovative curriculum tailored to the needs of a very rural population, fall from good to special measures in a matter of months. The shift from a complex vocational offer towards a much greater focus on academic subjects created so many problems that the school simply fell apart. It can, of course, be argued that senior leaders should have seen the changes coming and that, however rural the population, pupils still need access to the full range of academic opportunities, but the school's decline is indicative of a culture which is essentially hostile to vocational qualifications.

If a secondary school today is concerned about its Progress 8 score, it cannot avoid looking closely at the vocational courses it offers. Bearing in mind that there are only three open buckets, and many vocational courses demand twice the time allocation of GCSE courses, allowing too many pupils to take vocational options is a very risky business. Furthermore, the choice of such courses is now severely limited by the DfE's list of approved Level 2 specifications. For a course to score progress points, it must be included on the list. Schools where particular courses had been running successfully for years suddenly discovered that their course was not on the list and an alternative had to be found. And, of course, in order to fulfil the DfE's academic dreams, the alternative courses turned out to involve much more paperwork and much less practical activity. In other words, they weren't really vocational at all.

The consequence of all this is that far fewer vocational courses are now on offer in schools. This means that it has become increasingly difficult to ensure that the curriculum matches the needs of its pupils. However, the problem isn't simply one of limited subject choice; there is, as always, a series of more complex issues underlying any discussion of vocational courses in schools.

First, we shouldn't shy away from a very basic problem: Can vocational education really be delivered effectively in schools? This is not simply a matter of having the appropriate equipment and resources, but also a question of staff expertise. How many schools really have staff who are fully equipped to deliver vocational courses effectively? Most schools still offer a very limited vocational curriculum: it usually comprises one or two Business and Technology Education Council (BTEC) courses where paper-based work is at a premium and practical activities minimized. The most popular courses are probably business, health and social care and travel and tourism. These can be taught fairly easily in general classrooms and, more often than not, by teachers of other subjects who have space on their timetables.

No matter how strongly examination boards emphasize the academic rigour of their vocational courses, most schools include, for example, BTECs in their curriculum in order to cater to their weaker students. The consequence of this is that vocational education is immediately seen as something to be avoided by brighter pupils at all costs. It is surely time to be more honest, or perhaps less delusional, about vocational courses and acknowledge two painful truths: first, genuinely vocational courses should really only be taught in technical colleges where both the equipment and staff expertise are available, and second, the vocational courses on offer in schools are, in fact, courses for pupils who are not able to cope with the rigours of a full academic curriculum. Most of the BTECs currently delivered in schools are no more vocational than English and maths GCSEs.

For many school leaders, vocational courses are something of an embarrassment: they know they are not right, they know they are not really vocational, but they are also aware that there really aren't any viable alternatives. Most of us feel slightly uncomfortable talking up vocational courses when we know in our hearts that we should be able to offer something better and more appropriate.

Of course, we have to acknowledge the fact that some pupils simply cannot cope with nine or ten GCSEs. An alternative has to be provided. In some schools, additional support in English and maths is offered instead of an option subject or, increasingly, a language but, though seemingly a worthwhile endeavour, this doesn't give them the practical, hands-on experiences they really need. In schools with a predominantly academic curriculum, the practical choice is usually a design technology subject, but even here there are problems.

The design suite of subjects falls easily into the camel designed by a committee category. No matter how forcefully we argue that each of the subjects under the design umbrella involves similar skills, we all know really that food and textiles are very different from each other and dramatically different from product design or resistant materials. The real problem with design technology is that no one really knows what it is and, as a result, Design Technology (DT) departments are often the weakest areas in many schools. The business community is keen, quite rightly, to advocate the importance of design in industry, but somehow, the skills needed to equip the next generations of designers never seem to filter down into the GCSE specifications. Teachers of design also seem oblivious of the fact that most design in industry is now computer-based. For anyone considering a career in design, art graphics is really a much better option. The traditional DT curriculum doesn't really teach design skills at all.

Pupils undoubtedly need to be involved in practical activities simply to develop as fully rounded adults. Indeed, there have recently been calls from the Royal College of Surgeons for more practical activities in schools because trainee doctors no longer have the dexterity needed to learn surgical techniques. In most schools, leaders look to the DT department to teach practical skills and that is sensible enough. However, we really need to take a long hard look at the DT curriculum in order to make it fit for purpose. It is supposedly there to create the next generation of designers, but this is something it signally fails to do; it is really there to teach vital practical skills. The solution is obvious: schools need to be able to give pupils the chance to get involved in practical activities which are not necessarily examined. The current accountability structure militates against the obvious, however, with school leaders under increasing pressure to ensure that every moment of the school day leads to an externally examined course.

Design technology, though something of a mess, is not the real problem. The real problem is the government's current obsession with examined courses and performance measures. School leaders are forced to distort their curriculums in favour of examination subjects, and it takes a brave leader to withdraw significant numbers of pupils in order to offer them practical courses which may not attract progress points but which really fulfil their needs.

The importance of genuine vocational education has never been in doubt but a workable solution to the problem of academic credibility has yet to be found. Politicians often cite the experiences of students abroad where technical colleges seem to have equal status to academic institutions but anyone who has spent any time in any of these places, whether in France, Germany or Finland, has to acknowledge that there is still a sense among the population that the academic routes are still the most highly regarded.

It would be easy to list various government's failed attempts to create credible vocational routes, with city technology colleges, studio schools and T-levels being the most recent examples, but there is no getting past the fundamental problem. Western culture will always privilege the academic over the vocational. As far as schools are concerned, therefore, it is much more important to focus attention on developing practical skills rather than half-heartedly trying to offer vocational courses which are not really vocational at all and which everyone, if they are honest enough to admit it, considers second best.

Putting it all together

Constructing a school curriculum is no simple matter. School leaders need to consider a dizzying range of factors if they are to create a curriculum that genuinely meets the needs of every pupil against a background of extreme accountability and political interference. A useful checklist of things to consider might look something like this:

- Pupils' attainment on entry
- The local context of the school
- The competition – the distinctive nature of other schools in the area
- Provision for the core curriculum
- Coverage of the national curriculum
- Fulfilling legal requirements – RE, PE, etc.
- Adjustments to Key Stage 3 to reflect key aspects of the local area
- Broadening the range of options at Key Stages 4 and 5
- The relevance and importance of the Ebacc
- How well the curriculum responds to the demands of Progress 8
- Avoiding gaming
- Building challenge at all levels
- The financial viability of every course
- Time allocations for every subject
- The availability of staff with appropriate skills
- Independent advice and guidance
- The importance of choice
- A two-year or three-year Key Stage 3
- The importance of the arts
- Vocational or practical courses
- Provision for pupils with special education needs and disabilities and other significant groups

- Alternative provision using external agencies, if necessary

- Progression routes

- Evaluation mechanisms to check the curriculum's effectiveness

- Inspiration and pupil well-being

- Lifelong learning

This is by no means a comprehensive list but does serve to indicate the complexity of the undertaking. Creating an effective curriculum is possibly a school leader's most challenging task. It is, however, one of the most engaging and enjoyable aspects of the job. The excitement generated by innovative practice is a powerful school improvement mechanism. The excitement of teams of teachers striving for something better for their school is both inspiring and hugely beneficial to the pupils in their classes.

In *Leadership that Lasts*, Robert Hill identifies ten principles of school leadership which are thought to be essential if leaders are to continue developing.[6] Number 8, which states that sustainable school leaders must strive to renew themselves, is perhaps one of the most important and powerful features of leadership today. The excitement of conceiving a new idea and then generating enough enthusiasm to see it realized undoubtedly gives schools and their leaders a significant and long-lasting positive charge which surely must be to the benefit of teaching and learning in all schools.

The importance of narrative

So far, we have focused on the nature of the curriculum, its contents, its challenges and the political constraints that make it such a demanding undertaking. It is now time to move on to think about how the curriculum, once established, should be delivered.

While school leaders focus on outcomes governed by Progress 8 and the Ebacc, it is inevitable that their attention will be drawn to the destination and not the journey. On the other hand, the recent removal of Key Stage 3 levels presents us with a golden opportunity to look again at the curriculum and begin to see it as a narrative rather than a discrete series of units to be delivered en route to terminal examinations. Over the past few years, teachers have tended to look at GCSE specifications, or the contents of the Key Stage 2 tests, before working down the year groups to ensure that everything is in place to meet examination board requirements. At the secondary level, the unnatural division of Key Stage 3 and Key Stage 4 encouraged the notion of a curriculum in stages, with blocks of learning building up to examinations, often with little or no connection evident between the discrete elements. This is true within subject areas but much more so across the curriculum.

Anyone who has looked at pupils' books on a learning walk or as part of a book scrutiny cannot fail to be struck by the seemingly random nature of the content of many of them. Science books are full of notes of experiments, with little evidence of the development of skills or attempts to build on prior knowledge; history and geography books jump from topic to topic; and English literature books are often characterized by less than dramatic leaps from *Tom's Midnight Garden* to *Of Mice and Men* to *Macbeth*. One cannot help wondering what pupils make of all this. The curriculum to them must seem like wildly random sets of knowledge to be learned and then forgotten.

It is always difficult to urge school leaders to turn away from examined outcomes towards a wider consideration of the purpose of the curriculum, especially in those schools where a good inspection can mean the difference between employment and unemployment, but there are times when leaders have to be brave enough to focus on what really matters. In this case, it is the learning at the heart of the curriculum not the tests at the end of it. And, of course, if the learning is well directed, stimulating and relevant, pupils are likely to be better learners and better prepared to demonstrate their learning whatever the examinations throw at them.

In the age of digital entertainment, there is much we can learn from the way both teachers and pupils consume media content. And the culture of the box set provides an excellent analogy for curriculum design in schools.

First, box sets are extended narratives. Like Years 7 to 11, they often stretch out over extended five-year periods, with complex narrative arcs and interweaving subplots. They are designed to capture and retain audience interest, and they work hard to ensure that viewers stay with them. Teachers tend to plan the delivery of required content with very little thought regarding the narrative journey or the need to retain and cultivate their audiences. There is a lot to be learned from Tyrion Lannister, Saga Norén, Tony Soprano et al.

To design a curriculum that students find engaging it must be interesting. This is not just a question of content but of teaching styles. In the same way that strong narratives present us with different characters, a range of settings, various twists and turns in the plot, varying pace and shifts from tragedy to comedy, good teaching draws on a wide range of techniques to ensure that pupils are both attentive and inspired. Good teaching can undoubtedly help to deliver even the driest subject matter but a good television series teaches us that content is a key driver of the narrative. Moreover, that content must be coherent, directed and interlinked. Once we start thinking about the curriculum in terms of narrative, or, in simple terms, a storyline, it quickly becomes clear that many of the stories we currently tell our students are incoherent, disconnected and, sometimes, incomprehensible. We need, therefore, to start thinking differently: instead of looking at terminal exams and working backwards, we should perhaps think about what we want pupils to learn and then consider effective narratives to engage and sustain their interest.

One particularly useful feature of the box set is the 'Previously on. . .' section at the start of the programme. Far too often we assume that a topic has been learned and we move on. So why not start lessons with a recap not just of the last lesson but of lessons delivered months ago in the same way that television dramas often remind us of scenes that happened in early episodes that we may have forgotten and that we now need to recall ensuring that we fully understand what is going on in the narrative. Checking on pupils' learning is often left to the summative assessment at the end of the course; regular checks both at the start of lessons and during lessons are much more effective in embedding learning. And if we are serious about educating pupils, learning needs to be recursive so that nothing is forgotten and everything is seen as contributing to the storyline.

The most effective box sets feature engaging characters who stick in the memory. They act as anchor points in the narrative and appear again and again so that we really get to know them. If they are sufficiently developed, they can disappear for weeks on end and yet never leave our memory. Tyrion Lannister, in *Game of Thrones*, for example, is one of the most prominent characters in the series, yet he is absent from the screen for long periods. In the original novel sequence, he doesn't even appear in the fourth novel, *A Feast for Crows*. And yet we remember him. In each subject area there are surely key themes, key events, keywords or vital skills, to which we should return regularly so that, like Tyrion, they engage our attention and stay in the mind.

As viewers, we are always ready to ask the question, *What happens now?* The best lessons leave pupils asking *What's next?* and looking forward to the next instalment. Narrative theorists refer to this as a 'proximal function' so that we are led on to the next thing naturally and without any loss of attention. How often as teachers do we think about ensuring that pupils are encouraged to think about what's next so they are both prepared for it and look forward to it? We could even try the odd cliffhanger at the end of the lesson: 'If you want to know what's really clever about this theory, come back tomorrow.'

Some box sets offer us incredibly complex narratives – but they are not complex at the start. Anyone who has struggled to follow the twists and turns of the fourth series of *The Bridge* will appreciate just how complicated supposedly simple television entertainment can be. And yet, these narratives are not complicated to begin with. The complexity builds. The narrative becomes more complex as we are ready to cope with it and when the scaffold is sufficiently secure for us to grasp what is going on. How effectively do teachers build complexity into curriculum design and how often do they ensure that there is sufficient support to ensure that everyone can follow what is going on?

In her recent blog, Christine Counsell, explores the notion of a narrative curriculum in some detail.[7] She considers the question of the relationship between the key ideas, or the key learning points, and all the other things that go into making a curriculum enjoyable and engaging. She describes this as the 'core' and the 'hinterland.' The core could well be the key topics which a pupil needs to pass an exam, but it is the hinterland, the other stuff they learn along the way, that truly engages their interest. The battle for the seven kingdoms in *Game of Thrones* may be the story on which the rest of the plot hangs, but it is the characters and events along the way that stick in our memory and make the journey enjoyable. *The Bridge* is fundamentally a crime drama, but it is Saga's complete lack of social skills we recall first. In planning a truly engaging curriculum, it is important not to underestimate the importance of the hinterland as it is there that the real learning often takes place.

It is even worth considering the importance of the final credits as part of the box set analogy. Praise is a vital part of the learning process, but how effectively do we integrate opportunities to acknowledge good work into our curriculum planning?

Finally, we also need to think beyond our own subject and think in cross-curricular terms. Amazon perhaps provides food for thought here: 'If you enjoyed this, you'll really like this.'

It may be sad to relate that according to a recent survey 64% of people would rather watch a box set than read a book, but we must acknowledge the power of a medium that can engage the attention of mass audiences by delivering narratives as complex as those provided by Shakespeare or Dickens.[8] If teachers could develop curriculums as powerful as box sets, think of the possibilities. Ygritte's withering remark in *Game of Thrones*, 'You know nothing, Jon Snow,' should perhaps be the starting point.

Key points

- The curriculum taught in schools today is largely unchanged from the one taught 50 years ago.
- A curriculum is much more than simply a list of subjects, it is a coherent narrative involving both skills and knowledge.
- The core curriculum occupies a significant chunk of the timetable, but there is still room for innovation.
- There will always be a tension between meeting the needs of pupils and performance measures.
- Game playing may achieve short-term gains, but it is unlikely to lead to lasting school improvement.
- Strong curriculums take into account a wide range of factors including pupil data, local contexts, other schools, employment opportunities, geography and so on.
- Choice and challenge are key elements of successful curriculum plans.
- IAG is essential to ensure that pupils make the right curriculum choices.

- Leaders need to work hard to ensure that the arts are not neglected in schools.
- Vocational courses have also suffered due to the influence of performance tables, but they are clearly the right choice for many.
- Box sets provide a useful analogy for successful curriculum design.

Practical ideas

- Use the checklist from the 'Putting it all together' section of this chapter to review your school's curriculum.
- Ask heads of department to consider whether their curriculum plans develop a definite narrative or whether they are simply a list of topics to be covered.

Notes

1 R. Williams. 1965. *The Long Revolution*, London: Penguin, p. 188.
2 J. White et al. 2004. *Rethinking the School Curriculum*, Oxford: Routledge Falmer, p. 180.
3 From a presentation given by Sean Harford at the Ofsted/NASUWT BME Consultation Conference, 27 January 2018 ICC Birmingham.
4 A. Spielman. 2018. https://www.gov.uk/government/speeches/amanda-spielman-launches-ofsteds-annual-report-2017/18
5 E. Easton. 2016. *Social Mobility and the Skills Gap*, London: Creative Industries Federation.
6 R. Hill. 2006. *Leadership That Lasts: Sustainable School Leadership in the 21st Century*, London: Harcourt/ASCL.
7 C. Counsell's Blog. https://thedignityofthethingblog.wordpress.com
8 The survey was conducted by Censuswide on behalf of Sky Box Sets in April 2017, and 1,000 British people were questioned on their viewing habits.

The myth of governance

I have met very few head teachers who do not complain about governors, about the decisions they make, about the time they waste and generally about their lack of effectiveness as school leaders. I think it is fair to say that head teachers as a group are unlikely to be regarded as strong advocates of current governance structures, yet how often are their concerns voiced in the press or in academic literature? I cannot recall having read an article which was really critical of governance and certainly not one written by a head teacher. This is, of course, unsurprising. Governors are the head teacher's employers, they are in charge of appointments and, most telling of all, they conduct the head's performance management reviews. They are also responsible for disciplinary procedures. In other words, to criticize the governors is to criticize the people who determine your salary and who, ultimately, have the power to dismiss you. Head teachers, on the whole, are careful individuals, so it is hardly surprising that the inadequacy of governance is a topic they tend to shy away from in print.

Of course, every head will be able to tell you about the good governors – and there are lots of them – but stories of poor governance are too commonplace to ignore. It is therefore of vital importance to consider the effectiveness of governance in any thorough discussion of school improvement. It is also important to explore ways of managing governors to ensure that their impact on the school is positive. They are, after all, responsible for the school development plan, and with the rise of academy trusts, they are becoming increasingly powerful.

The role of governors

It is probably true to say that until teachers and other staff are appointed to senior leadership roles, they are likely to have very little to do with school governors, unless, of course, they choose to put themselves forward as staff governors. It often comes as something of a shock to discover how much power they have and how much potential influence they can have on the day-to-day running of the school.

For new head teachers, the steepest learning curve they face often involves dealing effectively with governors. For the majority of staff, however, governors are shadowy figures who have a somewhat nebulous relationship with the school and who are rarely, if ever, seen during the school day. With multi-layered academy models, where schools have local governors as well as a central trust, this relationship is likely to be even more distant.

For most staff, reading the Department for Education's (DfE's) guidance on the role of governors is an eye-opening experience as I suspect that very few have a real understanding of just how much power is invested in the governing body of a school. The DfE's Governance Handbook[1] describes the three core functions of governing bodies:

- Ensuring clarity of vision, ethos and strategic direction
- Holding executive leaders to account for the educational performance of the organization and its pupils and the performance management of staff
- Overseeing the financial performance of the organization and making sure its money is well spent

It then explains that effective governance is based on six key features:

- Strategic leadership that sets and champions vision, ethos and strategy
- Accountability that drives up educational standards and financial performance
- People with the right skills, experience, qualities and capacity
- Structures that reinforce clearly defined roles and responsibilities
- Compliance with statutory and contractual requirements
- Evaluation to monitor and improve the quality and impact of governance

It is only when you get to the detail that you begin to appreciate the comprehensive nature of the governor's role. What follows is a selection of the duties outlined in the handbook.

Strategic leadership:

- A clear and explicit vision for the future set by the board which has pupil progress and achievement at its heart
- Strategic planning that defines medium to long-term strategic goals, and development and improvement priorities
- Processes to monitor and review progress against agreed strategic goals
- Mechanisms for enabling the board to listen, understand and respond to the voices of parents/carers, pupils, staff, local communities and employers

Accountability:

- Rigorous analysis of pupil progress and attainment information with comparison against local and national benchmarks and over time
- Clear processes for overseeing and monitoring school improvement and providing constructive challenge to executive leaders
- A transparent system for performance managing executive leaders,
- Effective oversight of the performance of all other employees and the framework for their pay and conditions of service
- A regular cycle of meetings and appropriate processes to support business and financial planning and
- Effective controls for managing within available resources and ensuring regularity, propriety and value for money

People:

- Use active succession planning to ensure the board, and the whole organization, continues to have the people and leadership it needs to remain effective

Structures:

- Clear separation between strategic non-executive oversight and operational executive leadership which is supported by positive relationships that encourage a professional culture and ethos across the organization

Compliance:

- Awareness of, and adherence to, responsibilities under education and employment legislation
- Plans to ensure that key duties are undertaken effectively across the organization such as safeguarding, inclusion, special education needs and disability (SEND), and monitoring and oversight of the impact of pupil premium and other targeted funding streams
- For academies, adherence to the requirements of the Education Funding Agency's *Academies Financial Handbook* and the trust's funding agreement and articles of association
- Understanding of, and adherence to, responsibilities under the Equalities Act, promoting equality and diversity throughout the organization including in relation to its own operation

Evaluation:

- Processes for regular self-evaluation and review of individuals' contribution to the board as well of the board's overall operation and effectiveness

- Documentation which accurately captures evidence of the board's discussions and decisions as well as the evaluation of its impact and which complies with legal requirements for document retention.

Governors therefore have great power. They are responsible for the vision of the school; improvement planning and target setting; analysis of pupil progress; performance management; teachers' pay; property management; setting and overseeing the budget; appointing and disciplining staff; succession planning; adherence to legislation; safeguarding, inclusion and SEND; and monitoring the pupil premium.

And head teachers think they are in charge.

Of course, the really interesting descriptor relates to the relationship between the head and the governing body which refers to the clear separation between strategic non-executive oversight and operational executive leadership, in other words, who is responsible for what. It is here, of course, that much of the tension lies in the relationship between head teachers and governors: strategic leadership can too easily drift into operational leadership until roles become blurred and leadership founders. In most schools, particularly in the secondary sector, the majority of the roles outlined earlier are delegated to senior leaders or, if not directly delegated, become the responsibility of leaders. It is here that we get to one of the key problems of governance: governors have the powers but, in many cases, not the expertise to carry out the complex list of duties legally ascribed to them. Senior leaders are the experts, even if the DfE's handbook barely acknowledges this obvious truth, and it is they who effectively carry out the duties of the governors on their behalf.

Who are the governors?

Depending on the nature of the school, governors will have a variety of titles, even though in effect their roles are exactly the same. These include the following:

Academy Trustees – directors under company law and trustees under charity law of either a stand-alone academy trust or a multi-academy trust

Academy Members – these are akin to the shareholders of a company

Chair of Governors – the leader of the governing board

Co-opted Governor – someone from the community who has the skills and experience which the governing board require

Foundation Governors – individuals whose appointment to the governing board is approved by the diocese responsible for the school

Local Authority (LA) Governor – a maintained school should include one LA governor. They do not have to work for the LA, but their appointment is always approved by the local authority

Parent Governor – a parent elected by other parents

Staff Governor – a member of staff, usually elected by the staff, to ensure that staff views are represented on the governing body

These are the job titles, but who are they in practice? This is a question which cannot really be properly answered because every governing body is different, and because once we consider the nature of individuals, we are in danger of moving into the realms of anecdote and prejudice. We can, however, make some general points, some of which will doubtlessly be considered controversial (more so if you are a governor, less so if you are a senior leader), about the types of people who volunteer to become governors.

The word *volunteer* is a good place to start. Why would you volunteer to become a governor? To an objective observer, the opportunity to sit on committees that sometimes drag on until late in the evening, grappling with complex and demanding problems, may not seem to have much appeal, especially as it is all unpaid. There are, of course, lots of people who see the role as a chance to give something back and a way of supporting the local community. However, the fact that governors are all volunteers results in one of the key issues regarding the make-up of governing bodies – their lack of diversity.

One of the key requirements of the governing body as set out in the Governor's Handbook is to ensure a 'diversity of perspectives,' but it is fairly obvious that individuals who have the time and financial security to volunteer are likely to be from a particular social class and, more often than not, retired. A survey of the age profile of governing bodies across the country would doubtless confirm that the majority of governors are of a certain age and of a particular class.

Retired community members who want to give something back, or perhaps want something useful to do, tend to occupy the appointed rather than the elected slots on the governing body. They are usually partnership governors or foundation governors, for example. However much they deny it, simply because of their age and social class, they are likely to adopt a more conservative approach to governance. This is not ageist, or an attempt to promulgate any particular set of values, but merely an assertion of the reality of the situation. Older members of the community dominate governing bodies. It would be unfair to point to upstanding members of the public who become governors to bolster their social standing in the community, but these people undoubtedly exist. They have chaired the local Rotary Club, joined the Lions, kept quiet about their membership of the Masons and then moved on to become the chair of governors. Fortunately, they are often fairly harmless: their bid for social status achieved, they tend to let head teachers get on with the job.

Some governing bodies, particularly in cities, are lucky in that they are able to attract highly skilled professionals or local business representatives whose employers encourage them to undertake community roles. These individuals can help to add a level of dynamism which many governing bodies lack. The majority of governors do not, unfortunately, have the same level of expertise.

Parent governors are undoubtedly the most problematic members of the board, at least as far as head teachers are concerned. While many of them put themselves forward out of a genuine desire to support the school, many are motivated by vested interests and concerns for their own children. I suspect that every head teacher is able to talk about a particular parent whose sole aim in joining the governors was to promote the interests of their own sons or daughters. Parents with unresolved grievances are quite common, particularly if they think that their children are not being taught properly or if their concerns about bullying have not, in their eyes, been appropriately addressed by the school.

Once elected, governors tend to fall into two camps: the committee members and the enthusiasts. Committee members tend simply to turn up and contribute very little; enthusiasts throw themselves into the life of the school, sometimes to good effect, but more often than not they do so in ways which end up taking hours of staff time. The enthusiastic chair of governors is perhaps the most difficult individual to deal since he or she has a huge amount of power which, in the wrong hands, can end up impacting negatively on the development of the school and its day-to-day activities.

One of the key roles of the head teacher is therefore management of the governors. A carefully managed governing body can be a real asset to the school; a badly managed set of governors can do a great deal of damage. And as with every aspect of school improvement covered so far, governor management takes time. It is yet another example of the gradual art of school improvement.

How qualified are governors?

If you were to stand back and consider the nature of school leadership from a completely objective standpoint, I think you might begin to wonder how on earth anybody came up with a governance structure like the one currently imposed on schools. Every school in the country has a qualified team of professionals responsible for leading and managing the educational development of large numbers of pupils. These are usually highly qualified individuals who have degrees, postgraduate qualifications, teaching and leadership qualifications and years of experience. They have been through rigorous assessment procedures, and they are monitored closely by a variety of external agencies, including, for example, the Office for Standards in Education, Children's Services and Skills (Ofsted). So, with a team such as this in place, why would you think it a good idea to impose an additional layer of governance with immense powers, comprising individuals who have very little, if any, understanding of schools and education?

To the casual observer, the idea of assembling a group of between 10 and 20 people who know next to nothing about education or classroom pedagogy and telling them they are in charge must surely seem like lunacy. I am sure there are many teachers and head teachers who would agree wholeheartedly with this judgement, though they would perhaps be reluctant to say so out loud.

It is this mismatch between the extent of governors' responsibilities and powers, and their evident lack of expertise which is at the root of so many school improvement issues. It also accounts for the amount of time head teachers and other senior leaders have to spend briefing governors about the basics of educational management. From any objective point of view, this is a loopy system. There is, of course, a need for checks and balances in the system, and head teachers must be held accountable, but is this really the best way to do it?

One of the most worrying aspects of governance is the lack of control schools have over the appointment process. Governors effectively set their own constitutions, it is up to them who they co-opt as governors, and there are very few checks in the system to ensure that elected governors are fit to take on such powerful roles. Parent governors are elected, and the governing body is unable to change the outcome of the election unless the governor concerned is disqualified from serving as a governor. This is set out in law. So even when everyone in the school is aware that the parent concerned is unsuitable – and this could be for a variety of reasons including an obvious axe to grind, local knowledge of poor behaviour, a history in the community of aggressiveness, or a record of slating the school on social media – it is almost impossible to stop him or her becoming a governor. If someone has been elected, unless the person is disqualified to stand, he or she is automatically a parent governor from the time the outcome of the election is declared. They are required to apply for a Disclosure and Barring Service clearance within 21 days. The law does give reasons why someone may be disqualified from serving as a governor, but things have to be incredibly serious for this to apply.[2] In effect, an individual would have to have been convicted of causing a disturbance on school premises to be disqualified.

When you compare this to the application and interview processes schools employ in order to ensure that they appoint the right staff, the differences are stark. It is entirely possible for people to be elected to sit on governing bodies who have very little knowledge of education, very dubious backgrounds, and the sole aim of undermining the leadership of the school. Would any head teacher in the country appoint someone like that to any position in the school, let alone a leadership role?

The Governance Handbook stresses the need for governing bodies to appoint individuals with the skills needed to run a school, but how often does this actually happen in practice? Those schools fortunate enough to be able to attract retired education professionals onto their boards tend to have more effective governing bodies. All schools seek to attract solicitors, accountants and architects so that they can draw on free advice when it is needed, but it is people who have expertise in education who really make the difference.

It is very frustrating as a head teacher to have to spend so much time preparing materials for governors; it is even more frustrating to find yourself responding to very basic suggestions which you have, of course, already considered but which enthusiastic governors, keen to get involved, like to propose. Again and again, you find yourself wondering, 'Do they really think I wouldn't have thought about that?' When you have patiently responded to the 15th good idea which you and your leadership team have already considered months ago, you then begin to ask, 'Have they no appreciation of the professional capabilities of the leadership team actually running the school?' Of course, this is rarely the case, but it can feel as if it is. More often than not, governors ask questions to demonstrate their engagement and interest; it is immensely frustrating nevertheless.

It would be fascinating to conduct some genuine research into how much time head teachers spend dealing with governors, and then to consider the impact of that time. For many, much of it is dead time which could be spent more productively on dozens of other activities. If you think about the time a head spends with the chair of governors, on attendance at committee meetings and meetings of the full governing body, on reports that need to be written with suffocating regularity, with the casual visits of governors to see what's going on in the school, and helpful emails suggesting all sorts of old ideas and so on, it would probably add up to hundreds of hours a term. Simply writing a regular report to governors can take hours.

Governors, of course, can be useful, and there are some occasions when they are needed – exclusion panels, disciplinary hearings and so on – but unless they are properly trained and managed, they can often end up doing more harm than good. Governors on interview committees are particularly problematic as they often have no real understanding of the role candidates have applied to undertake and therefore tend to make decisions which are wildly out of step with the rest of the panel.

Governance in practice

The current system of governance is undoubtedly deeply flawed and clearly not fit for purpose, but we are stuck with it. We therefore have to look for the positives and adapt our leadership styles accordingly. With careful management, the governing body can become an ally and an important means of support. Relationships need to be nurtured, responsibilities understood and the boundaries between strategy and management made crystal clear. This is not an easy task, but it can be done.

It helps to be prepared. Much of the material to be discussed at governors' meetings is prepared by the head and the leadership team. The more thorough the preparation, the better the outcomes of the meeting. It is also useful to think about the questions governors are likely to ask: sometimes questions simply require further explanation, sometimes they are about nitpicking details designed to catch you out. After a while, you become familiar with the particular foibles of your own governing body and the questions therefore become easier to predict. If you can predict the questions in advance, you can provide the answers. This is an effective way of allowing the business to move along, and it has the added bonus of assuring governors that you know what you are doing. Some things are best left off the agenda, and after a while, you learn not to seek governors' approval for everything. A new head teacher is likely to be keen to seek support from the governors for a huge number of issues; experienced heads tend to seek support only where necessary. I am not suggesting that you keep them in the dark or try to hide things from them, I am merely pointing out the advantages of careful management of the agenda.

Increasingly, governors rely on support networks to guide them. There are usually local authority organizations for governors to join and there is the increasingly powerful National Governors' Association (NGA – not to be confused, of course, with the National Rifle Association, the NRA, which cynics suggest may share similarly authoritarian aims). These now offer standard agendas and calendars of activities for governing bodies to follow. A wise head is aware of these organizations and keeps up with their recommendations. This allows him or her to predict what governors are likely to want included on the various agendas. Most head teachers elect to be governors themselves, although they don't have to be, and this ensures that they have access to the same materials as every other governor.

An awareness of what is likely to be on the agenda, and some thought regarding the likely questions to be asked, will ensure that you enter meetings with a real advantage. In this way, you will be able subtly to direct the meeting and avoid the embarrassing situation of being asked questions you can't answer.

New governors

Remember that new governors, in particular, are likely to have a very limited understanding of education and the day-to-day running of the school. The world of education is fairly unique in that everyone has been to school, and therefore, everyone has an opinion about how things should be run. Very few people recognize that there is a huge difference between being the customer, as it were, and the provider. The experience of teaching is dramatically different from the experience of being a pupil in a school, but all adults consider themselves an expert on the system because they have been through it. This can make life very difficult for teachers and senior leaders, and it is therefore up to them to make the differences apparent. In other words, part of the role of the leadership team is to educate the governing body and help them to understand the complexity of teaching and the demands of school leadership. Once again, this is far from simple.

New governors appreciate support. This can be very basic, but it is often worth spending time to establish a good relationship from the outset. A welcome tour by the head teacher and a discussion of the issues facing teachers are essential. It is also useful, though rarely done, to take governors through the lesson planning process to show them just how skilled a job teaching actually is. They will have memories of their favourite teacher, whom they will regard as the exemplar of correct teaching, as well as memories of some terrible teachers. Many governors find it hard to move beyond this dichotomy, and they assume that your school will be full of similar archetypes. You need to show them how teaching has moved on. I am often encouraged to reflect on the fact that some of the terrible teachers I endured as a child would never be allowed to set foot in the classroom nowadays.

The planning discussion is a very useful exercise and often quite an eye-opener for new governors. If you sit down with them and explain the process in a series of steps, they begin to understand the complex nature of contemporary classroom pedagogy. You might walk them through the following topics:

- The teacher's awareness of attainment on entry. They know a pupil's previous performance, they know if he or she has special needs and they know if they belong to a particular group of which may need additional support
- The range of pupils in a class: those who enter with high prior attainment, those joining the school with low prior attainment; those with special needs; looked after children; disadvantaged children and so on.
- The importance of gender and the need to be aware of it when choosing classroom materials
- Potential discipline issues which have to be considered when planning the lesson
- The importance of the curriculum demands, whether the national curriculum at Key Stage 3 or examination specifications at Key Stage 4 and in the sixth form
- The importance of checking prior learning – what did the class learn last time?
- Any assessment activities and how these are moderated
- The importance of clear aims for the lesson: not just lesson objectives but much clearer pedagogical aims. What will the pupils in the class have learned by the end of the lesson?
- The lesson planning process: starters, main activities, activities to check learning and so on
- The types of activities teachers may consider using: everything from teacher talk to pair and group work
- What resources will be needed: card sorts, PowerPoint presentations, video clips, paper, card, pens, and so on
- What support materials need to be created to help those with special needs: e.g. coloured paper, enlarged print, among others.
- Differentiation – through questioning, through one to one support, with the help of specially prepared materials
- Briefing the teaching assistant
- Ensuring that questions to check learning are built into the lessons and that plans may need to be adapted depending on student progress

- Setting homework
- Ensuring that the lesson moves at an appropriate pace
- Ensuring that pupils are challenged and engaged

Anyone who hasn't been in school for some time is very unlikely to have thought about much of this. It is therefore a really powerful way of getting new governors to think about both the complexity of teaching a single lesson and the skill of the teachers involved.

The next step is to explore the demands of leadership. This is frankly not as important as establishing an understanding of teaching and its complexities, but it will give governors a sense of how much head teachers and their leadership teams have to think about on a day-to-day basis. So, talk them through the aspects of leadership they will grasp easily – budget setting and monitoring, buildings, appointments and performance management, among others – but also ensure they are aware of the importance of the leadership of teaching and learning. Explain the curriculum, assessment, reporting, the performance tables, the inspection process, how the quality of teaching is monitored, line management and so on.

In too many schools, governor induction comprises a chat with the head, a tour of the school and attendance at a few committee meetings. If, however, you take the time to outline both the demands of teaching and the complex nature of leadership, you are much more likely to end up with governors who appreciate just how professional the organization they have joined actually is. Reminding governors that they are dealing with highly skilled professionals and not two-dimensional versions of hopeless teachers they remember from the past is a vital leadership task. Moreover, it needs to be done on a regular basis. It is essential for governors to understand that they are dealing with professionals as highly trained as doctors and lawyers.

Outlining the complexities and demands of contemporary teaching and school leadership needs to be balanced by an understanding of the needs of new governors. They quickly find that the role is much more demanding than they expected. They therefore need help and support. The best way to do this is to make sure everything is explained clearly, and that background information is always available.

A good place to start is with the simple stuff that people who work in the profession assume everyone knows. For example, how many governors are given lists of acronyms when they take up their roles? To take part in a meeting where the head is talking about Key Stage 3, P8, continuing professional development (CPD), Design Technology (DT), Personal, Social and Health Education (PSHE), and dozens of other everyday acronyms with which educational professionals are all familiar, will leave a new governor confused and bewildered. Similarly, governors need to understand what the curriculum looks like, how pupils are assessed, what examinations will be taken, what support is on offer and so on. A new governor will be on a very steep learning curve, so a supportive head teacher is vital. If you are involved in helping them get to grips with their new role, they are much more likely to offer support when the time comes rather than challenge.

Briefing notes are often useful. If you sketch out the parameters of a discussion before a meeting, it allows you to take control and exert considerable influence over the meeting. If you simply turn up unprepared and not really ready to talk about an agenda item, the discussion could go anywhere. Experienced head teachers use briefing notes to guide discussions towards the outcomes they favour the most. In other words, here are some choices, though this is obviously the best choice.

Reporting to governors

The head's report is one of the best ways of taking control of the agenda. A comprehensive report will give the information governors need to feel that they are on top of things as well as reassuring them that the leadership team is on the case. An example is included in the appendix. A good report should cover the following topics:

1. The context of the school, including pupil numbers and staffing

2. Pupil achievement: examination performance, progress towards targets etc.

3. SEND/Pupil Premium (PP)

4. Behaviour and safety, covering exclusions, attendance, pastoral issues, pupil well-being, safeguarding

5. Teaching and learning, with sections on assuring the quality of teaching, performance management, progress with the learning plan, CPD, the curriculum and extra-curricular activities

6. Leadership and management: initiatives to promote learning, involvement in other projects such as teaching schools or collaborative work

7. Resources: the budget, premises, capital projects, health and safety

8. Other matters, including events for governors to attend

A detailed report will not only cover key agenda issues. but it will answer most of the questions governors are likely to ask. It will also give them the information they need to talk to inspectors should the need arise. There is no avoiding the fact that these kinds of reports can take hours to prepare, but they serve a purpose beyond satisfying the needs of governors: they ensure that head teachers regularly review each topic discussed and stay on top of the detail themselves. This turns accountability on its head. Governors have to hold the head to account, but the best head teachers hold themselves to account first, making the relationship with the governors much less threatening and much more manageable.

A carefully designed head's report should link in neatly with both the learning plan and the self-evaluation form (SEF). The plan outlined earlier covers most of the areas you would expect to see in an SEF and comments explicitly on progress against the objectives as set out in the learning plan. Thus, we are adding another layer to the school improvement process which both complements the work done by teachers and extends it into the realms of governance. From the classroom teacher's performance management objectives, via the departmental learning plan, up through the CPD programme and the departmental review process, there is a golden thread which ties everything to the whole school learning plan. The thread then extends to include the governors via the head's report, ensuring that the learning plan is a live document at every level in the school.

The importance of policies

Writing and maintaining school policies are huge undertakings, especially when they can seem more akin to a bureaucratic exercise than a genuine attempt to outline the procedures, practices and values of the school. The DfE's publication *Statutory policies for schools 2014* includes in its introduction a somewhat optimistic reference to the 'ongoing commitment to reducing bureaucracy for schools,' before listing dozens of documents that need to be in place in every school and reviewed regularly.[3]

Head teachers recognize the importance of policies, even if they refer to many of them very occasionally and some never at all. They can also be overwhelmed by the pressure to write, review and update them on a regular basis. A glance at the list of the policies set out in the DfE guidance makes the point. Schools need to have up to date policies covering the following areas:

- Charging and remissions
- Special educational needs
- Teachers' pay
- Data Protection
- Admissions arrangements
- Governors' allowances
- Minutes of, and papers considered at, meetings of the governing body and its committees
- Equality information and objectives
- Register of pupils' admission to school
- Register of pupils' attendance
- Child protection policy and procedures

- Early Years Foundation Stage
- Statement of procedures for dealing with allegations of abuse against staff
- Supporting pupils with medical conditions
- Capability of staff
- Charging and remissions
- School behaviour
- Sex education
- Special educational needs
- Teacher appraisal
- Teachers' pay
- Data protection
- Health and safety
- Admissions arrangements
- Accessibility plan
- Behaviour principles written statement
- Central record of recruitment and vetting checks
- Complaints procedure statement
- Freedom of Information
- Governors' allowances
- Home-school agreement document
- Instruments of government
- Minutes of, and papers considered at, meetings of the governing body and its committees
- Premises management documents
- Equality information and objectives (public-sector equality duty) statement for publication
- School information published on a website
- Register of business interests of head teachers and governors
- Staff discipline, conduct and grievance

They also have to ensure the following information is readily accessible on the school website:

- School contact details
- Admission arrangements
- Ofsted reports
- Exam and assessment results
- Performance tables
- Curriculum
- Behaviour policy
- School complaints procedure
- Pupil premium
- Year 7 literacy and numeracy catch-up premium
- PE and sport premium for primary schools
- SEND information
- Careers programme information
- Equality objectives
- Governors' information and duties
- Charging and remissions policies
- Values and ethos
- Requests for paper copies

Plus, for academies and free schools:

- Annual reports and accounts
- Trustees' information and duties

Although important, policies are yet another distraction from the school improvement agenda, and it is here that governors often prove to be of most value to the school and the leadership team. The regular review of policies should be a key part of the governing body's annual agenda – they are, after all, ultimately responsible for ensuring that they are all up to date. This allows them to develop an area of genuine expertise and encourages them to think about a huge range of issues relating to the day-to-day management of the school. It also means that senior leaders are given the time to concentrate on teaching and learning secure in the knowledge that policies are up to date and fit for purpose. Of course, heads must also check them regularly simply in order to keep up to date, but they don't need to spend hours scrutinizing the detail. A more cynical observer might also add that governors who are busy with policies have less time to interfere with the leadership of the school.

Critical friends

The notion of school governors as 'critical friends' has been around for some time. Originally a term used in education to described groups of teachers working together to support each other by offering positive criticism, it is now most frequently used in the context of school governance. In *The A-Z of school improvement: principles and practice,* Tim Brighouse and David Woods describe a critical friend as an external person

> who understands and is sympathetic to the purpose of the school, knows its circumstances very well, is skilled in offering a second opinion about an issue. Critical Friends are seemingly effortlessly skilled at asking questions. They bring to that questioning task a mastery of inflection and timing, so that questions are never damaging.[4]

Governors should therefore be offering a blend of support and challenge, taking care never to make their questions damaging. The relationship between governors and senior leaders should ideally be positive and professional. The governors' role is therefore both external, in the sense that they are looking at the school from an objective standpoint, and internal, since they are part of the school and a key element of its leadership. This can be a difficult balance to strike. A chair of governors, for example, who becomes too closely involved in the day-to-day running of the school or who has a particular personal agenda can easily act more like a critic than a friend. Often, this is done with good intentions: he or she gets so involved in the school or becomes so worried by the statutory duties of governance outlined earlier that it can be difficult to adopt the appropriate distance from the school's leadership team. When this happens, head teachers and leaders find working with governors most challenging.

Head teachers need to be wary of allowing themselves to drift into situations where the governors become more and more demanding until they are not supporting school leaders but actively undermining them.

It is absolutely essential for head teachers and senior leaders to be firm on the difference between strategy and day-to-day management. This distinction is made clear in The Governors' Handbook: 'Boards should play a strategic role and avoid routine involvement in operational matters.'[5] This is a distinction which is difficult to establish: exactly what is strategic and what operational is hard to define. Once again, we are back to gradual development. A new head will obviously need more guidance from governors and will certainly be under greater scrutiny. Once trust is established, however, governors should adopt an increasingly light touch, allowing the leadership team to get on with the day-to-day management of the school. They should also be prepared to recognize the head's expertise, acknowledging that his or her understanding of strategy is likely to be more compelling than theirs. In reality, it is the head teacher who devises a school's improvement strategy; the governors' role is to question and monitor but ultimately support it. It is hard to imagine a governing body with a sophisticated understanding of both the school and the educational landscape which matches that of the head teacher. The head teacher is the professional; governors are amateurs. Whatever the DfE guidance states, it is surely the head teacher who is best placed to determine the strategic direction of the school.

In multi-academy trusts, where lines of leadership are often much more complex than in stand-alone maintained schools, distinctions between strategy and day-to-day management are often quite stark. Schools which are members of trusts often have head teachers, or heads of teaching and learning, who are based in schools and responsible for day-to-day management. They then have executive heads, to whom they are accountable, who are responsible for the management of several schools. They, in turn, must report to local boards and trust boards responsible for strategy. In this way, the head teachers in the schools inevitably become divorced from strategic decision making. In other words, theirs is an emasculated role, with leadership diluted to mere management. When this happens, it is not difficult to see why schools led by managers begin to lose their way. Moreover, heads brought up in this kind of system move on to executive leadership without the strategic skills needed to exert genuine influence on governors. There are too many examples now of schools around the country following strategies set by distant trust boards where the leaders actually working in the schools have very little say over strategy. Without this vital knowledge of context, improvement priorities cannot properly be identified, and leaders cannot really lead.

Establishing a balance between governors' strategic duties and those of the head teacher is the key to successful leadership. Only when the parameters of this relationship are understood by all concerned – not necessarily explicitly, this kind of understanding is much more likely to be implicit – will genuine school improvement be possible. A school where the governors and the leadership team are at war is a school at war with itself. A symbiotic relationship is vital. It is not, however, the relationship set out in the bald, authoritarian terms of The Governors' Handbook. It is much more nuanced than that. It is a relationship where the governors respect the expertise of senior leaders and work with them to monitor and to hold them to account in ways that are rigorous yet supportive.

Where the relationship between governors and senior leaders has reached this kind of accommodation, the notion of the critical friend becomes a reality. The relationship between governors and the head teacher is particularly important in this regard, not only in terms of working together to drive the school forward but also in offering the head teacher much-needed support.

Although I cannot imagine too many teaching staff getting out their handkerchiefs at this point, it is important to acknowledge the loneliness and isolation of the head teacher's role. However personable or charismatic he or she proves to be, head teachers are in charge, and this means making decisions which are bound to upset colleagues they work with closely. Head teachers regularly make decisions which others don't like, whether they relate to the budget or the curriculum. Head teachers have to discipline staff, help determine their pay, write their references, decide whether to promote them or not and sometimes have to make them redundant. It is hard to consider someone with this much power over your working conditions and career prospects simply a friend. Consequently, head teachers, and increasingly senior leaders, occupy an uncomfortable position in the school. They are surrounded by people all day long, they are often the centre of attention as all eyes turn to them for a decision, they laugh and joke with their colleagues, but they are always one or two steps removed. They may be admired and respected by their staff, but they are rarely considered their friends. When difficult decisions have to be made, they can feel very isolated indeed.

It is here that the critical friend is vital. Governors are in a position to befriend the head, to support him or her and to attempt to reduce this sense of isolation. This, too, takes time. Governors need to be fully aware of the demands of the head teacher's role and encouraged to bear this in mind in their relationships with him or her. Once trust has been established, once the balance between management and strategy has been settled, a genuine working relationship can be established which will be vital both to the head's well-being and the future prospects of the school.

Inviting governors into school

As already observed, most staff in schools have very little contact with governors. It is important, therefore, that when governors do come into school, their visits are properly managed. This is another potentially sensitive area and, in some ways, almost a microcosm of the strategy/management dichotomy discussed earlier. Governors need to come into school on a regular basis, and they need to talk to staff to get a clear understanding of what goes in the classroom, but they are visitors, not employees. Most important of all, they should not be commenting on what goes on in lessons.

Every governing body has a statutory responsibility to establish and monitor its school's policies and evaluate the effectiveness of the school and its curriculum. Governors are also held to account for their own school's performance. Inspectors assume that governors know the strengths and weaknesses of the school and will test that assumption during a school inspection. One of the best and most effective ways in which governors can get to know about their school is to visit during the school day and see it at work. Most schools appoint link governors, with the responsibility of liaising with particular departments. The link governor should be both a source of support to the school and a source of information for the governing body.

It is important for governors and leaders to establish clear guidelines so that potential conflicts are avoided. The simplest and most effective way of doing this is to use visit notes.[6] If every governor is asked to complete a brief visit note when he or she comes into school, not only is there a record of governors' engagement with the school to show inspectors but also a common understanding of appropriate protocols for such a visit. Governors should be clear about the objectives of their visits. A sensible set of objectives will look something like this:

- To develop links with a year group, subject area and/or school as a whole
- To establish and develop effective relationships with the staff
- To understand the environment in which staff work and teachers teach
- To have a greater understanding of students' needs
- To increase their first-hand knowledge of the school which will inform strategic decisions
- To evaluate the implementation of the school development plan
- To see policies and schemes of learning in practice
- To recognize and celebrate success
- To demonstrate that the governing body is contributing to the school's self-evaluation process
- To develop individual governor's roles in terms of their specific responsibilities, for example, special needs, literacy and so on

It is also important to stress the following:

1 Governors should not make judgements about the effectiveness of the teaching they observe.

2 Governors should not pursue a personal/parental agenda or seek to take advantage of their position.

3 Governors should always provide a written report.

4 Governors and staff must respect confidentiality arising from any aspect of the visit.

5 Any action points arising from the visit will be discussed and agreed by appropriate parties.

If governors follow these clear guidelines, then their visits are much more likely to be received positively by staff in the school. Whether they are then perceived to be of any real value is another matter. It is hard to see what teachers get out of a governor visit, unless they have an axe to grind or a particular issue they would like discussed at a governors' meeting. For many staff, a governor visit is yet another task to be performed; the real value of the visit is not only to the governor but also to the senior leaders working with governors who, having visited the school, are more likely to have a better understanding of its day-to-day operations.

Accountability and trust

There is no getting away from the fact that schools and their leaders have to be held to account. External accountability, if managed properly, is vital to effective school improvement. Whether governors are the best people to do it is a matter for debate, especially with so many other systems already in place. However, accountability should go hand in hand with trust, but it is here we get to one of the most significant problems affecting the teaching profession today. Part of the reason governing bodies don't always trust senior leaders is the toxic view of teachers promulgated by successive governments. As we have seen, ambitious politicians are keen to interfere in the education system because they see it as an easy win, and they also think that, having been through it themselves, they understand it thoroughly. This belief, as we saw in Chapter 1, has led to an era of constant change complemented by the frequent disparagement of teachers unsurprisingly resistant to so much change.

One of the most disappointing aspects of the various governments' view of teaching is their lack of understanding of how skilled teachers have become in recent years. If they were aware of this, they might begin to trust us a little more.

I was interested to read the findings of the *Global Teacher Status Index*[7] which found that UK respondents had a higher opinion of their country's education system than those in all the other major European countries. This extremely positive news was balanced, however, by the fact that teachers in the UK work longer hours than their peers in other countries around the world. Only in New Zealand, Singapore and Chile do teachers work longer hours. The report also observed that teachers earn around £5,000 less than the British public think they should be earning. What struck me about this report was how positive it was. Most head teachers today would, I think, find the support of the British public to be something of a surprise, especially given the lack of support shown by so many parents. It is encouraging to think therefore that, despite the seemingly constant political assaults on the profession, most people think teachers are doing a good job.

If this is the case, then perhaps we can be reassured that governors will hold similar views and that governing bodies can be encouraged to trust the teachers in their schools. More to the point, let us hope they can be encouraged to trust their school leaders to take charge of the school improvement agenda.

The essential duty of school governors is, ultimately, to let the professionals get on with the job.

Key points

- Head teachers are often reluctant to complain about or publicly criticize governors.
- The DfE's guidance demonstrates clearly the degree to which power is invested in governing bodies.
- Governors are generally amateurs with limited knowledge of education and pedagogy.
- Governing bodies lack knowledge and diversity.
- Managing the governors is a key leadership skill.
- New governors need to be carefully inducted into the school.
- The head's report to governors is a key document and a useful way of taking charge of the agenda.
- Governors can be used very effectively to consider and update policies.
- Governors can be important as critical friends, although these relationships have to be carefully cultivated.
- Leaders need to work hard to ensure that there is a clear distinction between governors' strategic duties and the duties of the head teacher.
- Governors should be regularly invited into school to develop a thorough understanding of how the place works, but these visits need to be carefully managed.
- The essential duty of governors is to let the professionals get on with the job.

Practical ideas

- Use the suggestions listed in the 'New governors' section of this chapter to construct a thorough induction programme.
- Revise the head's report to governors in the light of the suggestions made in the 'Reporting to governors' section of this chapter.
- Think about who is responsible for writing policies in your school; what role do governors have, and could this be enhanced to reduce the burden on teaching staff?

Notes

1 Governance Handbook. For Academies, Multi-Academy Trusts and Maintained Schools. DfE, January 2017.
2 The Constitution of Governing Bodies of Maintained Schools. DfE, 2017, p. 22.
3 Statutory Policies for Schools. DfE, September 2014, p. 4.
4 T. Brighouse & D. Woods. 2013. *The A-Z of School Improvement: Principles and Practice,* London: Bloomsbury Educational.
5 Governance Handbook. For Academies, Multi-Academy Trusts and Maintained Schools. DfE January 2017, p. 18.
6 An example of a visit note proforma is included in the appendix.
7 The Varkey Foundation. The Global Teacher Status Index, November 2018.

7 Inspection

The majority of education systems around the world have some kind of inspection regime. Their approaches differ from country to country, but there seems to be a general consensus that some form of monitoring is important in order to ensure that standards are maintained and quality assured. Some systems focus on regulation and compliance; others allow greater freedom, with the school's own self-evaluation procedures forming the backbone of the system. The UK inspection framework contains elements of both compliance and self-evaluation. It not only imposes regulatory checks but also stresses its developmental role.

In a recent article posted online, Bob Rothman outlined five international inspection regimes:[1]

- In Hong Kong, schools are required to develop an improvement plan based on a central development and accountability framework model. These are complemented by external school reviews carried out by the Education Bureau, with schools selected at random and notified three months in advance.

- In the Netherlands, all schools receiving public funding are inspected every four years with inspectors looking at the way funds are spent, the curriculum and attainment targets. Underperforming schools are inspected more regularly and more intensively.

- In New Zealand the Education Review Office conducts reviews based on an examination of data, school's self-assessment and site visits conducted by trained evaluators. The final report rates the school against national standards. How often schools are reviewed depends on their rating, with underperforming schools reviewed every year.

- In South Korea, schools are inspected annually using a Ministry of Education evaluation plan. Most inspectors are experienced teachers or school leaders, and they look at teaching and learning, the curriculum and student needs. Poorly performing schools are monitored regularly and supported to improve

- In Taiwan, schools are inspected according to a Ministry of Education evaluation schedule covering leadership and management. Leaders of underperforming schools receive coaching from academics to help them improve.

These are all high-performing education systems, and all seem to consider inspection as key to maintaining quality. Finland, on the other hand, is well known for having no formal inspection system. School inspections in Finland were abolished in the early 1990s. The activities of education providers are guided by objectives laid down in legislation as well as the national core curriculum and qualification requirements. The system relies on the proficiency of teachers. Education is evaluated locally, regionally and nationally, with a strong focus on self-evaluation.

While most teachers would, I am sure, prefer the Finnish approach; whatever system is employed relies heavily on a school's ability to evaluate its own performance. Even highly structured regulatory frameworks insist that schools take responsibility for their own performance. It is important therefore, in any discussion of inspection, to make it clear from the outset that inspection isn't simply about external monitoring or inspection visits; it is also about helping schools to quality assure their own performance and practices. Most teachers no doubt regard inspection visits as punitive rather than supportive, but school inspection is essentially a quality assurance process. The ultimate aim of every inspection regime is to assure the quality of education, in other words, to help schools maintain standards. This will strike many as a somewhat rosy view of inspections, but it hard to argue against the aims of inspection. The impact of inspections on schools and teachers' morale is, of course, another matter, but the purpose of inspection is, ultimately, to bring about improvement.

The way to neutralize the perceived threat of inspections, therefore, is to ensure that schools have robust self-evaluation procedures in place and effective improvement plans. School leaders who focus continually on school improvement, who evaluate their progress honestly and accurately, and who never lose sight of what is going on in the classroom, rarely consider inspection a threat. Indeed, many welcome the chance to have an external agency verifying their own judgements.

The need for inspection

Unpalatable as it may sound, there is clearly a need for school inspections. Indeed, given the increasingly chaotic nature of the education landscape in the UK, inspections have perhaps become almost essential if standards are to be maintained. Beyond the Department for Education (DfE), the inspection system is possibly the only remaining organization common to all schools.

With the decline of local authorities, the monitoring of the quality of teaching and learning is managed by schools in dozens of different ways. Free Schools and stand-alone academies, or 'orphan' academies (as they are delightfully known to the Regional Schools Commissioners [RSCs]), rely on their own systems, unless they work with teaching schools, buy in services from commercial companies or buy back services from the local authority (LA). Schools that are part of multi-academy trusts develop their own monitoring procedures, but these can vary wildly depending on the size of the trust. The larger, national chains have highly developed systems which have effectively replaced local authority school improvement teams; small trusts may rely solely on the expertise of the lead school. In some cases, individual schools have become completely isolated, with very little support available to them from anywhere.

In such a fragmented system, a common inspection framework is surely vital. An inspection may be the only occasion that some schools are subjected to any kind of formal evaluation. A few years ago, all schools would have been monitored by the LA and would have received visits from local authority officers. Head teachers worked with School Improvement Partners, and there were funded support mechanisms in place. All that has now disappeared so that stand-alone academies, small schools in rural areas and maintained schools in underfunded authorities can effectively disappear from view. Far too frequently nowadays, schools that were assumed to be doing well are suddenly revealed to be struggling. It is only through the school inspection system that underperformance in these schools comes to light.

The self-improving system has been widely promoted, but it will be successful only if all schools are involved. At the moment, it includes only those schools that choose to work together, leaving too many alone and isolated. Despite its obvious benefits, the self-improving system has a serious flaw: if schools are given the autonomy to govern themselves, all schools need to be included, but the only way all schools can be included is by the creation of an overarching authority to ensure that everyone is involved. As soon as such an authority is created, it is no longer a self-improving system, and we are back to where we started with organizations that look remarkably like local authorities. The irony of multi-academy trusts is that they are now developing systems of governance which do indeed seem to be replicating LA structures. The only real difference being that schools in a multi-academy trust can be dispersed over much wider geographical areas rather than limited to county boundaries. A cynic might suggest that we have simply re-invented local authorities but made them much more difficult to manage by spreading them out across the country.

There are, of course, schools where governance and leadership are weak, and these need to be identified. There are also schools that were once considered good but which have become complacent. The DfE has attempted to identify complacent schools with its creation of the 'coasting schools' definition, but there are still far too many which don't fall into the coasting category but which are clearly coasting. The inspection system is able to identify schools where improvement has stalled, where progress is weak and where complacency has set in. It therefore performs an essential function in the education system.

The dangers of being satisfactory

The word *satisfactory* has long since disappeared from the inspection framework. Requires improvement is a much better descriptor, many would argue, as it suggests forward motion rather than stasis. It is nevertheless a dangerous category for schools. First, it implies that school leaders have taken their eyes off the ball. A school with strong self-evaluation mechanisms should have been aware that the quality of education was declining, that outcomes were poor, or that there were problems which should have been addressed. Head teachers in schools graded as requires improvement (RI) often have a raft of excuses at the ready, but unless they come with solutions attached, they are just that: excuses. This may sound high-handed and harsh, but although I would argue strongly that the quality of a school is measured by the quality of the teachers in the classrooms, it is the job of their senior leaders to support them with an energetic improvement agenda which never allows complacency to set in.

The second problem of an RI judgement is public perception. When parents are choosing schools, they are far less likely to choose one that requires improvement over one that is considered good or outstanding. No matter how unfair the judgement is considered to be by governors and leaders, the judgement sticks. Once parents choose to go elsewhere, numbers decline, funding falls and a whole host of new problems present themselves. Staff, however committed to the school, don't want to be considered second rate, so many of the better staff leave, and the leavers will inevitably include those who are hard to replace – physicists, mathematicians, linguists and so on. Once key staff members leave, the quality of teaching and learning declines. Soon funding becomes an issue, staffing a nightmare and public perception toxic. Without firm leadership which acknowledges the school's weaknesses and sets out a clear plan for improvement, the risk of an inadequate judgement begins to loom large.

The fear of falling into a category accounts for a great deal of the stress and pressure felt by school leaders today. However, by far the best form of stress relief is preparation. If leaders understand the inspection system, build their self-evaluation processes with regard to the inspection framework and make sure that any weaknesses in the school's performance are addressed in the learning plan, then an RI judgement is far less likely. Leaders able to pinpoint areas of weakness and who are open with staff about them will be able to work with their colleagues to bring about improvement; leaders who assume everything is okay because it was at the last inspection are the ones most likely to come unstuck when the inspection teams appear.

Glib as it may sound, the answer to the fear of inspections is to accept that inspections are essentially a natural part of the school improvement process. School improvement is a continuum covering the learning plan, continuous professional development, examination performance analysis, the monitoring of teaching and learning in the classroom, performance management, external validation and inspection. The inspectors may be anonymous visitors and thus external to the school, but they are very much a part of your school's improvement agenda.

The dangers of being outstanding

When the government built an exemption from inspection for schools graded outstanding into the statute, many regarded this as a grave mistake. In hindsight, it is hard not to agree. With some schools not inspected for more than ten years, a significant number have had no external validation at all, apart from performance in public examinations. In most of these, leadership teams have kept up: they have continued to move the school forward, always aware of the inspection framework even though they know they are exempt from its strictures. That is probably why they were considered outstanding in the first place.

The danger of an outstanding judgement is, of course, complacency. It is easy for leaders to look at their examination performance and assume that everything is fine, but this kind of attitude slides quickly into a reduction in the drive for further improvement. Leaders relax, and standards decline. Most worrying of all is a lack of attention to the regulatory framework. If this happens, safeguarding procedures, for example, can easily lose their rigour, and children end up being put at risk.

Grammar schools are perhaps most in danger of complacency: with a highly selective intake, excellent examination results are almost inevitable, and if results remain good, the assumption will be that everything is okay. Often, however, it isn't: teaching becomes routine and characterized by a lack of challenge, administrative procedures slacken and the school begins to drift. In this case, however, parental support rarely flags. I am always amazed by the faith of the middle classes in the excellence of grammar schools. Their views are based on a combination of the conviction that grammar schools are fundamentally better than other schools plus admiration for the school's excellent examination performance. It rarely seems to occur to them that if you select only the brightest pupils, success in examinations is almost inevitable.

The real danger of an outstanding judgement, however, is the failure to take advantage of it. Schools which do not have the prospect of an inspection hanging over them should be free to push the boundaries of school improvement. Sadly, the opportunities to innovate and go beyond outstanding, which lay behind the original decision to exempt selected schools from inspection, have far too often been ignored in favour of tried-and-tested approaches. An outstanding school should be an innovative school, with a sophisticated learning plan aimed at continually improving the quality of teaching and learning in the classroom.

The limitations of inspection

Inspections are necessary, and if viewed in a positive light, they are a vital part of the school improvement agenda. However, they have their limitations, the most significant of which is the fact that once an inspection judgement has been delivered, that is the end of the process, unless, of course, the school falls into a category when further inspections and monitoring visits are inevitable. Most international systems work in this way, with ongoing support provided only for those schools where underperformance has been identified.

Inspection reports tend to identify only two or three areas for improvement when it is probably true to say that inspectors, if given the opportunity to do so, would be able to identify a whole host of ways in which the school could be improved. This, of course, applies equally to good and outstanding schools, not just those requiring improvement as all schools have room for improvement. At the very least, inspectors could take part in very valuable school improvement discussions once the judgement has been determined. We often overlook the fact that inspectors have unique access to schools: they can go virtually anywhere and ask virtually anything. They have access to a huge range of documents and, during their brief visits, nevertheless manage to gather an enormous amount of information. An experienced inspector will therefore have a considerable bank of knowledge on which to draw, and their advice could be invaluable. Moreover, most inspectors nowadays are experienced practitioners, and many are experts in their fields.

In most systems, the role of inspectors is to judge not advise, and this is a shame. I quite like the analogy of taking your car to the garage: you don't tend to ask the mechanics simply to identify the fault and then return the car; you assume they will fix it. It would be interesting to see the impact of a system where the inspection team was able to visit a few days later and work with the leadership team to discuss school improvement. The main stumbling block here, of course, is objectivity. Inspectors must go into schools without any preconceptions about the quality of education practice they are likely to encounter. If inspectors began working closely with schools, their objectivity could well be compromised. Perhaps in a more open, collaborative system, such an approach might be possible; for the moment, however, inspectors must maintain their distance.

Another limitation on the effectiveness of inspections relates to the accuracy of the judgements. I think it is fair to say that there are few occasions nowadays when inspectors could be accused of getting things seriously wrong. There will always be errors, and some degree of inaccuracy is inevitable in any system, but most inspection regimes now have rigorous quality assurance procedures to ensure that judgements are accurate. Of course, any discussion with a group of head teachers will result in one or two of them sharing their concerns about an inspection where they are convinced that inspectors have got it wrong, but most would admit that nowadays wildly inaccurate judgements are rare. Nothing is black-and-white, and an inspection judgement will ultimately be based on a range of evidence. It can never be definitive. It is the role of school leaders, of course, to ensure that the evidence they present is as compelling as possible and that the work they have done to improve the school is reflected in what goes on in the classrooms visited by inspectors.

The inspection framework itself also imposes limitations since it sets out the areas for inspection. Recently there has been a change of approach, with less emphasis placed on data and more on a child's experience of school. When Amanda Spielman took up her post as Her Majesty's Chief Inspectors for Schools, she took a particular interest in the curriculum, focusing on what pupils learn rather than simply how well they perform in public examinations. This approach has been broadly welcomed by the teaching profession, but it is unlikely that any inspection will ever entirely disregard attainment and progress. However strong the focus on the quality of education in the school as measured by pupil engagement, the strength of the curriculum and the opportunities afforded by the school to enable its pupils to prepare to go out into the world properly equipped, performance data will still play a key part in any judgement. The inspection schedule is therefore restricting in that is necessarily limited. Inspectors cannot consider everything. This is undoubtedly a limitation, but we must be realistic about what can actually be assessed objectively. Current inspection frameworks are, after all, fairly comprehensive in their scope.

Preparing for inspection

The notion of preparing for an inspection is something of a red herring: a school should always be prepared. There are dozens of publications, and hundreds of commercial courses, all aimed at helping senior leaders prepare for an inspection as if they were preparing for a particularly stressful party. Inspections should not be considered to be one-off events which have to be prepared for a few days in advance and then forgotten once the thing has taken place. If inspection is seen as a natural part of the school improvement process, then preparations for the actual inspection should be minimal, focusing on preparing staff rather than preparing documentation.

This doesn't mean, of course, that senior leaders should relax and wait for things to wash over them, but there is no need for them to rush around like headless chickens. In schools where an inspection triggers widespread panic, there is clearly something wrong with their approach to school improvement. There are some sensible checks to undertake, however, as no matter how good a school's self-evaluation mechanisms actually are, mistakes still occur. It is also wise to ensure that any evidence you might wish to present is readily accessible.

A checklist might look something like this:

- Are all safeguarding procedures in place? This will include the following:
  - Checking that the single central record is accurate and up to date
  - All statutory policies are easily accessible on the website
  - The name of the designated safeguarding lead is on the website and all staff know who he or she is
  - All are staff familiar with the latest version of *Keeping Children Safe in Education*?

- All safeguarding records are easily accessible so that if inspectors ask to see staff files, information on students off-site, attendance records, training records, referrals to social services and so on, they can be found immediately?
- Evidence of safer recruitment training
- Details of any pupils who are the subject of protection plans, looked-after children, children missing in education and so on
- Risk assessments
- Records of exclusions
- Site security information
- Information on safeguarding in the curriculum
- Information on female genital mutilation and prevention
- E-safety protocols

- Is the self-evaluation form up to date? Is it honest and accurate?
- Are governors appropriately briefed? As discussed earlier, if the self-evaluation form (SEF) is up to date and the head teacher's reports are thorough, this should be easily accomplished.
- Is the school improvement plan complete and available?
- Is the staff list up to date? Indicate newly qualified teachers, trainees, absences, temporary staff and those subject to support plans or disciplinary proceedings.
- Are timetables available and are they accurate?
- Do you have records to show how the quality of teaching and learning is monitored in the classroom?
- Are governors' minutes available?
- Do you have reliable information on the progress of current groups of pupils? Is it accessible? Is it based on accurate assessment and moderation procedures? Will it be reflected in what inspectors see in the classroom?

The most noticeable feature of this kind of checklist is the safeguarding section. Schools are much better at safeguarding nowadays, but far too many are still caught out by poor safeguarding practices, and these can lead to a poor inspection judgement before any other aspect of the school has even been considered. A strong leadership team is aware of this and takes pains to ensure that the school's safeguarding procedures are thorough and up to date. Given the priority it is afforded in the inspection process, there is really no excuse for leaders to be lax about safeguarding. Many of the requirements are administrative and easily fulfilled; everything else is about awareness. It is hard not to see a leadership team which neglects safeguarding as anything other than incompetent.

Once safeguarding has been checked and self-evaluation documentation assembled, the focus should be on people. Staff need to be prepared. They should be reminded of the basics as outlined in the school's policies: if the policy says that children line up outside the room before lessons start, they should do that; if the teaching and learning policy states that learning objectives are displayed on the board, they should be; if the assessment policy refers to particular feedback styles, these should be used. The point here is that inspectors will not be looking for particular styles – remember that there are no preferred styles in current inspections – but they will be looking for consistency. One of the most important messages to send to staff as they prepare for an inspection is the need for consistency. In good schools, staff all pull in the same direction. Pupils know what to expect in the classes they attend, and their teachers apply policies consistently across the school.

The next point to make is about what inspectors will be looking for. They won't be looking at the teachers, they'll be looking at their pupils. The focus will be on the progress pupils are making in lessons, not the skills of the classroom teacher. Staff should be encouraged, therefore, to work on demonstrating progress rather than trying to demonstrate their dazzling teaching skills. Inspections are about progress, not the performance of teachers. How many staff will believe that is another matter, but the point needs to be made.

Inspections are often caricatured as threatening and intimidating, as if some kind of dark force was about to settle on the school. In practice, this is rarely the case. It is useful therefore to remember to focus on the human aspects of the process. If you are honest and open, if you have identified issues and explained clearly what you are doing about them and if you work with the inspectors rather than against them, you will probably find that an inspection is much less arduous than you expected it to be. Honesty is key to a good inspection. A head teacher who tries to hide problems, who presents overly optimistic data and then who behaves defensively merely demonstrates to the inspection team that there are issues in the school which aren't being properly addressed. A head who not only acknowledges but also actively points out the issues, before outlining the mechanisms in place to sort things out, is much more likely to impress.

And, of course, make the inspectors feel welcome. Find them a comfortable room, ply them with coffee and sandwiches and make the information they require both easily available and easy to comprehend quickly. Staff should be encouraged to be equally welcoming: a friendly school is usually a good school.

Over-preparing

As anyone who has prepared for a public performance of any kind will tell you, it is possible to over prepare. You can get too tied up in preparations and too worried about outcomes, the result of which is a poor performance. This is true of inspections. The irony here is that the inspection providers often get the blame for creating unnecessary stress in schools when the stress has, in fact, been created by the schools themselves.

Over-monitoring is an increasingly common problem in schools, but it is often the result of the determination on the part of the leadership team to bring about improvements. As always, the quick-fix culture is part of the problem: schools requiring improvement, or with serious weaknesses, have to be sorted out quickly, and this means that leadership teams are tempted to try to tackle everything at once. Consequently, tight systems of control are imposed, and in some cases, quite unreasonable demands made on staff.

Data monitoring is a good example. In order for leadership teams to monitor progress, they need good systems in place to check how much progress pupils in each class and each year group are making. If assessment systems are robust and if predictions are accurate and moderation process embedded in the school, it is possible to track pupil progress with a fair degree of accuracy. This is normally done by asking staff to grade pupils two or three times a year and then comparing those grades with previous grades and associated targets. In some schools, however, staff are asked to measure progress much more frequently, with 'data drops,' as they are called, sometimes requested as often as once a month. With this degree of pressure, the systems inevitably begin to buckle. Teachers tend to report the data leaders want to see rather than reporting accurate data. Moreover, if data drops are too frequent, pupil progress simply cannot be measured accurately. Pupil progress is not straightforwardly linear, and it can often take most of the year for teachers to be able to determine with any certainty how much, if any, progress pupils have made.

An inspection team presented with a mountain of data which doesn't correspond with what has been observed in classrooms is very unlikely to give much credibility to leaders' assurances that pupils are now making much better progress than before and that outcomes are therefore certain to improve next year.

Schools where staff are monitored too closely and too frequently are schools where staff experience high levels of stress. There is obviously an urgent need to get underperforming schools back on track as quickly as possible – pupils have only one chance at education after all – but if the approach is too rapid the effect will be deleterious rather than positive. Staff subjected to constant monitoring not only feel under incredible pressure to perform, they feel that school improvement is about imposition and not teamwork.

Preparations for an inspection can be similarly overdone. In some schools, once the inspection has been announced, members of the leadership team fly around the school in a desperate attempt to ensure that all staff are on board and, of course, fully compliant. Consistency is key to a good inspection but insisting on compliance is not necessarily the way to ensure it. If the leadership team insists that lesson plans are completed for every lesson, using often quite burdensome planning templates; that detailed notes on pupils are made available to inspectors; that lessons follow common patterns; and that all books are brought up to date and marked thoroughly, the response is likely to be that staff feel overwhelmed before the inspectors even arrive. All of this should have been done as part of the ongoing school improvement process; trying to impose it all at the last minute is dooms it to failure.

Leaders are much better off checking that teachers are ready and that they feel comfortable. They should be reminded that the inspectors are looking at the whole school and not at individuals; they are looking at pupil progress and not specific lessons. The quality of teaching over time is the judgement they will be making, not the quality of single lessons. Staff should also be encouraged and reminded that their teaching is always of good quality. They should be reassured that the process will focus on the leadership team much more than on them as individuals. If school leaders approach an inspection with confidence, staff will do so too.

Of course, simple reminders are helpful: make sure you think about what you expect pupils to have learned by the end of the lesson and that you are checking on their progress regularly; make sure you are aware of the various pupil groups in your classes; don't talk too much and give pupils a chance to show what they know. Above all, remind them about their safeguarding responsibilities and check that they are familiar with *Keeping Safe in Education*.

School inspections last one or two days. They are essentially monitoring visits. It is far too easy to regard inspections as make or break events, where the future success of the school and everyone in it depends upon the outcome of the inspection. Of course, a 'requires improvement' judgement or, worse still, 'special measures' will have a dramatic impact on the school and its community, but in reality, these are few and far between. For the majority of teachers in the majority of schools, an inspection visit is a positive experience. If it is approached as such, it is more likely to be a positive experience. Above all, it is a visit which must be seen as part of the school's own improvement agenda and ultimately a validation of its learning plan.

Key points

- Most countries around the world have some kind of inspection regime.
- There is clearly a need for inspections, and inspection should be seen as part of the school improvement process.
- Schools which settle for satisfactory put themselves at risk of failure.
- The biggest threat to outstanding schools is complacency.
- All inspection systems have their limitations.

- Schools should always be prepared to be inspected; inspections should not be regarded as events to be dreaded but as a natural part of the improvement cycle.
- Over-preparation is potentially as damaging as a lack of preparation: schools should take care not to place too much emphasis on data and complex monitoring systems.

Practical ideas

- Use the checklist in the 'Preparing for inspection' section of this chapter to see how prepared your school is to be inspected.
- Institute a regular review process to ensure that all staff have a good knowledge of safeguarding procedures.

Note

1 B. Rothman. *Inspection Systems: How Top Performing Nations Hold Schools Accountable*, Top of the Class Newsletter, National Center on Education and the Economy (NCEE). May 2018. http://ncee.org/2018/05/how-top-performing-nations-hold-schools-accountable/

# Pupils, not systems

One of the unique ironies of the teaching profession is that successful teachers move steadily farther and farther away from the classroom. The first steps on the ladder offer one or two free periods a week, and that translates to one or two fewer lessons a week. Heads of departments, the real subject experts, teach even fewer lessons. In many schools now, not only does the head teacher not teach, but some members of the leadership team avoid teaching too. The better you get at teaching, the less of it you do.

The natural corollary of this drift away from the classroom is less and less contact with children. It is unsurprising, therefore, that senior leaders often embark on complex improvement programmes without really considering either their impact in the classroom or the views of the pupils involved. Real improvement planning is about teaching and learning, but these are not abstract concepts. Teaching means teaching individuals in the classroom; learning means helping real pupils learn the things they need to know.

In order to assess the quality of teaching and learning, the obvious thing to do is to ask the pupils themselves. This is not as straightforward as it sounds, however. Most schools nowadays attempt to consider the views of pupils; 'pupil voice' is a widely promoted improvement strategy. In too many, however, this is done in fairly systematic ways which ultimately tell you very little about what really goes on in school and, in particular, in the classroom.

The traditional school council is now a feature of most schools across the country but, in many ways, it is one of the least effective school improvement vehicles. Most school councils attract the brightest and the most involved students who are keen to cooperate with 'authority' and who look forward ambitiously to professional careers. Homework, for example, is not an issue for them, nor, generally, is achievement. They find it easy to engage with the educational pedagogy presented to them and, very quickly, they effectively become establishment figures. As teachers we make the councils in our own image, and they quickly begin to reflect our own ideas back to us.

Having chaired dozens of school councils set up along traditional lines, I must confess to finding the meetings quite often dull and uninspiring. Schoolchildren are remarkably conservative; they tend to accept things the way they are, and consequently when asked to suggest improvements or to find fault, they tend to opt for what can only be described as timid, incremental change. In councils where elections have taken place, you tend to end up with two delightful pupils from each year group, each chosen because they get on well with their teachers and their peers. They are usually quite bright and articulate, and they are often very middle class. They respect authority so are wary of saying anything likely to offend or rock the boat, and they are generally happy at school. Children who are happy with their lot are often reluctant to change anything. The council members I have worked with in the past enjoy coming to school, they do well in lessons, they play musical instruments and they do lots of sport. They do their homework, they look smart in their uniforms and they are supported by their parents. In other words, they are model students, and they model the system as it operates in school.

Discussions with school councils like this tend to convince you that everything is going well. They complain about the loos and the food in the kitchen and daringly suggest that we might consider sweatshirts instead of blazers, but they don't really give you an insight into what it is like to be a child in your school. You might get a glimpse of what it is like to be a happy, compliant, bright child who accepts school as a natural part of life; what you won't get is any idea of how less-well-adjusted pupils regard the school.

The Alternative School Council

In an effort to address this, a few years ago I set up the Alternative School Council. This council emphasized the need to hear not just the constrained voice of the 'good' students but the lost voice of the minority. The key elements were the following:

- It was not elected like the main council.
- Members were chosen by heads of year who are asked to pick two disaffected or disruptive students who would not be afraid to express their opinions.

As you can imagine, this caused some surprise in the staffroom, particularly when they saw who was on the list. Many wondered why on earth I would want to listen to 'that lot'; some genuinely thought it wasn't a good idea to put so many 'wrong-uns' in a room together at the same time. Who knows what might happen.

There were practical difficulties to overcome. The initial meeting was something of a farce: of the ten students chosen to attend, three had been excluded, one was absent and one forgot. Obvious, really, but a salutary reminder of the kind of students we are dealing with here. After a few false starts, however, I managed to ensure that I had a good number of students in the room – this was essentially done via a system of substitutes and some arm-twisting.

It isn't easy to engage these kinds of students in discussions which are essentially about pedagogy. They shuffle uncomfortably, they miss the point, they ramble and some of them just enjoy the sound of their own voice. All of them, however, were pleased to be there. For many of them, this was the first time they had been in the head teacher's office for any reason other than to be told off. They were also pleased with the sense of status they had suddenly acquired. They were part of the head's special group of advisors. For some of them, the attention made a huge difference in their attitude towards school and their behaviour in lessons. I didn't consider this when I set up the group, but as more and more teachers commented on their involvement, it began to dawn on me what effect being a member of the group actually had on those involved. These are students who are not used to being consulted, the truly disenfranchised. Just being asked by the head what they think and having that opinion valued improved their self-confidence and contributed to an undoubted boost to their self-image. One particularly difficult student offered to act as a mentor to a lower school pupil to help him avoid going the same way as he had done. In addition, the alternative councillors enjoyed the respect of their peers in the same way that the traditional councillors enjoy the prestige of their elected posts.

Often the meetings falter and sometimes break down. The students involved find it hard to express themselves and cannot articulate the issues that really concern them. Occasionally, however, points are made which raise issues never considered by most school councils. At the start of one meeting, for example, a student was anxious to talk about a member of staff who had just upset her. Despite the injunction that the council does not talk about particular staff, she kept worrying away at the point, and it was evident that her frustration was growing. Finally, she was able to express what she was really getting at. She was a poorly behaved student and she knew she was, but she wanted to change. Every lesson for her, however, began with a warning or a teacher moving her to sit on her own. No one seemed to be prepared to recognize the fact that she wanted to change. Finally, she said, 'Why can't every teacher start every lesson as if it is a new lesson?' When this exchange was conveyed at a staff meeting, there was a long silence as teachers thought about the profound implications of what the girl had struggled so hard to say.

Once the confidence of the group grew, I began really to learn about what it was like to be in the classroom, what it was like if you were struggling with your work and the teacher didn't seem to be able to help and what it was like to be criticized for simply not understanding. These were not simply sentimental observations, however; they led to detailed discussions of classroom practice. They made us, as a staff, really think about our teaching in relation to disadvantaged students, those with special needs, and those who simply found school a real struggle. Instead of talking in abstract terms about pupil premium students, we found ourselves discussing ways to engage those pupils whose voices we had heard probably for the first time. And as we considered the power of pupil voice when it confronted us in this manner, we also began to consider whether there were any other voices in the school we were not hearing.

Teaching and learning and the school council

One of the ways to ensure that both groups of pupils – the traditional elected council and the alternative council – really began to contribute to the school improvement agenda was to insist that meetings focused on teaching and learning. I made sure that we did not get bogged down with the usual fare: the loos, the dining hall, social spaces, uniform and so on, and I encouraged pupils to think about how they were being taught and what they were being taught.

This led to a really interesting series of discussions about what a good lesson should look like. What made it particularly interesting was that I asked teachers exactly the same question and then put the two side by side in both council meetings. This resulted in further discussion and, in the end, the drawing up of what the councils regarded as a fairly definitive list titled *What makes good learning in a lesson at our school*:

- Practising a new skill
- Use of visual learning
- Being encouraged to remember things your own way
- Putting ideas/concepts in real-world contexts
- Students teaching each other, providing that everyone takes part and the class is under control
- Teachers avoid lecturing but if they do pupils should be reminded to take notes
- Positive, enthusiastic teachers and students
- A comfortable atmosphere in class
- Good relationships
- Ensuring that everyone is involved throughout the lesson
- No hands up
- Non-embarrassing strategies for those who don't understand
- Teachers fully aware of the range of ability in the class and providing for it
- Teachers providing work to stretch the brightest and providing support for the weakest
- A variety of activities helps but stopping and starting should be avoided, as should too much repetition
- Regular revision should be a part of the lesson
- The starter should be short and there should be a memorable summary at the end

- Questioning should be used to check learning
- Half termly tests are useful to reinforce learning
- Competition helps, especially among the brighter pupils
- Homework should reinforce what has happened in the lesson or it should prepare for the next lesson.
- A reward system supports learning
- Both students and teachers must be organized.

There is nothing earth-shattering here, only a reminder of just how sharp pupils are when thinking about learning. After all, they have spent thousands of hours in the classroom, and they know what works and what doesn't. This list was drawn up nearly ten years ago, but it is still relevant today. It is discussed regularly by both school councils, and it still surprises staff who haven't really thought about just how perceptive pupils really are. The students' list is used by teachers every year as the starting point for a discussion about what a really good lesson should look like. The teachers' version – *What does outstanding learning in a lesson look like?* – is included in the Appendix.

The students' list offers some salutary reminders: pupils admire good teachers and appreciate good teaching; they want teachers to be in control; they want to be engaged, and they want to know what they are learning and why; they want to get on with their teachers; they don't want to be embarrassed if they don't understand; and, above all, they want to learn.

On another occasion, as a result of a discussion about behaviour, pupils drew up their own classroom code of conduct. It is neither wildly original or particularly sophisticated, but it came from the students themselves:

The school council classroom code

We, the students of school, know that we are here to learn. We recognize that for lessons to run smoothly we need to do the following things:

- We like to wait outside classrooms sensibly until a teacher arrives.
- We wear our coats outdoors only.
- We stand quietly behind our desks until the teacher is ready.
- We recognize that is best to sit where the teacher asks us to.
- We don't get up and wander around without asking permission.
- We look after classroom furniture and equipment.
- We bring the appropriate equipment to lessons.

- We respect other people's belongings.

- We try not to shout out: we put up our hands or respond when asked.

- We never eat during lessons; we drink water to keep us hydrated (but we realize that in some rooms it is inappropriate).

- We are always courteous and polite to teachers, staff and other students.

- We leave the room as we would like to find it.

- We stand quietly behind our desks before leaving the room.

The lessons are for our benefit: we aim to enjoy them and take part!

There are two key points here that are easily overlooked when we consider teaching and learning and behaviour, in particular: pupils clearly want to learn, and they want everyone to be well behaved. Although they push the boundaries all the time, fundamentally they understand the need for rules and expect staff to impose them. I have often found it amusing to discuss uniform with pupils whose shirts are hanging out, whose ties are not done up, whose skirts are far too short and who are clearly wearing items of clothing not permitted under the school's uniform rules only to discover that they are, in fact, fierce advocates of uniform and wouldn't countenance its abolition.

Pupils respect staff who teach well and impose order. What they don't like is teachers who are unfair. If the rules are applied fairly, then the majority of pupils are content.

Pupils as leaders of learning

Although I really don't like to think about education in commercial terms, it is interesting to think about pupils as consumers. We certainly shouldn't consider education as a commodity, even if it has long been considered as such by private schools and is increasingly become commoditized by the larger multi-academy trusts, but it is helpful to think about pupils as consumers of learning. In which case, it is important to ensure that our teaching, like all good products, is fit for purpose and appreciated by the customers in the classroom. How interesting then, to turn the table and get the pupils themselves to become the providers rather than the consumers. This is an exercise that throws up all sorts of interesting questions.

A few years ago, following a discussion in the school councils about the demands of teaching, pupils came up with the idea of trying it themselves. The result of the discussion was what became known as 'Takeover Day,' a day during which staff were encouraged to let pupils in their classes teach the lessons themselves. We are all used to students doing presentations in lessons or leading short episodes, but to ask pupils to teach a whole lesson was something of a revelation. Most pupils decided to get together in groups, but some brave souls volunteered to lead lessons by themselves.

It was a remarkable day. As I toured the school, looking into as many lessons as I could, it struck me just how seriously pupils were taking things. There were lessons going on all over the school, and the majority of them were calm, focused and engaging. The day itself was a real success, but it was the subsequent discussions which proved to be the most valuable. When asked to give feedback on how they thought their lessons had gone, pupils were able to talk at length about the demands of teaching, about the things they hadn't thought about, about the necessity of keeping people interested and, something experienced teachers don't often think about, about the length of the lessons. One of the most interesting observations was that, as pupils, an hour's lesson didn't seem that long; as teachers, an hour seemed to stretch on endlessly, with most pupils struggling for material after about 20 minutes.

As far as the pupils were concerned, the most important learning to come out of the day was an appreciation of just how difficult teaching actually is. Subsequent discussions looked at how lessons are planned, how classes are kept on task, how teachers know how long things should take, working out exactly what needs to be learned and so forth. It would, of course, be impossible to measure the long-term impact of this exercise, but there can be no doubt that the pupils learned huge amounts from trying out teaching for themselves which, in turn, must surely have led to a greater sense of engagement in lessons generally.

Another striking example of both the value and the power of student voice can be seen when pupils are involved in staff appointments. Again, this is something they take very seriously, and as with the alternative council, it is important to include pupils from across the spectrum and not just the shiny, well-behaved A-grade types. Even pupils whose behaviour staff feel leaves a lot to be desired tend to rise to the occasion. The most effective way of arranging student interviews is very simple: between eight and ten pupils are brought together and told they are going to interview a selection of candidates for a particular teaching appointment. Briefing is minimal because it is generally unnecessary. They need to be told to get to know the candidates but not to embarrass them, find out what they are like as teachers and get a sense of whether they would fit in. Above all, they need to answer the question, Would I want to be taught by these people?

Only on one occasion have I felt it necessary to ask pupils not to ask a particular question again, even if it did turn out to be an excellent discriminator. One overly enthusiastic group finished each 20-minute session with 'and finally, tell us a joke.' This, for some of the candidates, proved to be an excruciatingly embarrassing moment, and it had to be explained to the students that this was unnecessarily cruel. On the other hand, the better candidates took it in their stride and answered the question.

In order to capture the details of each meeting, we usually ask a governor, or a member of the support staff, to sit in the corner and record what happens. Pupils are also asked to give feedback after they have interviewed everyone and decide who they would appoint. What I always find fascinating, though it's probably not surprising, is that they nearly always choose the candidate who is subsequently appointed. In fact, they are able to talk about candidates with a remarkable degree of sensitivity and insight: they recognize straight away those who are trying too hard to be their friends, those who will have discipline problems and those whose heart really isn't in it. As consumers of learning, they have an excellent understanding of who is best to provide it. I sometimes wonder whether we really need to go through the whole day-long interview process when we could simply ask the students.

As discussed in Chapter 4, student voice should also be a key part of departmental reviews. Here, of course, it is school leaders asking the questions with each set tailored to align with the focus of the review and the department concerned. The sorts of questions asked might include the following:

- What do you enjoy about your lessons in this subject?
- Do you actively engage in your lessons? What can influence this?
- How do you know if you are making progress? Do you know what steps to take to improve?
- What are the things your teachers do, and what are the things you do in lessons that best help you to learn?
- Is there anything you think hinders your learning?
- What have been the biggest challenges since you started the course?
- Tell me what typically happens in a lesson?
- What kind of feedback does your teacher give you, and how do you respond to it?

It is these kinds of questions which elicit really interesting answers. Pupils know they are not allowed to talk about particular teachers (though it is, of course, often evident who they are talking about), but they really appreciate the chance to give their opinions on what happens in lessons. Although their comments are usually well received by the members of the departments concerned, there are always one or two surprises. It is the surprises that really make departments think. Good departments usually have a fairly good idea of where their strengths and weaknesses lie, but it is always useful to get a glimpse into what pupils really think and alter course accordingly.

It is these kinds of interactions with pupils that give teachers and leaders a real insight into how children learn. Most schools use some kind of annual questionnaire, but the real value of such exercises is debatable. They are useful in giving school leaders a general sense of what is going on in the school and particularly useful at highlighting aspects of the school's ethos that need strengthening. For example, questionnaires are helpful in identifying the scale of bullying in a school, or the extent to which pupils feel safe. However, for detailed information on what goes on in the classroom, and the quality of learning in the school, activities like those discussed above are likely to be much more informative.

Pupil pursuits are not normally discussed as a feature of student voice, but they often prove to be a really useful way of finding out what it feels like to be a student in the school from their point of view. In that sense, you are giving them a voice, if somewhat indirectly. For this kind of thing to be of real value, it must be done properly. In other words, you must spend all day following the same pupil around. This doesn't mean you have to stick to the student like glue, and he or she should be released from the torture of having a senior leader by his or her side at lunch and at break, but to appreciate the student's experience of school fully you cannot cut corners. Pupil pursuits often involve two or three lessons or a series of lessons spread over the week; the only way to do it properly, however, is to attend every lesson for the whole day.

For staff who undertake a full-scale pupil pursuit, it can be a real eye-opener. I remember clearly getting to the end of my first pupil pursuit and wondering how on earth pupils in the school learned anything at all. Although I had done it as a child myself, the experience of a day in school struck me as almost overwhelming. I was fascinated by the way the boy I followed was able to switch in an instant from talking about Macbeth to considering the intricacies of wave motion before rushing to the changing rooms to put on his physical education kit and then getting back into the classroom for an hour of language learning. There were times when I was thoroughly engaged with the lesson, and others when I was tired and bored. I was also fascinated by the way pupils seem instantly to adapt to the various teachers they encounter as they move through the day. In some lessons, the class worked quietly and seriously; in others, the atmosphere was much more energetic. The same pupils responded in dramatically different ways depending on the way the teacher conducted the lesson. Most notably, of course, pupils who were badly behaved in some lessons proved to be compliant and fully engaged in others.

It was something of a rollercoaster ride. From marvelling at the way one teacher carefully explained what struck me as a really difficult concept in science, so that everyone in the room seemed to grasp it straight away, to shuffling in my seat in frustration as a technology teacher laboriously explained how to cut up a piece of wood safely. At one point, I really felt like walking to the front and sawing it in half myself just to get the lesson moving, a feeling I am sure I shared with the rest of the class.

An appreciation of a student's day really changes the way you think about teaching, and it makes you think about how you structure your own lessons. It also gives you a remarkable insight into how children learn, as well as intense admiration for the way in which they cope with so much.

Parents

Most guides to school improvement focus quite rightly on teachers and pupils, but they also include lengthy discussions considering the importance of parental involvement. However, the role of parents strikes me as somewhat overstated and, in many ways, tangential to the improvement agenda. Unlike teachers and pupils, they are not part of the school. They support it, they are interested in it and they want to know how effective it is in educating their children, but they are at one step removed. Their knowledge of the school comes via their children. Their knowledge and their understanding of what happens in the classroom is therefore filtered and, in most cases, filtered quite heavily.

Nor should be shy away from the fact that, nowadays, parents have become much more critical and much more likely to complain. In some cases, this is fully justified; in many, it is an overreaction. Their complaints are always prompted by genuine concerns for their children's welfare, but it is increasingly the case that they have very little confidence in schools and their leaders. Standards of professionalism in schools have never been higher, and much greater attention is paid to student welfare than ever before, yet parents seem increasingly distrustful. The reasons for this are complex – the rise of social media has certainly contributed to new levels of criticism and unkindness to others – but the government must take the lion's share of the blame. When the country's leaders are clearly contemptuous of teachers, it is not difficult to see why parents adopt the same stance.

Strong parental support is, of course, vital. Schools need to know that parents are encouraging their children to learn and that they value education. This isn't always the case, however, and schools then have to work hard to convince both children and their parents of the value of education. Where parents really feature in the improvement process, however, is in helping their children to learn, and that is where school leaders need to devote their energies. Once again, if the focus is kept firmly on teaching and learning, then improvements are possible.

Engaging parents therefore is not simply a matter of regular communication, open evenings, and newsletters as these are essentially marketing tools. What really matters are those events and activities which focus directly on learning. The most obvious of these are parents' evenings, where teachers get the opportunity to explain how pupils are doing and, if they are wise, to involve parents in their children's work. These are often frantic occasions, however, with some exchanges lasting little more than a few minutes. Really effective parental engagement needs to take place over long periods.

Most schools nowadays put on evening sessions designed to warn parents about the dangers of drugs and other health issues, but sessions aimed directly at what goes on in lessons are few and far between. Of course, there are options evenings and sixth-form open evenings, and lots of schools now offer sessions aimed at helping parents to encourage their children to revise and how to support them through stressful exam periods. The most effective forms of engagement, however, are based not on general topics like revision and which subjects to choose but on subject content.

A good example is maths. Lots of parents say they would like to help their children with their maths homework but complain that maths is very different now and not at all like the maths they studied when they were at school. Some schools have decided as a result to run maths classes for parents which mirror the maths studied by the children in class. I must confess to finding these particularly enjoyable. I quite often look through the windows in the doors of the maths rooms to see parents shuffling uncomfortably and clearly thinking, 'Don't ask me.' In the end, of course, they enjoy these sessions and leave feeling better equipped to help their children. As always, of course, it is the parents of those who need the least help who attend, and one of the priorities of any school leadership team intent on school improvement is to work out imaginative ways of attracting less supportive parents to attend. These sessions inevitably involve a lot of extra work for the staff involved, but the pay-off is that parents often leave incredibly impressed by their skill and much less likely to complain. As with almost every aspect of school improvement, if the focus is teaching and learning, things will improve.

Academic pupils, happy pupils

When senior leaders engage with pupils and really try to understand what it is like to be a pupil in their schools, they are driven to consider fundamental questions about the purpose of schooling. The current obsession with performance tables and accountability measures would seem to suggest that, as far as the government is concerned, schools are all about passing exams. As soon as you start listening to pupils, it quickly becomes clear that schools are about much more than that. We all know that when we think back to our own school days, it is rarely the lessons we remember; it is all the other stuff. And it is the other stuff that ultimately powers the academic agenda. If pupils are happy, if they enjoy coming to school, if they feel safe and if they are given lots of opportunities to get involved, they will succeed academically.

One particularly memorable moment in an alternative school council meeting sticks in my mind. Both the school council and the Alternative Council were told that we were about to conduct our annual curriculum review and they were asked to design a new curriculum from the ground up. Imagine you could study anything you want, they were told; what would your day or week look like? The traditional school council, of course, set about the task with enthusiasm and eventually came up with a timetable which looked virtually the same as the one they followed every day.

The Alternative Council members meanwhile took a while to grasp what they were being asked to do and quibbled over whether it was their job to consider such things. Their ultimate conclusion, however, was telling: 'It doesn't really matter what subjects we do,' said one small girl, 'we just want teachers who are kind to us.'

Key points

- Effective school improvement depends on pupil involvement.
- Too often, the pupils who sit on the school council are the brightest, most biddable students who reflect teachers' own ideas.
- An 'alternative school council' offers real insights into what it is like to be a child in your school.
- Schools councils should talk about teaching and learning, not about the state of the loos or the choices in the dining hall.
- Pupils should be encouraged to contribute to discussions around teaching and learning; they know better than anyone what it is like to be in lessons.
- Pupil interviews are key to successful departmental reviews and a vital part of the school improvement process.
- Parental involvement in schools should be focused directly on learning.
- Above all, pupils value fairness and kindness.

Practical ideas

- Set up an 'alternative school council' in order to hear the voices of the disadvantaged and the dispossessed.
- Ask pupils to create their own version of 'What makes a good lesson in our school?'
- Ask pupils to create their own classroom code.
- Ask pupils to design a poster titled 'What makes a lesson outstanding?'
- Involve pupils in every interview and consult them on all key decisions.

Appendix

Societal expectations of schools and school leaders

Between 1 September and 31 October 2018, the following problems were identified as things that schools should either be responsible for or help to sort out. All of them were widely reported in the media. They appear in the order in which they were reported.

- Not enough children have the opportunity to participate in sports days.
- Schools should encourage more ethnic minority children to play rugby.
- The Royal Horticultural Society urged schools regularly to involve children in gardening.
- Teachers should know to what extent their schools are affected by asbestos.
- Schools 'need to change their entire culture' as the hierarchical way in which they are run, including children being streamed into sets based on their abilities, encourages bullying.
- Schools should be designed so that their hours match the hours of working parents.
- Children should be taught critical learning skills and political and social awareness.
- Schools should ban mobile phones.
- Schools shouldn't ban mobile phones.
- Boys and girls should be allowed to wear either trousers or skirts to school.
- Schools should reduce the number of exclusions.
- Teachers should not express political views.
- Schools should end period poverty.

- Staff should be inclusive to lesbian, gay, bisexual and transgender (LGBT) children.
- Schools should remove hazardous gauze mesh from science labs.
- Schools are using exclusions inappropriately.
- Schools should reduce the use of streaming.
- Schools need to counteract the fact that children's minds are dulled by iPads.
- Religious Education should be renamed Religious and World views to reflect diversity.
- Primary schools should use the National Crime Agencies teaching package on online sex abusers.
- Single-use plastics should be part of the curriculum.
- Schools should teach pupils about the importance of sleep.
- Children should be educated about the signs and symptoms of cancer.
- Teachers should prepare children for disappointments.
- Child abusing reporting should be a regulated activity.
- Banning dreadlocks is discriminatory.
- The post-16 curriculum must be broadened.
- More attention needs to be paid in schools to mental health.
- The recommendations of the Women and Equalities select committee should be implemented in full in schools.
- More attention should be given to pupils with special educational needs (SEN) to cut down on exclusions.
- Darcey Bussell called for schools to teach more physical education (PE).
- Schools should be more aware of child carers.
- Schools should not use exclusive suppliers.
- Schools are to be encouraged to join Connected Classrooms through Global Learning.
- Video games aimed at exploring coercive violence to be introduced in schools.
- Children should not be over-protected as this leads to mental health issues.
- Schools need to teach transgender issues more effectively.
- Children should be taught about terrorism.

- Children should be taken on trips to mosques to tackle Islamophobia.
- All pupils should complete at least 25 hours of volunteering.
- Teachers need to crack down on classroom messaging apps.
- The National Society for the Prevention of Cruelty to Children (NSPCC) wants schools to teach more about what constitutes abuse.
- Schools should be able to spot children used as drug mules.
- Schools leaders should ensure that pupils know what they want to do before they leave school.
- Schools should avoid off-rolling.
- All primary schools should be twinned with a farm.
- Schools should explain and monitor 'county lines.'
- Schools should not overwhelm parents with information.
- Schools should encourage parents not to have outdated and snobbish attitudes to vocational education.
- All pupils should walk a mile every day.
- Evolution is being taught the wrong way around – more guidance on evolution and genetics needed.
- All schools should encourage pupils to play chess.
- Schools shouldn't band children from bringing water or squash into school
- More schools should set up pigeon racing clubs.
- Schools should support their former pupils at university.
- PE teachers need to be better trained.
- Schools should use more cover supervisors.
- Schemes to reduce childhood obesity should be targeted at ethnic minority pupils.
- More pupils should be studying STEM (science, technology, engineering and mathematics) subjects
- Schools should plant more trees.
- More schools should extend their days.
- Schools to supply more data on off-rolling.
- Schools should debate the merits of homework.

- Schools should have policies on the healthy use of social media.
- More pupils should be encouraged to study languages.
- Schools need to teach pupils to focus as they are losing the ability to focus thanks to modern technology.
- Teachers need to be aware of the sleeplessness crisis.
- Roads near schools should be closed to traffic.
- STEM subjects should be rethought to appeal to girls.
- Children should be taught to count in 12s, not 10s.
- There should be a greater emphasis on black history in school textbooks.
- Schools should boost competitive sport with the help of the Premier League.
- Schools should run breakfast clubs.
- Prince Harry doesn't want children to play Fortnite.
- Schools should do more to promote apprenticeships.
- Trans inclusion issues to be taught in schools.
- Schools should ditch processed red meat.
- Schools should prepare pupils for the rise of robot technology.
- Teachers need to be aware that Russian cyber trolls are targeting teenagers.
- All schools should text pupils for dyslexia.
- More effort needs to be put into promoting music in schools.
- Pupils should be taught about slavery.
- Forest schools should be part of more school curriculums.
- Schools should not have expensive uniforms as these result in selection by wealth.
- Schools should teach Team Leadership.
- Schools should track children's happiness and mental health through regular checks and tests.
- All teachers should be able to spot brain injury and concussion.
- Children should not be forced to sing hymns.
- Children should be taught about the legacy of the British Empire.
- Schools should ensure pupils are aware of the risks of gambling.

- Fitness should be as important as maths and English.
- Schools should take measures to combat extended screen time.
- Schools should encourage pupils to be bilingual.
- Schools should do more to encourage pupils to walk to school.
- Pupils should be trained to deliver CPR.
- Schools need to convince pupils that Oxbridge is for pupils 'like them.'
- Pupils should be encouraged to read fiction several times a week.
- Teachers should draw attention to black, minority and ethnic (BME) writers when compiling reading lists.
- Sailing should be part of the national curriculum.
- Pupils need to be taught more about modern slavery and county lines.
- Schoolchildren should be educated about menopause.
- Schools should broaden the focus of Remembrance Day to include all who suffered.
- Schools should not give sanctions to pupils who don't do their homework.
- Schools need to be more aware of food allergies.
- School leaders need greater powers to search pupils for guns in school.
- Teachers should be encouraged to work in areas of disadvantage.
- Personal finance should be taught in schools.
- Pupils are to be encouraged to do more work on the Holocaust.
- Schools must try to reverse the decline in music education.
- Schools need to teach emotional intelligence as well as knowledge.
- Teachers should teach children how to be kind to animals.
- Dance should be a curriculum subject for all children to improve their fitness.
- Maths should relate more to everyday life situations.
- More teachers need to be trained in identifying and working with pupils with attention-deficit/hyperactivity disorder.
- Teachers need to do more work to convince girls that STEM subjects are for them.
- Schools should devote more time to practical skills to counteract the screen culture.

Line management meeting minutes: The Elysium Academy

Subject: _____   Date: _____

Staff: _____   Line Manager: _____

Progress and Standards	
Intervention – vulnerable & Disadvantaged students	
Day-to-day management	
CPD/Developing teaching and learning in team	
Curriculum/Assessment developments	
AOB	

A vision for The Elysian Academy

The aim of the leadership team is to ensure that The Elysian Academy provides the best possible experience for its pupils and to continue to develop the school so that it is recognized as one of the best in the country.

In academic terms, the intense focus on pedagogy and outstanding classroom practice will lead to excellent progress for every pupil. This means that every child is recognized as having individual needs and aspirations and none are overlooked: the weakest are fully supported, those in the middle are stretched and never treated as average, and the brightest are inspired to aim for the top universities and the most demanding professions.

Elysian should always achieve excellent ratings in whatever performance measures the government chooses to adopt, with pupil progress being the most important consideration.

Elysian's vision is not a narrowly academic one, however, and it is the ambition of the school to develop the most comprehensive and effective pastoral support systems, the most engaging and varied extra-curricular programme, and, above all, a learning environment which is both safe and welcoming to all.

In order to achieve this vision, the leadership team strives to ensure that every decision is focused on teaching and learning, every appointment secures the very best teacher or member of the support staff, and every lesson is taught to a standard that says, 'This is truly an outstanding school.' The aim is to ensure that there are no underperforming subjects and that each pupil will experience the same high-quality teaching in every area of the curriculum.

An outstanding school needs to be equipped to respond to change, it needs to be driven and it needs to embrace innovation which makes a difference, not innovation for its own sake. The best schools continually reinvent themselves, but they do it within a strong framework of good practice, traditional codes of conduct, fair and supportive working practices for staff, and simple good sense. They are also in it for the long-term and recognize that there are no quick fixes in the pursuit of excellence.

In addition, a school's vision must be confident enough to welcome criticism, share good practice, and work openly with other schools and academic institutions.

Finally, Elysian's vision embraces both breadth and depth in education, recognizing the importance of core subjects like English, Maths and Science but also valuing and promoting the arts and humanities as fundamental to the creation of a civilized society. It also aims to give students and, indeed staff, the confidence to embrace a digital future which includes rather than excludes traditional study, cultural history and good citizenship.

The Elysian Academy

A model self-evaluation form (SEF) with suggestions and examples

The School: Begin with a brief outline of the school and its context. **The Senior Leadership Team:** Note any key changes. **Governance:** a brief outline **Students:** Include attainment on entry data and attendance data. Include actions to improve attendance and persistent absence.	**Sources** Ofsted Reports IDSR

The Quality of Education: attainment and progress – the school's track record of performance over the past three years.

School Judgement: always make a judgement. Don't dither – be accurate. **Benchmarks for achievement at Key Stage 4** ▪ Overall achievement is. . . ▪ Attainment . . . ▪ Progress . . . **Achievement by groups at Key Stage 4** ▪ Groups are. . . ▪ Pupils with high attainment on entry. . . **Achievement in Core Subjects** ▪ Attainment and progress in Maths, English and Science remains. . . **Achievement at Key Stage 5** ▪ Attainment and progress – Good overall but with . . . outcomes for disadvantaged students

Achievement (Unvalidated) **Include key data:** - E&M Basics (standard pass) and (strong pass) – FFT (High) target - P8 calculated using, for example, the ASCL data set/ Internal calculations etc. - Areas of underperformance and actions to address them. The actions are key here. - Areas of outstanding performance. - FFT estimates for the following year. Current predictions with caveats. **Previous achievement (Validated)** - Attainment and Progress figures - Basics with standard pass and strong pass or better (against FFT targets) - % 5EM (standard passes). - IDSR P8 figure against national and with a percentile ranking. - Rankings for individual subjects: Eng P8 (rank: th), Ma P8, Ebacc P8 with elements. Science VA (rank:) and Humanities (rank:) Languages (rank:) Comment on underachievement. - ALPs analysis if available.	*GCSE results* *Alps report KS4* *Internal P8 calculations (using ASCL/4Matrix data set) Performance Tables Check* *FFT Aspire data* *IDSR*
Current achievement by groups (Unvalidated) **Disadvantaged pupils (number):** (Internal/ASCL) P8 from Internal IDSR Progress figures for in Eng, Maths, Sci, Ebacc, Other **SEND (Statement) (number):** (Internal/ASCL) Progress figures **SEND (Support) (number):** (Internal/ASCL) Progress figures Comment on progress and actions to improve weaknesses. **Past achievement by groups (Validated)** Progress made by disadvantaged pupils, most able, etc. HPA, LPA etc. Gender. EAL etc. Comment on progress and actions to improve weaknesses.	*Performance Tables* *Alps report KS4* *Internal P8 calculations* *FFT Aspire data* *IDSR report* *GCSE results analysis*
Current Achievement in Core Subjects (Unvalidated) Mathematics, English, Science, Ebacc elements. **Past Achievement in Core Subjects (Validated)**	*GCSE results* *Alps report KS4*

Appendix 161

Current Achievement Key State 5 (Unvalidated) Performance at A level % of entries at A*–A, % of entries at A*–B, % of entries at A*–E – comment on performance APS grade per entry: 3-year T score if you use ALPS. Individual subject grades worthy of comment. Actions to address weaknesses **Past Achievement at Key Stage 5 (Validated)** IDSR VA VA (disadvantaged) APS per entry: % of pupils achieved at A*/A -etc	*A-level results* *Alps report* *School Performance Tables* *IDSR*

Quality of Education

School Judgement:

The curriculum is well designed, comprehensive and appropriate
- *The curriculum meets the needs of all pupils*

Teaching engages and challenges so all pupils make progress
- *Teaching is at least good in all subjects*

Teaching enables pupils to improve their basic skills
- *The explicit teaching of basic skills (particularly writing) is a feature in the most effective lessons*

Assessment is used by teachers and students so 'gaps' are identified, and action is taken to close them
- *Formative assessment (characterized by rich questioning and enabling pupils to reflect upon what they are doing well and how next to improve) remains a strength*

Reading is given high priority in the school
- *There is a strong focus on reading and cross-curricular literacy*

The curriculum is well designed, comprehensive and appropriate Comment on the breadth and depth of the curriculum Comment on **Implementation** and indicate **Impact**	
Teaching engages and challenges so all pupils make progress Comment on the quality of teaching, with specific examples and accurate data. Comment on **Issues** and indicate **Actions**.	

Teaching enables pupils to improve their basic skills Comment on action taken to improve basic skills.	*NGRT reading tests*
Assessment is used by teachers and pupils so 'gaps' are identified and action is taken to close them Comment on the effectiveness of assessment.	*Subject evaluations*
Reading is given high priority in the school Comment on reading programmes, cross-curricular approaches, etc.	

Personal development

School Judgement:

Spiritual, moral and cultural development
- *Students' spiritual, moral, social and cultural development is outstanding and is promoted across the curriculum*
- *There is a comprehensive Citizenship programme which covers equalities, FBV, healthy living etc.*

Careers
- *The school runs a comprehensive and individually tailored careers programme*

The personal development of students is given high priority Careers information/preparation for the next stage/ Healthy living Citizenship Equalities	*Ofsted Report* *Kirkland Rowell survey*
Careers Comment on the range and nature of the programme, and next steps	*Gatsby benchmarks*

Behaviour

School Judgement:

Students feel safe and behave well
- *Pupil behaviour is . . .*
- *Effective systems promote outstanding behaviour in the majority of lessons, it is never less than good*
- *Robust systems ensure that health and safety matters remain a high priority*

Students choose to attend
- *Attendance is . . .*
- *Rates of persistent absence are . . .*

Students feel safe and behave well	Ofsted Report
Exclusion rates	Kirkland Rowell survey
Bullying	
Behaviour and Behaviour for learning.	
Comment on pupil safety.	
Pupils choose to attend	*Attendance reports*
Comment on attendance and interventions	

VIth Form

School Judgement:
Students make the most of their opportunities post 16 and there is a relentless focus on raising achievement
- *The Sixth Form is inclusive and students achieve well*
- *Leadership is . . .*

Students make the most of their opportunities post 16 and there is a relentless focus on raising achievement	Ofsted report
	VIth form evaluation
Comment on context.	
Achievement and outcomes	

Effectiveness of leadership/management

School Judgement:

Self-evaluation systems and CPD work to improve teaching and learning
- *Self-evaluation and provision of CPD as tools to improve T&L are. . .*

Leaders at all levels demonstrate drive and ambition for students to fulfil their potential
- *Leadership and management are . . .*
- *There is clarity at every level about school priorities and how these might be achieved*
- *In all subjects leaders know their students' strengths and weaknesses and ensure improvement activities seek to address those weaknesses*

Governors have the expertise to challenge and support the leadership team so that improvement priorities can be realized
- *Governors recognize their core role and support the school's work to drive up standards*

Self-evaluation systems and CPD work to improve teaching and learning Brief outline of self-evaluation systems and CPD. Discuss its effectiveness and impact.	*Training Programme and staff feedback*
Curriculum Comment on the effectiveness of the curriculum. How does it meet pupil needs? Breadth? Intent, Implementation, Impact.	
Governors have the expertise to challenge and support the leadership team so that improvement priorities can be realized Brief comment on the effectiveness of governance.	*Governor meeting minute/ visit notes*

Working with the community – The views of pupils, parents, carers etc.

School Judgement: **The school is popular and valued by the local community** ▪ *The school is oversubscribed in most year groups and there remains great competition for places* ▪ *The school is a caring community that is keen to engage with its parents and other stakeholders*

The school is popular and valued by the local community Comment on Parent View and other surveys.	*School Council minutes* *Kirkland Rowell*

Key issues for the school

Subject leaders are encouraged to draw learning plan priorities from actions A through L that follow. Heads of year should focus their learning plan priorities by adapting actions H to K. Priorities M to O relate to whole-school actions for the coming year.

Key issue 1 – improve the quality of learning

To achieve this, we will need to:

A **Ensure lessons make learning relevant to students**, foster curiosity and build a love of learning

B **Refine questioning skills that secure more rapid progress in lessons**, for example by using strategies that improve student retrieval or recall of facts or that check comprehension

C **Narrow the word gap that exists between our most and least successful students** by explicitly teaching 'tier 2' as well as 'tier 3' words

D **Improve student skills when applying (or transferring) knowledge** by including a greater range of decision-making or problem-solving activities in lessons

E **Make progress more visible** in lessons by explicitly teaching students, particularly in Key Stage 5, metacognitive and memory recall skills as well as supporting their note-taking and organizational skills

F **Further refine teacher's use of instructional language** so that it both recognizes mistakes as a positive learning tool and lessens the stress associated with constant reference to examinations

G **Continue to adapt, renew and in light of intense budgetary pressures, protect our curriculum** so all students are engaged by their lessons and better prepared for the ongoing changes to assessment systems in all Key Stages

Key issue 2 – raise attainment and secure sustained progress

Many of the actions above will lead to improved performance by our students. In addition, we need to:

H **Improve teaching in Key Stage 5** so ALPs scores at A level increasingly align with those recorded at GCSE

I **Revise lessons, particularly at Key Stage 5 so that they reflect the nature of our intake** – stretching and supporting where it is needed

J **Challenge and close gaps still further between different groups of students** by ensuring when differentiating learning is 'scaffolded down' and not up

K **Ensure that identified vulnerable groups and those making slow progress** in each year group are supported both within and beyond classrooms so more of them fulfil their potential

L **Improve the quality of student's written responses by extending their vocabulary** so that they improve in using their knowledge more flexibly and so that they respond to examination and task rubrics more successfully

Key issue 3: sustain improvement across the school

To sustain the pace of improvement in the school by engaging in the development of education locally, nationally and internationally.

To achieve this we as a school need to:

M **Reduce costs, making further efficiencies so that we can continue to offer an outstanding education to our students** whilst maintaining the ongoing, severe real terms fall in our budget

N **Further develop staff skills as researchers** so that we have ever more robust methods that enable us to determine which teaching strategies are most effective at closing gaps in student learning and also which methods are not

O **Support the raising of standards in the region** as we extend our position as a support school and membership of Sport England's National Teacher Support Network

Examination Performance and Targets

Subject x department learning plan

GCSE 1			
	Target 2018	Actual 2018	Target 2019
GCSE 4+ %	86	81.1	87
GCSE 5+ %	73	68.6	74
GCSE 7+ %	33	23.1	32
A Level A*–A %	28	0	42
A Level A*–B %	65	55.6	75

GCSE 2

	Target 2018	Actual 2018	Target 2019
GCSE 4+ %	84	84.6	85
GCSE 5+ %	71	66.9	71
GCSE 7+ %	29	29	28
A-Level A*–A %	22	16.7	–
A-Level A*–B %	59	41.7	–

Targets

Focus 1: Improve teaching in Key Stage 5 by introducing greater differentiation and explicitly teaching key skills.	
Action	**Impact**
Use trio/collaborative learning time to: • Devise strategies at KS5 to model and scaffold essay structure for exam answers. • Lesson observations used to check use of the strategies and student responses. Explicitly teach note-taking skills to improve quality of student learning and aid effective revision. • Use homework to consolidate learning and recall. • More frequent checking of student notes. Delay teaching some content until key skills and concepts have been learned.	• Improvement in student performance in assessments leading to improved grades. • Improvement in conversion of Ds to Cs in all 3 A levels. • Improved student organization and engagement in learning. More effective revision leads to more students achieving expected progress or above. • Better quality responses lead to higher grades.

Focus 2: Narrow the word gap that exists between our most and least successful students by explicitly teaching 'tier 2' as well as 'tier 3' words.	
Action	**Impact**
At KS4 amend SoW to more explicitly teach key vocabulary from GCSE texts and exam questions.	• Improved student vocabulary leading to greater understanding of texts and exam questions.

Focus 2: Narrow the word gap that exists between our most and least successful students by explicitly teaching 'tier 2' as well as 'tier 3' words.	
Action	Impact
• Devise starters to pre-teach vocabulary for set texts and ensure student understanding of key tier 2 and 3 words. • Lesson observations used to observe teaching of vocabulary. At KS3 explicitly teach etymology in Year 7 lessons. • Creation of word walls/windows in Reading classrooms to display word families. Use of 'Word of the Week' across the department.	• Improved student ability to decode unfamiliar vocabulary when reading. • Improved student engagement and confidence when meeting new vocabulary.

Focus 3: Improve the quality of students' written responses by extending their vocabulary and building in more regular practice of writing skills.	
Action	Impact
Devise 200-word writing challenges for Year 9 homework, to be extended across KS3/4. • Specifically teach and practise skills, such as varied sentence lengths and punctuation, more regularly. • Use of punctuation triangles to aid students when writing. Use trio/collaborative learning time to further develop use of structure strips throughout KS3 and KS4.	• Regular short writing practice leads to improved quality of writing and performance in end of year exams. • Improved structure of student responses evident in both reading and writing assessments.

Department self-evaluation

Learning plan

1 Improve the quality of learning – continue to adapt and renew our curriculum, making progress more visible.

- Having successfully seen the first cohort through the new GCSE and A Level courses, the team has continued to refine and adapt schemes of work to improve performance and enhance student engagement.

- Trio and collaborative learning time has been used to devise structure strips at KS4 to help students respond more effectively to exam questions and to develop the use of 'NOW task' feedback sheets across both KS3 and KS4.

- Quotation hexagons were trialled successfully, particularly with higher sets, to help develop more analytical and focused responses.
- A bank of starters to help students learn quotations for the exam was devised with a focus on interleaving to enhance recall.
- Vulnerable students, particularly in Sets 3, 4 and 5 were identified throughout the year and intervention was targeted at improving specific areas of weakness, particularly those identified in the Mocks.
- All Year 11 students were provided with a structured revision programme to be followed at home and after-school club from February half-term.
- A large bank of revision resources for GCSE has now been created and made available to students via group email and Moodle.
- Collaborative marking of the Mocks was successfully trialled, ensuring a fair distribution of workload across the department. It was well-received by students who viewed it as being more objective and good preparation for the summer exams.
- Assessments at KS3 are now being completed/stuck in exercise books making progress and identified areas for improvement clearer to both students and parents.

2 Ensure lessons make learning relevant to students, foster curiosity and build a love of learning.

- A new Level 2 course has been introduced in Year 10 Set 7 and two units out of three have been completed.
- Exam board 'Stretch and Challenge' resources were used with the top sets in Year 11 during preparation for the GCSE exams. As these were not released until the middle of the Spring term their use was limited this year, but greater use will be made of them next year.
- All Set 1 and 2 teachers have been provided with a guide to aid preparation of lessons that help students develop the analytical skills required for Grades 7–9.
- Scripts at different grades from last summer's exam were purchased and reproduced to help students understand the requirements for different grades and recognize how responses can be improved.
- Staff have continued to create and share resources, ensuring that work is relevant and engaging for students.
- Extended lesson activities continue to build a love of learning, such as the after school clubs and trips and visits, etc.

3 Revise schemes of work at Key Stage 3

- Greater differentiation has been built into the Key Stage 3 schemes of work.
- Practice of the more challenging Paper 2 skills has been built into the Year 9 curriculum with students completing a Paper 2 exam at the end of the year.

This has involved the use of more examples in lessons. This means that all Year 7, 8 and 9 complete GCSE style end-of-year exams, with exam skills across both papers embedded into teaching at Key Stage 3.

- Writing homework tasks to be introduced consistently throughout Y9 from next September onwards.
- Contextual information is more consistently embedded into units of work rather than treated as an 'add on.'
- The department has continued to raise challenge at Key Stage 3 by moving some topics from Year 8 to Year 7.
- Good examples of student writing have been collected over the year and will be used to create the first annual magazine in September.

Key issues arising from examination performance

1 For the second year running, the number of 9–8 GCSE grades was extremely pleasing across both examinations (25 in Subject 1 and 22 in Subject 2 out of 169 entries). The number of Grade 9s was well above the national average of 2.6% – Subject 1 7%; Subject 2 6%.

The exam board's Enhanced Results Analysis shows that our Grade 9–5 results were 21% above other centres.

Results in Subject 1 were slightly lower than Subject 2 whereas nationally results in Subject 1 are higher (All centres, Grades 9–4: Subject 1 62%, Subject 2 73%).

There were some unexpected results (both higher and lower than expected) in both subjects when compared to individual students' consistent performance over the past two years, suggesting there may still be some worrying anomalies in the quality of marking at GCSE.

Key issue: Continue to ensure there is a balance between the teaching and assessment of skills for both exams and impress on students the importance of revision for the exam.

2 ERA shows that our results in all three A-Levels were all above other centres, particularly at the higher end:

Subject 1 A*–C 83% Other centres 75%

Subject 2 A*–C 100%   Other centres 75%

Subject 2 A*–C 82% Other centres 77%

Results were pleasing with all apart from 1 of the 12 students achieving at or above their expected grade.

Key issue: To convert A grades to A*s through more in-depth teaching of essay structure.

Subject 1 results were lower than last year but generally in line with expectations, although 3 of the 9 students achieved one grade below the minimum expected grade. Several students were only two or three marks below a grade boundary. Student grades were affected by the moderator reducing students' marks in some cases, which was unexpected as all marks had been validated last year and the same criteria and standard had been applied this year. The marks were the one area where we under-performed in comparison to other centres (School 67%; all centres 74%).

Key issue: To improve the standard of the assessments, particularly AO1.

Results were also pleasing with 2 of the 11 students achieving an A* and all apart from 2 achieving at or above their expected grade.

Key issue: To continue establishing effective learning plans – clear guidance from the exam board and updated commercial resources have only recently become available.

Progress

1 **Progress Overall:**

		GCSE v FFT			GCSE v TA			GCSE Results											
	No	above	at	below	above	at	below	9	8	7	6	5	4	3	2	1	U	9–4	9–5	APS
Subject 1	169	27%	31%	42%	23%	33%	44%	7%	8%	14%	20%	18%	18%	11%	3%	1%		85%	67%	5.45
Subject 2	169	22%	26%	52%	23%	35%	42%	6%	7%	10%	18%	27%	12%	11%	5%	2%		81%	69%	5.23

2 **Key Stages 2–4** – Average point score 5.78

Subject 1:	27% of students achieved above FFT
	31% of students achieved at FFT
	42% of students achieved below FFT
Subject 2:	22% of students achieved above FFT
	26% of students achieved at FFT
	52% of students achieved below FFT
Subject 1 ALPS Grade 3	
Subject 2 ALPS Grade 5	

Key issue: Attainment in Subject 1 has fallen below attainment in Subject 2, suggesting that student revision in this area needs to be improved. Ensure the balance between the subject focus in lessons is correct and that revision skills are actively taught from the beginning of Year 11.

Key Stages 4–5

A Level 1 ALPS grade 4

A Level 2 ALPS grade 5

A Level 3 ALPS grade 5.

3 Pupil Premium:

Of PP students, 82% achieved a standard pass at GCSE; 66% achieved at or above their FFT indicator.

SEN: 83% of SEN K students achieved a standard pass; 64% achieved at or above their FFT indicator.

Key successes and strategies to build on those successes

1 High level of attainment at GCSE and A-level.

   Strategies: Further fine-tuning of approaches to teaching skills, particularly those that focus on effective revision skills and encourage student independence.

2 Teaching of the skills required for GCSE appears to be particularly effective with student attainment 22% above that of other centres at Grade 9–4. Continue to build on that success through further embedding of the required skills at Key Stage 3.

Subject department learning plan

Italics = examples. please replace with your info in black! please stick to this format – do not change format in any way

EXAMINATION PERFORMANCE AND TARGETS

TABLE TO *BE ADDED IN SEPT*

TARGETS *Choose 3 target areas from the whole school key issues grid (primarily actions A-G and where appropriate H-L) and then consider how you can address them in your department. Your plan might look like this:*

Focus: Improve the detail and focus of student's written responses so they fulfil examination rubrics more successfully

Action (*realistic and practical actions that involve a clear* **research-plan-do-review** **cycle**)	Impact (*how will you know your actions have been worthwhile – how will your students/ staff/ results be different at the end of this work?*)
Use trio/collaborative learning time to: • Scrutinize returned Y11 higher examination papers in team meetings to determine specific skills that need improving in paper 1 • Share resources that promote examination skills such as decoding questions and that link points more effectively • Agree marking criteria for assessing extended writing – run a baseline test in Sept and re-run in Jan to gauge progress • Jointly plan lessons in department meetings which promote extended writing skills	• All team members know which aspects of examination performance students were insecure in (results breakdown) • Resources have been planned and used that close specific learning gaps • In observed lessons students review their progress – via self-evaluation questions applying the Solo taxonomy principles • Written answers have shown improvement between Sept and Jan (when responses are marked against our revised criteria)
• Trial approaches with classes • Use paired observation and work scrutiny to determine the extent interventions have been effective – focusing specifically on A*-A students	• X% of students achieve 7+ at GCSE in recent examinations (a rise of Y%)

Focus: Build regular opportunities in lessons for students to reflect upon how and what they have been learning

Action (*realistic and practical actions that involve a clear* **research-plan-do-review** **cycle**)	Impact (*how will you know your actions have been worthwhile – how will your students/ staff/ results be different at the end of this work?*)
• Share and read literature on questioning and memory. Focus on findings of Robert Bjork and Deborah Meier • Use reflective questions in Y8 classes as well as comments in books that result in more teacher-student dialogue about progress • Plan lessons which promote student understanding of how their memory works and how they might expand their schemas (also known as schemata) on targeted topics • Apply findings, where appropriate to teaching across Key Stage 3 in summer term	• Teachers become more skilled at providing effective feedback • In observed lessons students make rapid progress because teachers use questions that promote retrieval and encourage students to reflect upon how they have or haven't succeeded in the lesson (Trio observations) • Feedback (observed in teacher-student conversations or through book scrutiny) consistently elicits a response and students have to think to make that response • Book scrutiny conducted in department meetings in Jan and July reveals that these approaches are embedded features of classroom practice

Focus: Adapt and renew our curriculum in KS4

Action (*realistic and practical actions that involve a clear* **research-plan-do-review** *cycle*)	**Impact** (*how will you know your actions have been worthwhile – how will your students/ staff/ results be different at the end of this work?*)
• Attend new examination specification course/ webinar	• New programmes of study and teaching sequences in place

• Disseminate key messages with team
• Build new teaching materials and programmes of study for classes that
  o Include new content and skills
  o Enable time for students to reflect upon learning and thus gauge the progress they are making
  o Engage students and enable them to progress in line or above expectations
• Interview Y10 students to assess their understanding of how they can achieve their expected grade (comparing responses from a sample taken in Sept to May)
	• Interviews show students can articulate (specific skills to develop, knowledge that must be retained etc.) their learning and progress more effectively in May than in September
	• Teacher forecasts at the end of Y10 are in line with expectations

Subject department self-evaluation

Learning plan

Write a brief summary of your Department's progress against each of your targets from last year's Learning Plan.

1

2

3

Key issues arising from examination performance

Identify the key issues evident from the detailed analysis of your department/ year group – for example, lack of A*s, underperformance of boys, concerns over coursework and so on.

1

2

3 etc.

Progress

Analyse the progress made from Key Stage 2 to Key Stage 4 and Key Stage 4 to Key Stage 5 by students in your subject, commenting specifically on the progress of Disadvantaged (Pupil Premium) students

1 Progress Overall:

2 Pupil Premium:

3 SEND:

Key successes and strategies to build on those successes

1

2

3 etc. if necessary

Part 2 – General self-evaluation – September

This section to be prepared for the head/line manager in preparation for the September results meeting **but not included** in the learning plan document. This will be the basis for the results discussion.

Write a brief summary of your department's overall performance using the following questions adapted from Ofsted's Evaluation Schedule.

1 How good is student attainment in your department? This section should include a detailed class by class analysis of your headline examination results compared to previous years and where possible national results sets. Please identify any issues arising (e.g. underperformance off boys, or lack of top grades etc.) and any action points. Make specific reference to the achievement of particular groups within your subject area (e.g. Disadvantaged/PP students SEND, students with high, middle or low PA (prior attainment), boys/ girls etc.).

2 How good is student progress in your department? This section should include a detailed class by class analysis of your examination results compared using ALPs GCSE analysis of each class and/or % of students in each class matching or exceeding their FFT (high) target. You need to show how pupils have progressed from KS2 to KS4, and from KS4 to A-Level. Is their progress in line with those

targets. Make specific reference to the achievement of particular groups within your subject area (e.g. Disadvantaged/ PP students SEND, students with high, middle or low PA [prior attainment], boys/ girls etc.).

3 How effective is learning in lessons in your department? This section should include reference to the data above as well to your records of lesson monitoring. You must make it clear how you monitor learning in your department.

4 How effective is assessment in your department? Give clear examples of how you ensure that progress in years and between teachers is tracked, identifying areas for development. You may wish to use the outcomes of any recent review. Focus particularly on how assessment is used to inform progress.

Head of year X self-evaluation

Learning plan

Write a brief summary of your Year Group's progress against each of your targets from last year's Learning Plan.

1

2

3

Key issues arising from examination performance/teacher assessments of your year group

Identify the key issues evident from your detailed analysis of your year group – for example, lack of top grades, underperformance of boys or girls, concerns with progress made by groups with high, middle or low PA (prior attainment) and so on.

1

2

Progress

Analyse the progress made by the students in your year group commenting specifically on the progress of Pupil Premium students (e.g. by comparing their position in Eng and Ma against the school progress flight paths in Sept to Jun/July)

1 Progress Overall:

2 Pupil Premium:
- Student X:
- Student Y:

- Student Z:
- Etc

3. Send

Key successes and strategies to build on those successes

1

2

3 etc. if necessary

Part 2 – General self-evaluation – September

This section to be prepared for the Head/Line Manager in preparation for the September results meeting but not included in the Learning Plan Document. This will be the basis for the results discussion.

Write a brief summary of your Year's overall position using the following questions adapted from Ofsted's Evaluation Schedule.

1. How well do pupils achieve in your Year? This section should include a detailed analysis of examination results/teacher assessments compared to FFT (High) targets/School Progress Flight Paths. Please identify any issues arising (e.g. underperformance of a gender group, or lack of top grades in some Ebacc subjects, concerns with progress made by students with SEND or high/middle or low PA and so on and any action points).

2. How much progress do pupils make in your year group? With reference to the data, identify how pupils have progressed from Key Stage 2 to Key Stage 3, from Key Stage 3 to Key Stage 4, and from Key Stage 4 to A-Level. Is their progress in line with estimates according to the School Progress Flight Paths? Make specific reference to the achievement of particular groups within your subject area including Disadvantaged/Pupil Premium students

3. How effective is learning in your Year Group? This section should include reference to the data above as well to findings from your lesson monitoring records. You must make it clear how you monitor learning in your year group.

4. How effective is assessment in your Year Group? Give clear examples and identify areas for development. Focus particularly on how assessment is used to inform progress.

The Learning Plan Cycle

May — SLT identify key issues for following year + long-term issues

June — 4 days' whole-school CPD at hotel based on key issues

July — Depts./HOYs explore key issues and draft 3 focus areas

August — Exams

September — Plans revised in the light of results. Data targets added.

September — Previous year's plan fully evaluated

September — Head/line manager meet every HOD/HOY to review results

September — SEF revised – full SEF and SEF in a page

September/October — Learning plan published and presented to governors

September/October — Performance management meetings

September/October — CPD/teacher research programme for the year constructed

October Onwards
- Plan monitored – including sixth-month review
- Link governor visits
- Line management – fixed agenda item
- Challenge coordinator support
- SLT observations
- HOD/HOY observations shared in Dept. reviews
- Good practice shared in CPD sessions
- Staff and dept. meetings

Continual Focus on Teaching and Learning
- Regular T&L conversations
- Response to data
- National developments
- Identified issues
- CPD
- Research/reading
- TSA conferences
- Schools council
- Dept. reviews
- Challenge coordinators' feedback

Challenge Coordinators | Governors' School Improvement Group | Staff Forum | SLT Thursday Meeting | Line Management | Teaching School | Maths Hub

Line management

Purpose

- To build successful departments and outstanding leadership
- To monitor student progress in subjects and in year groups
- To identify approaches that would address where progress is not being made
- To revisit and assess the extent planned actions in classrooms are improving student progress
- To develop consistent approaches to key teaching priorities
- To share best practice (two-way process)
- To discuss management issues and agree on next steps
- To listen to the challenges of leadership
- To offer help

Frequency

- 1 hour per fortnight
- Smaller departments may meet for 1 hour on a monthly basis
- With newly appointed subject or year leaders – meetings may be jointly held so best practice is modelled

Audience for minutes

Written by the line manager for (in order of priority):

- Subject leader
- Team
- Line manager
- Head teacher

Typical headings used for discussion:

1. Progress and standards
2. Progress of disadvantaged groups
3. Development of teaching and learning
4. Lesson drop-ins
5. Leadership of the team
6. Management – weekly/day-to-day issues
7. AOB

Line management meeting minutes – Departments

Subject: _____ Staff: _____ & _____ Date:

Progress and standards	
Intervention - vulnerable & disadvantaged students	
Day-to-day management	
CPD/developing teaching and learning in team	

Curriculum/assessment developments	
AOB	

Line management meeting minutes – Year Heads

Subject: _____ Staff: _____ & _____ Date:

Progress and standards	
Group/individual student monitoring and intervention (PP, SEND, LAC, Behaviour/ Attendance)	

Progress and standards	
Tutor team leadership/management	
CPD/Development of T&L	
AOB	

The Elysian Academy
Teacher Research – our CPD Structure 2019–2019

Summer Term

Hotel based whole staff training

- Sets whole school priorities
- Explores new classroom and research approaches
- Promotes deliberate practice as a method of refining teacher skill

Dept. evaluation and action planning

- Evaluate effectiveness of research/development in current year
- Agree dept. priorities (linking them to the whole school, where there is underperformance, findings from dept. reviews)
- Draft the Learning Plan

Autumn Term

Department meetings are used for:

- **Sharing examples of best practice** linked to the team's learning plan priorities – e.g. how to close the word gap by teaching tier 2 vocabulary or by planning and teaching lessons that build students' transferrable skills
- **Deliberate practice** of classroom skills – questioning, promoting student reflection or building greater engagement in KS5 lessons
- Revising and **updating your curriculum** and aligning assessments to the 9 to 1 grades
- **Moderating the team's marking** and analysing performance data

Trio and collaborative work (in the directed time allocated) is used for:

- **Initial evidence gathering** via joint observations, work scrutiny, pupil interviews or questionnaires, data analysis and reading pertinent research
- **Trialling in classrooms** those strategies that are anticipated to help students learn more effectively
- **Further evidence gathering** to gauge how these approaches might or might not be helping different types of students in the affected classrooms (using 3 Monday meetings set aside for this)
- In some instances, **re-trialling of strategies** with refinements made
- **Disseminating findings** to the team setting out clearly what works and why and what doesn't – report writing by July 19
- N.B. Part time staff contribute to collaborative work in negotiation with their subject leader.

Performance management is used for:

- **Setting individual targets** for teachers that link directly to those activities taking place in departmental meetings, via trio work and as result of Monday night research sessions
- Monitoring by the line manager that each of the team is deliberately practising and developing those skills essential to the priorities in the team plan being realised
- N.B. PM target setting for part-time staff is similarly linked to priorities, but targets can be fewer

Monday night leadership research is used for:

- sharing research on **pedagogy** with all teachers. In 2018–19 sessions will link to those priorities shared so far
- Supporting teachers' **small-scale research** undertaken in their trio groupings
- **Writing about the findings** from small-scale trio research
- N.B. part-time staff are always welcome to come to all these sessions. However, where they opt to attend just some they must always attend the sessions in blocks of three. i.e. Leadership sessions 1 to 3/ Trio sessions 1 to 3.

Department Priorities
Trio/Collaborative work
Performance management
Monday night research sessions

Spring Term

Summer Term

Initial, early evaluation of CPD activities helping to inform the next cycle of work.

Head's report to governors

1. School context

i Pupil Numbers

- *Current number on roll.*
- *Sixth form numbers*
- *General comments on admissions, applications, numbers in each year group etc.*

ii Staffing

- *List current staff issues: appointments, promotions, retirements*
- *Recruitment issues*
- *Pay progression*
- *Maternity leave*
- *Budgetary implications*

2. Pupil achievement

- *Autumn term: analyse the summer's examination performance immediately after the exams and then in response to national figures when published*
- *Throughout the year, provide data on the current progress of key examination cohorts*
- *Include details of specific groups: disadvantaged, LACs, higher prior attainers, EAL etc.*
- *Report on school specific data like ALPS, FFT or 4Matrix*
- *Focus on progress as well as attainment*
- *Discuss performance of particular departments and any action plans to correct underperformance*
- *Highlight areas of outstanding performance*

ii SEN/PP

- *Include detail reports on the progress of SEN/PP pupils*
- *Consider EHCPs*
- *Support plans*
- *Attendance of vulnerable groups*
- *Annual reviews*

3. Behaviour and safety

i Exclusions

- *Include up to date exclusion figures for permanent exclusions and fixed term*
- *Include details of any SEND/PP exclusions*
- *Pupils educated off-site monitoring details*

ii Attendance

- *Attendance figures for the last academic year plus current attendance*
- *Include details of attendance figures for vulnerable groups*
- *Include details of pupils with attendance below 90% and the actions being taken*

iii Pastoral

- *Any pastoral issues to be discussed*

iv Safeguarding

- *Comment on updates for safeguarding procedures.*
- *Checks on the Central Record.*
- *Check on governor training, including safer recruitment*
- *Updates on staff training*
- *Comments from the DSL*

4. Teaching and learning

i Monitoring the Quality of Teaching and Learning

- *Discuss reviews of results following examinations*
- *Departmental reviews*
- *Performance management*
- *Learning Plan construction, updates, progress etc.*
- *Evaluation of teaching*
- *Updates on learning walks, external reviews etc.*
- *Response to Ofsted Areas for Improvement*

ii CPD

- *Year plans with regular updates*
- *Training days*

- *Details of specific CPD for individual staff*
- *Research/Trio working*
- *Collaboration with other schools*
- *Governor involvement in CPD*

iii Curriculum

- *Proposed curriculum developments*
- *Monitoring and evaluation of curriculum changes*
- *Choices at GCSE and A-level*
- *Financial viability of courses*
- *Staff issues*
- *Updates on changes to specifications and how departments are coping, including discussion of resources and CPD*
- *Assessment: updates. How effective is the current system? How is it evaluated?*

iv Extra-curricular

- *Outline current highlights*
- *Trips and visits*

5. Leadership and management

i Initiatives to promote learning and well-being:

- *Progress with the Learning Plan*
- *Current leadership issues*
- *Response to national changes*
- *Support for disadvantaged and vulnerable groups*
- *Policy updates*

ii School specialisms, for example, Teaching School or Maths Hub

6. Management of resources

i Budget

- *Comment on progress with budget and projections for the next year*
- *Savings*

- *Expenses*
- *Pupil numbers and their impact on the DSG*
- *Staffing considerations*
- *Departmental accounts*

ii Premises/Accommodation

- *Building projects*
- *Cleaning*
- *Catering*
- *Accommodation issues*

iii Health and Safety

- *Include reports from the Health and Safety Committee*

7. Other

- Detail school events to which governors are invited
- List key events coming up

The Elysian Academy

Record of governor's visit

Governor's name, link and role:	Date of Visit:
Focus of visit: e.g. Department, year, class, etc.	
Sources of information: e.g.: Head teacher, departmental meeting, head of department, class teacher, looking at resources, etc.	
What area of the School Learning Plan was seen or discussed?	
In order to demonstrate that the Governing Body is contributing to the school's self-evaluation process, please summarize any points that need to be taken forward for discussion:	
Signed:	Date:
Date reviewed by the Governing Body:	

What does outstanding learning in a lesson look like?

Before the lesson –

- Teachers plan challenging, objective-led, learner-centred lessons.
- Teachers consider the needs of their students and plan accordingly.
- Teachers consider how far their students' learning can be taken over the course of an hour.
- Teachers ensure that the learning in the lesson links into an overarching programme of study.

At the start of the lesson –

- Students demonstrate high levels of engagement and curiosity.
- Students are settled and ready to be challenged by the learning.
- Students want to learn, and they want to find out.
- Students know the focus for their learning and how they might demonstrate this at the end of the lesson.
- Teachers share learning objectives/ key questions, and these are talked about with students in terms of 'How will you know you have had a good lesson/ been successful?'
- Students might even be given the opportunity to set the learning objective/key question or respond to this by agreeing to a set of success criteria for the lesson.

As the lesson progresses –

- Students do most of the challenging work because teacher explanation doesn't dominate.
- There are high levels of student activity that help them to build their learning.
- Students are able to build their ideas through paired, group and whole-class discussion.
- Where students have difficulty, they are confident to ask for purposeful guidance (teacher questioning ensures that the conversations are more than just ones where students claim to be stuck with the teacher giving them the answer).
- Since the students are learning through activity there is a chance for the teacher to work with targeted individuals or groups on particular things that they might be finding difficult.
- At key points in the lesson students are asked to reflect upon their learning, assess their performance and pick out what might need to be learnt next (mini-plenaries). This might lead to an adjustment in the next part of the lesson.

- Students are aware that they are not simply learning new facts about the subject they are also given the chance to discuss certain generic skills that they might need to use again in another subject.
- Students are invited to ask questions, and this can, if appropriate, take the learning in unexpected but useful directions.
- Students can be asked to become the teacher to develop the learning of others
- Students recognize the value of learning collaboratively; they are encouraged to use the appropriate social and emotional aspects of learning (SEAL) skills to help them.
- There is a buzz in the classroom.

As the lesson ends –

- It is visibly or audibly apparent that students have made progress during the lesson. This might be through questioning, mini-whiteboards, a review of work completed and some peer assessment.
- Where appropriate, a plenary requires the students to either demonstrate or apply new learning from the lesson.
- Students check their learning and have strategies to use to help them to retain it.
- Praise is given for achievement, not just effort.
- Students are sometimes asked to suggest what needs to be found out in the next lesson.

After the lesson, reflecting on learning with colleagues –

- Teachers review not their own performance in a lesson but talk about how all or certain pupils made progress in the hour. (They want to talk about progress, not performance.)
- Teachers use the word *learn* more often than they use the word *work* or *do*.
- Teachers can begin to identify how certain things they do lead to the improved learning of all or certain groups of their pupils.
- Teachers consider their pupils' needs when deciding how to plan their next lessons.

Endnote

Philip Reeve's compelling novel *Mortal Engines* is set in a steampunk world thousands of years in the future. A terrible global war has destroyed most of civilization, leaving chaos and confusion in its wake. Instead of towns and villages, giant 'traction cities' on wheels roam the earth, literally consuming smaller cities in order to replenish their supplies of fuel and resources. This strikes me as a powerful metaphor for education in the UK today. Giant multi-academy trusts roam a landscape ravaged by years of governmental neglect 'consuming' small schools as they go. The Regional School Commissioners no longer approve of stand-alone academies, and small academy trusts are increasingly urged to join with others to survive. Maintained schools that have not yet succumbed to academization; they live in fear that they will be swallowed up, their resources stripped, their staff transferred or discarded, and their distinctiveness lost in the guts of monstrous commercial behemoths.

A fanciful comparison, I accept, but one that perhaps forces us to think about the current status of educational thinking in this country. My hope is that this book goes some way towards turning the tide away from systems and back to the classroom. It is surely time for school leaders and, of course, politicians to think less about systems and more about learning and to realize that genuine, long-lasting change takes time. School improvement is a gradual art.

Index

Alternative School Council 141
arts education 95
A-Z of School Improvement, The (Brighouse and Woods) 121

Ball, S.J. 1
BBC 14
behaviour for learning 14
Blair, T. 4
box sets 102–104
Brighouse, T. 121
Bussell, D. 10

Carroll, L. 1
challenge coordinators 64–66
continuous professional development (CPD) 17, 34, 36, 53, 60–70, 118
Counsell, C. 104
critical friends 121
culture 4

Davis, M. 46
Department for Education 7, 10, 24, 25, 42, 50, 84, 91, 107, 118, 129
department reviews 71–74
digital leader 41–43
distractions 9–10
Dunford, J. 14

Educating Essex 20
English Baccalaureate 8, 86, 94, 95, 97

finance manager 35–37
Finland 129
Fischer Family Trust 53
Fortnite 10
free schools 86, 129
Frost, R. 30
Fundamental British Values 7

Game of Thrones 103–104
Gatsby standards 94
Global Teacher Status Index 125
Godwin, W. xv
Gove, M. 86
governors 106–126
grammar schools 90, 132
Great Yarmouth Charter Academy 14

Harford, S. 84
Hattie, J. 21–22
head of teaching and learning 11–13
head's report to governors 117
hero head 20, 32
High Status, Low Threat (Myatt) 21
Hill, R. 101
Hopkins, G.M. 44
Hultins, A. 27

Ibbotsen, E. 30
improvising 43
innovation 26–32, 85
inspection 9, 49, 128–139
inspection limitations 132

Journey to the River Sea (Ibbotsen) 30

Keeping Children Safe in Education 134, 138
Keywords (Williams) 4

leadership of learning 13
leadership team 32–41
Leadership that Lasts (Hill) 101
league tables 9, 87
Learning and Skills Council (LSC) 25
learning plan 50–56
Levin, B. 1
Long Revolution, The (Williams) 83

Martin, George R.R. xv
May, J. 75
Mortal Engines (Reeve) 191
multi academy trusts 27, 107, 122, 191
Murray, L. 26
Myatt, M. 21

National Governors' Association 114
National Professional Qualification for Headship 21, 62

Ofsted 24, 84, 88, 111
open classrooms 15
outstanding 132

parents 148
Parker, C. 44
PISA tests 8, 95
PixL 87
policies 118
politics 7, 125
progress 8 94, 97
pupil pursuits 148

quick fix 2, 14, 20, 87, 137

reading 29–31
Reeve, P. 191

Regional Schools Commissioner 7, 24, 27, 79, 80, 130
reluctant staff 74
requires improvement 131
Rethinking the School Curriculum (White) 83
Road not Taken, The (Frost) 30
Rothman, B. 128
Russell Group universities 8

safeguarding 134
satisfactory 131
school councils 140
science, technology, engineering and maths (STEM) 7, 95
self-evaluation form (SEF) 48, 118, 135
self-improving system 130
social media 43, 149
Specialist Leaders in Education 62, 78
Specialist Schools and Academy Trust 26
Specialist School Status 6
Spielman, A. 83, 92, 134
sport 5
Staff Forum 76
Stronach, I. 1

teaching schools 63, 77–80
This Much I Know about Love over Fear (Tomsett) 13
Tomsett, J. 13, 14
Trios 63–64

Visible Learning (Hattie) 21
vision 47–48
vocational education 97–100

Weick, K.E. 44
White, J. 83
Williams, R. 4, 8, 83
Woods, D. 121

For Product Safety Concerns and Information please contact our EU
representative GPSR@taylorandfrancis.com
Taylor & Francis Verlag GmbH, Kaufingerstraße 24, 80331 München, Germany

www.ingramcontent.com/pod-product-compliance
Lightning Source LLC
Chambersburg PA
CBHW081419230426
43668CB00016B/2290